Cartier
IN THE
20TH CENTURY

Cartier IN THE 20TH CENTURY

MARGARET YOUNG-SÁNCHEZ

WITH ESSAYS BY

MARTIN CHAPMAN

MICHAEL HALL

STEFANO PAPI

JANET ZAPATA

FOREWORD BY

CHRISTOPH HEINRICH

Frederick and Jan Mayer Director, Denver Art Museum

INTRODUCTION BY

PIERRE RAINERO

Image, Style, and Heritage Director, Cartier

THE VENDOME PRESS

NEW YORK

DENVER ART MUSEUM

COLORADO

CONTENTS

FOREWORD

BRILLIANT: CARTIER IN THE 20TH CENTURY IS THE most recent in a series of major art exhibitions that brings the cultural riches of Europe—in particular, France—to Denver. In 2012, the Denver Art Museum hosted *Yves Saint Laurent: The Retrospective*, a spectacular exhibition on one of the twentieth century's greatest fashion designers. The following year, the museum was the organizer and exclusive venue for *Becoming Van Gogh*, a lyrically beautiful and revealing show on the development of the painter's artistic identity, crucial portions of which took place in France. And in late 2013, *Passport to Paris*—a constellation of three exhibitions on French painting and drawing—inspired the Denver public. *Brilliant* is equally, if not more, ambitious: a breathtaking presentation of the Parisian Maison's rise to global preeminence, told through an array of stunning jewelry, timepieces, and decorative objects.

But in fact, Colorado's connection to Cartier extends back more than a century. The exhibition features a clock that belonged to Denver-born Evalyn Walsh, daughter of an Irish immigrant who struck it rich in 1896 at the Camp Bird gold mine near Ouray. When Evalyn and her husband, Ned McLean, traveled to Paris on their honeymoon in 1908, she went straight to Cartier to pick out a wedding present from her indulgent father and walked out of the rue de la Paix store carrying the 94.8-carat Star of the East diamond. A few years later, Pierre Cartier showed Evalyn and Ned the blue Hope diamond and recounted its captivating legend. Evalyn purchased that magnificent stone in 1912 and remained a Cartier customer for decades.

Cartier's success in catering to the taste and aspirations of new clients such as Evalyn Walsh McLean while retaining the loyalty of established elites was key to its growth and international expansion in the 1900s. It is also emblematic of the Maison's sensitivity to this tumultuous era's social, cultural, and economic changes, to which it continually responded with innovative products and trend-setting designs. "Cartier" is now a byword for luxury and quality around the world, equally recognizable in Denver, Rio de Janeiro, New Delhi, Hong Kong, Rome, and Paris. Cartier's story is chronicled by this volume and the exhibition it accompanies. Organized by Denver Art Museum curator Margaret Young-Sánchez, with expertise from Cartier's Heritage Department and many international jewelry specialists, the show, like the book, consists of seven thematically organized sections that take us from 1900 to 1975. "Aristocracy

ABOVE Evalyn Walsh McLean, about 1932, wearing the Hope diamond; necklace and chain supplied by Cartier New York in 1932.

and Aspiration" illustrates the years from 1900 to 1914, when Cartier specialized in exquisite platinum and diamond jewelry, clocks, tabletop accessories, and delightful hardstone carvings. This lavish era was brought to a cataclysmic end by World War I and the Russian Revolution. "New Outlook: Art Deco" presents jewels in the modern style pioneered by Cartier and showcased at the 1925 Exposition internationale des arts décoratifs et industriels modernes in Paris. The new look suited the uninhibited attitudes and daring fashions of the giddy 1920s. "Foreign Fascination" highlights Cartier's colorful jewelry, accessories, and timepieces inspired by the arts of India and Persia, ancient Egypt, and East Asia. Many pieces incorporate imported components, such as ancient Egyptian faience, Chinese carved jade, and Indian enamelwork. "Foreign Fascination" climaxes with Cartier's most extravagant products: panther-pelt accessories, luscious tutti frutti–style jewelry, and fabulously imaginative mystery clocks.

Cigarette smoking exploded in popularity during the first half of the century. Cartier's superbly decorated cigarette cases and holders, ashtrays, and table boxes for both men and women are featured in "Art of Smoking." While jewelry is commonly associated with women, Cartier has always catered to discerning men. Discreet jewelry, inventive pocket items, inscribed commemoratives, and stylish watches are the focus in "Masculine View." Cartier's "Age of Glamour," which extends from the mid-1930s to the 1960s, features stones in a glorious spectrum of colors set in both platinum and sleek yellow gold. These bold jewels were worn by cosmopolitan women who traveled the globe and made personal style into an art form, as documented in magazines and by some of the finest photographers of the time. The finale, "Icons of Style," focuses on five women who helped shape the fashion ideals of the twentieth century. Daisy Fellowes, the Duchess of Windsor, Princess Grace of Monaco, Elizabeth Taylor, and María Félix turned to Cartier for jewels that expressed their individual personalities and also epitomized their eras.

This exhibition and book were made possible by many extraordinarily generous organizations and individuals—most importantly, the Heritage Department of Cartier, headed by Director of Image, Style, and Heritage Pierre Rainero, under the leadership of Cartier International CEO Stanislas de Quercize and with the support of Cartier North America President and CEO Mercedes Abramo and her predecessor Emmanuel Perrin. The department's Cartier Collection houses the greatest assemblage of Cartier objects in the world, chosen for both historical significance and excellence in design. Splendid objects selected from the Cartier Collection form the backbone of this exhibition. Private collectors have loaned singularly beautiful and significant objects to the exhibition, immeasurably enriching our presentation. Exhibition designer Nathalie Crinière collaborated generously with the museum's curatorial, education, and exhibition staff to generate an installation that is both incredibly dramatic and highly informative. Jewelry experts and scholars Martin Chapman, Michael Hall, Stefano Papi, Margaret Young-Sánchez, and Janet Zapata contributed insightful essays to the book; Pierre Rainero graciously contributed an introduction. Mark Magowan, Alexis Gregory, and the expert staff of Vendome Press created an inspired design for this book.

This exhibition is presented by Joy and Chris Dinsdale and the Bank of Colorado. Support is also provided by contributors to the museum's Annual Fund Leadership Campaign and the citizens who support the Scientific and Cultural Facilities District (SCFD). To each of these individuals and organizations, who have been so remarkably generous in so many ways, I offer my heartfelt thanks.

Christoph Heinrich
Frederick and Jan Mayer Director
Denver Art Museum

ACKNOWLEDGMENTS

A MAJOR MUSEUM EXHIBITION CAN BE COMPARED to an opera production: each requires lengthy preparation and the cooperation of many skilled and creative professionals, most of whom are invisible to those who eventually enjoy their multisensory productions. Logistics experts and handlers; exhibition, graphic, and lighting designers; carpenters and construction crews; interpreters, fund-raisers, and marketing specialists are all essential. Most important, of course, are the performers (in this case, extraordinary Cartier jewels and objects), all contributing their individual brilliance and combining their voices to tell a compelling story. The exhibition itself is evanescent, on view for only a few months; fortunately, a record is preserved in this stylish book. I have been privileged to work with dozens of talented and dedicated professionals to bring this project to fruition; only a portion of them can be named here individually, but all are deeply appreciated.

Many experts shared their knowledge of both Cartier and jewelry history and helped me formulate the content and themes of this exhibition. They include Pierre Rainero, Pascale Lepeu, Michel Aliaga, and Violette Petit from the Cartier Heritage Department; Judy Rudoe of the British Museum; Richard Edgcumbe of the Victoria and Albert Museum; Lisa Hubbard and Alexandra Rhodes of Sotheby's; Geoffrey Munn; Harry Fane; Lee Siegelson; and Sarah Davis. Scholars Martin Chapman, Michael Hall, Yvonne Markowitz, Stefano Papi, Pierre Rainero, and Janet Zapata not only shared their expertise but also contributed fascinating texts to the book. Many institutions and individuals agreed to loan unique, extraordinarily beautiful objects to the exhibition. I received wonderful generosity from the Cartier Collection, especially Pascale Lepeu and Caroline Kranz, and the good offices of Bernhardt Berger and Gregory Bishop. Russell Feather and Jeffrey Post of the Department of Mineral Sciences at the Smithsonian Institution's National Museum of Natural History, Hubert Bari of the Qatar Museums Authority, Hervé Irien of the Palais Princier de Monaco, Barbra Streisand, and several private collectors who wish to remain anonymous shared with us their amazing treasures.

Database management, transportation, insurance, customs paperwork, and compliance with international regulations were expertly handled by the Denver Art Museum's registrar Lori Iliff, with key assistance from Laura Paulick-Moody, Sarah Cucinella-McDaniel, Anna Estes, and Jana Gottshalk, as well as the Cartier Collection's highly professional Nadia Cretignier. The impressive resources of the Cartier Archives in New York, Paris, and London, and the documentation center in Paris, were graciously extended by Renée Frank, Violette Petit, Marina

Wright, Geoffrey Bishop, Jenny Rourke, Michel Aliaga, Hélène Godard, Anne-Hortense Dupont-Wavrin, and Gäelle Naegellen. Xavier Gargat generously and patiently explained the complex jewelry production process to me and other museum staff, giving us a new appreciation for Cartier's great historic jewels. He also provided advice essential to the interactive "workshop" area of the exhibition and loaned his personal jeweler's tools. The museum's education team, in particular Melora McDermott-Lewis and Stefania Van Dyke, were full partners in envisioning and formulating the exhibition's extensive and diverse interpretive components to help visitors appreciate the jewels and grasp historical and social context. Nathalie Crinière of Agence NC in Paris, and her talented staff (especially Anne Lebas and Maud Martinot), designed the magnificent installation, working cooperatively and sensitively with decorator Monique Saner and Denver Art Museum staff. These included Jill Desmond, who provided encouragement as well as organization and coordination, David Griesheimer, Tony Fortunato, Steve Osborne, and John Lupe. We received invaluable advice from the curators and staff of the Grand Palais in Paris, especially Laurent Salomé, Laure Dalon, and Vincent David.

The gorgeous book that accompanies *Brilliant: Cartier in the Twentieth Century* was produced in cooperation with Vendome Press, renowned for outstanding jewelry and design publications. Denver Art Museum head of publications Laura Caruso expertly managed the many detailed processes required to assemble texts and images and supplied crucial advice and editorial input. Anna Estes organized object information, correspondence, contracts, photographs, and image rights—tasks that require meticulous attention to detail. Sarah Cucinella-McDaniel, assisted by Liz Wall, Laura Bennison, and Mary Davis, procured image rights, while Jeff Wells and Christina Jackson consulted on image quality and handled electronic transfers. Cartier supplied outstanding photographs of works in the Cartier Collection. David Behl and Peter Lynde shot excellent new photographs of private collection objects, and Sotheby's generously shared images made for its use. At Vendome Press, we benefited from the expertise and enthusiasm of Mark Magowan and Alexis Gregory, the sensitive editorial skills of Jacqueline Decter, and the design talents of Celia Fuller.

My husband, Fernando Sánchez, and daughters, Cecilia and Claudia, supported me throughout the lengthy preparation of this exhibition and book. My colleagues in the New World Department, Donna Pierce, Julie Wilson, and Jana Gottshalk, helped me balance competing demands. Anna Estes, project assistant for the exhibition, supported multiple aspects of both exhibition and book—an impressive juggling act. The kind and imperturbably gracious Renée Frank of Cartier shepherded *Brilliant* from its inception, doing everything in her power to ensure its success, and I am deeply grateful. Finally, I especially wish to thank Cartier's Stanislas de Quercize and Pierre Rainero for their unswerving encouragement and support, as well as Denver Art Museum director Christoph Heinrich for entrusting me with this project and for inspiring the entire team to strive for a level of excellence worthy of Cartier's great legacy.

Margaret Young-Sánchez
Frederick and Jan Mayer Curator of Pre-Columbian Art
Denver Art Museum

ABOVE Design drawing of *Flower basket* pendant (see fig. 112, page 114, for a similar piece). Cartier Archives.

Cartier
Cartier
Joaillier
London W.
175-176
New Bond St

PIERRE RAINERO

INTRODUCTION

CARTIER AND TWENTIETH-CENTURY DECORATIVE ART

A DISTINCTIVE VISION

"A PARTICLE OF GOD"; "A FLASH OF THE LIGHT THAT created the world";"spirit made matter to be held between the fingers, the invisible made substance and stone": these are the gemstone-inspired metaphors that the great poet Paul Claudel used in *The Mystique of Precious Stones*, a book-length poem he wrote in 1937 for his friend Pierre Cartier. Four years earlier, the poet's son had married the jeweler's daughter, sealing the union of two families and, symbolically, of two art forms destined to come together—not least because both, prior to either interpretation or appropriation, distill pure emotion.

By imparting a mystical dimension and spiritual significance to precious stones and the art of their assembly, Claudel, among other things, emphasized what sets jewelry apart among the decorative arts: a jewel is a declaration of faith. This is not only because the creation of its sublime materials is shrouded in mystery but also because we offer jewelry and accept it out of love. We wear it as a message, a declaration, an offering, a talisman. Jewelers work in an ever-present symbolic and poetic dimension that designers of furniture and other functional objects rarely touch upon. In this, jewelry is a truly singular art form.

The House of Cartier, moreover, through its unique style—characterized by a quest for refinement, true emotion, and authenticity—has always emphasized originality. This did not prevent the firm from inscribing its creations within the artistic and cultural landscape of its time. But it did so in a manner all its own: countless examples from the history of the firm illustrate its original approach, including the many creations of the 1920s inspired by faraway civilizations. Consider, for example, the six brooches in the exhibition that draw on ancient Egypt and place them alongside architectural and decorative works of similar inspiration produced in the same period. In city streets, in the apartments of Paris and New York, and aboard ocean liners, the Egyptomania of art deco materialized in buildings and decor that blended elegance and kitsch in a pastiche of

OPPOSITE The model Capucine leaving the Cartier boutique at 13, rue de la Paix. Cartier Archives.

the stylistic elements of Nile Valley temples and tombs. Grauman's Egyptian Theatre in Los Angeles (1922) and the Louxor cinema in Paris (1921) are spectacular examples. Cartier's creative spirit, however, was of another kind entirely. Drawing inspiration from distant lands, its approach was neither pastiche nor imitation; instead, it set out to recapture the authenticity of universal and timeless emotions. This explains the frequent use of *apprêts*, a term used at Cartier to refer to authentic items—such as faience components—that Pierre's brother Louis purchased from antiques dealers and reinterpreted in the form of jewelry.

The quest for the essential became a hallmark of the firm from the moment Louis Cartier took over the direction of jewelry creation in 1899. Applying a classically influenced aesthetic and philosophy, he consistently stripped away anything he considered superfluous in order to arrive at the essence of beauty. It was a Platonic approach, similar to the one that leads Socrates, in the famous *Greater Hippias* dialogue, to ask the sophist: "What is the beautiful?" By way of answer, Hippias can only recite examples of beauty: a gracious maiden; gold, for its ability to ennoble all things; the virtues of a happy life. But for Socrates, these examples fall short of defining the nature of what is beautiful, and he finally renounces his quest, acknowledging the truth of the proverb "Beautiful things are difficult." Cartier's exceptional craftsmanship resembles this subtle exercise, in which rigorous aesthetic principles combine with imaginative inspiration to arrive at the essence of beauty.

View of Cartier on the rue de la Paix, Paris, about 1924. Watercolor on card by Robert Desouches. Cartier Archives.

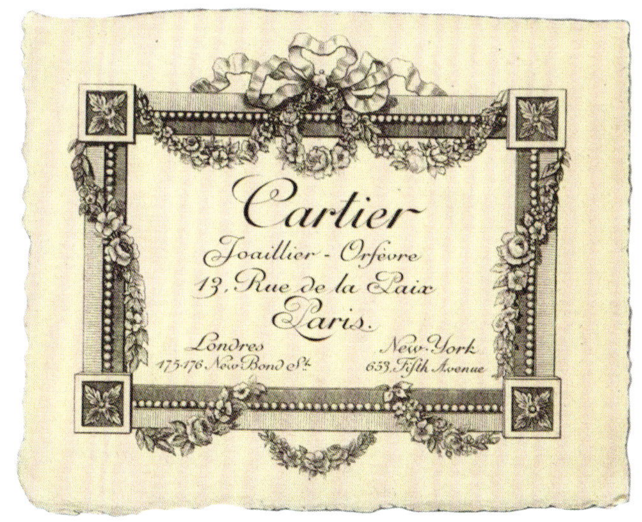

LEFT Alfred Cartier (second from right) surrounded by his sons. From left to right: Pierre, Louis, and Jacques, 1922. Cartier Archives.

ABOVE Cartier invitation, including the addresses of its Paris, London, and New York boutiques. Cartier Paris, 1918. Cartier Archives.

A NEW AESTHETIC

This new approach emerged in the first years of the 1900s with the garland style, the name given to Cartier's innovative and virtuoso use of diamonds, platinum, and millegrain settings to reinvent and refine eighteenth-century French neoclassicism in the form of sparkling, fluid, and ethereal jewels. These would lay the foundation for Cartier's international reputation. References to Louis XVI style were also incorporated into bejeweled decorative and functional objects, such as the enamel desk clocks that were gradually stripped of their traditional classical decorations—garlands, acanthus and laurel leaves, tassels, and bows—to achieve the spare elegance of a circle in a square. As early as 1904, Cartier also began producing abstract jewelry with geometric styling. This established the firm as a pioneer of the modern style, not only within the field of fine jewelry but also within the history of art in general.

The House of Cartier anticipated not only the streamlined minimalism of the modern but also the future of another functional object: the wristwatch, to which Louis Cartier turned his attention in 1904—a quarter of a century before wristwatches achieved broad popularity. This time, especially with his men's watches, he not only gradually stripped away superfluous decoration but also undertook an aesthetic process focused on the object's *function*, namely, to show time on the wrist. The jeweler was never more a *designer* than in that moment, as he pondered the key elements of this function: the attachments that link the watch and strap. The union of the two achieved formal and functional perfection in the Tank, which debuted in 1919, refining concepts first articulated in the Tonneau (1906) and the Tortue (1912). Throughout the firm's watchmaking history, the wristwatch has been a privileged indicator of the radical changes that have swept society. Thus, for example, the radically destructured Crash captures the energy of swinging London in the late 1960s while the massive Pasha de Cartier expresses the 1980s trend toward objects that display taste and power.

BEYOND FASHION

In the 1920s, the growing influence of Jeanne Toussaint—who would be appointed director of fine jewelry in 1933—marked an evolution in Cartier's style, though its fundamentals would never be called into question. "The panther," as Toussaint came to be known, was a woman of elegance, forceful character, and bold taste. With a confident, feminine approach that was groundbreaking for jewelry design at the time, she brought about the reinstatement of figurative elements at Cartier, especially floral and animal motifs. Through her independent turn of mind and visionary grasp of the profound social changes of the period after World War I, she embodied the triumph of the *garçonne*, or flapper, and of modern women in general, with great refinement. With the creation of long *sautoir* necklaces perfectly adapted to straight dresses, she responded aesthetically and functionally to the new silhouettes put forward by her fashion designer friends Jeanne Lanvin, Elsa Schiaparelli, Jean Patou, and Lucien Lelong.

Toussaint also understood and shared the desire of women to assert themselves beyond the dictates of fashion. Influenced by sculpture, she thought up bold, three-dimensional ornaments, either abstract or figurative, that would previously have been inconceivable accessories for women of society. They were manifestos for an emancipated womanhood, freed from constraint, that challenged the narrow limits of "good taste." In 1926 she debuted naturalist brooches featuring wild beasts, such as tigers and panthers that were coiled to jump—and perhaps even bite. The House of Cartier also expressed this new audacity through stunning color combinations that mixed diamonds with emeralds,

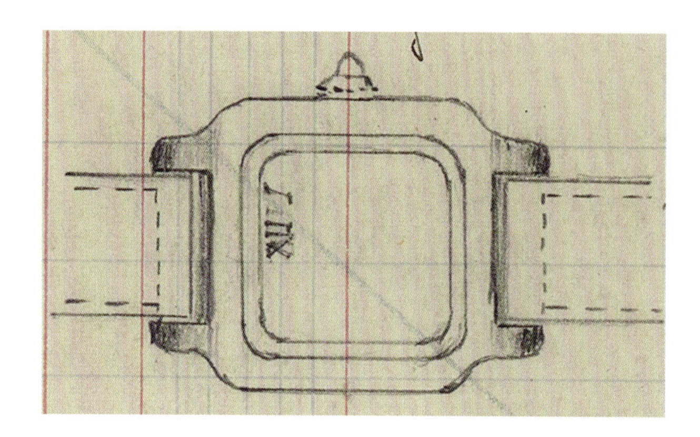

ABOVE Drawing of a Santos watch from a 1911 stock ledger. Cartier Archives.

RIGHT Crash wristwatch, Cartier London, 1967. Cartier Collection.

rubies, and sapphires engraved with floral motifs in the Indian manner. This style, later given the name tutti frutti, overturned the conventions of jewelry design.

This same period saw the launch—in 1924—of one of Cartier's most iconic creations, first popularized by Jean Cocteau: the Trinity ring and bracelet, made of rolling bands of white, rose, and yellow gold. Once again, Cartier had pioneered an innovative and versatile creation, both simple and extremely refined, that responded to a new and very down-to-earth desire: to be able to wear the same piece of elegant jewelry from morning to evening, regardless of the occasion.

It was also in this period and in the same modern spirit that Cartier set the trend for other designers by

OPPOSITE Jeanne Toussaint posing for a style shoot in the 1920s. Cartier Archives.

Jean Cocteau wearing two Trinity rings.
Cartier Archives.

Nail bangle, 1971, designed by Aldo Cipullo for Cartier.
Cartier Collection.

developing multipurpose accessories made from precious materials: letter openers with watches embedded in the handles, calendar pens and watch pens, and even a watch-lighter-pen combination.

MODERN POETRY

Large, bold jewelry that allowed women to assert their individuality remained a Cartier mainstay until at least the 1950s and reappeared in the 1980s with the relative "masculinization" of the executive woman. In the wake of World War II, still under the aegis of Jeanne Toussaint, a further dimension emerged: humor. It reflected the joie de vivre of the postwar era with a satirical note inherited from the Zazous—outrageously dressed jazz aficionados who frequented the basement bars of Saint-Germain-des-Prés in Paris. A similar whimsy found its way into the world of design, notably in George Nelson's Coconut lounge chairs, Verner Panton's classic Panton chair, and Jean Royère's Polar Bear sofa. At Cartier, Toussaint offered clients delightful gold jewelry that was sculpted with imagination and humor: gold was woven, twisted into fine strands or cords, and transformed into mesh and flexible gas-pipe coils. And yet Toussaint never lost the thread of Cartier's distinctive style, with its fluid movement and refined elegance. Even after her departure in 1970, Cartier continued in the same spirit, looking beyond the world of jewelry to find inspiration in everyday life and returning with the nail-shaped bracelet and Love, a flat bangle fastened with a screwdriver—a "handcuff" evoking inseparable love.

Although they emerged from different, specific contexts, the Trinity, Nail, and Love bracelets remain iconic decades later. They offer ample proof that the great emblems of the House of Cartier are less a reflection of their times than of the aesthetic principles that make Cartier creations timeless and universal: refinement and elegance.

OPPOSITE Model wearing Cartier jewelry in the March 15, 1955, issue of *Vogue*. Condé Nast Archive.

MARGARET YOUNG-SÁNCHEZ

ARISTOCRACY AND ASPIRATION

CARTIER IN THE EARLY TWENTIETH CENTURY

IN 1900, PARIS REIGNED AS THE WORLD'S UNDISputed cultural capital, and the House of Cartier, already one of the city's leading luxury firms, was poised to become the most prestigious jeweler of the twentieth century. Despite political turmoil and economic instability throughout the nineteenth century, Paris's cachet as an artistic center never faltered. Painters, sculptors, musicians, and writers gravitated to the city, drawn by its gracious avenues and parks, grandiose monuments, and thriving cultural scene. Travelers from around the world made Paris a destination, seeking to experience the sophistication and pleasure for which the city was famous: "How gay were those years at the turn of the century when in Paris there gathered a cosmopolitan society come from Rome, Berlin, St. Petersburg, Vienna and London, with the sole object of spending money and finding amusement! There were parties every night, and the days were crowded with sightseeing, racing and shopping."[1] The grand Exposition universelle, staged in Paris in 1900, confirmed France as a cultural and commercial epicenter, with splendid new exhibition halls hosting more than fifty nations' displays of agricultural, manufacturing, and artistic achievement. From its premises near the fair, Cartier was determined to capitalize on the presence of millions of visitors and face down foreign competitors such as Tiffany & Co., from the United States, and Russia's House of Fabergé.

Cartier, a family-operated firm founded by Louis-François Cartier in 1847 and taken over by his son Alfred in 1874, aspired to a position of supremacy among Paris jewelers. Alfred's eldest son, Louis (who joined the firm as partner in 1898), and younger sons, Pierre and Jacques, injected new energy and talent, as well as personal charm, into the company. Louis was an innovator whose vision was to play a crucial role in shaping the firm's design philosophy and public image. Pierre became known as a connoisseur of fine stones and also as a talented entrepreneur.

OPPOSITE Olga, Countess Hohenfelsen, wife of Grand Duke Paul Alexandrovich, costumed for the 1912 Hungarian Ball in Paris. She wears a 1908 Cartier diamond-and-pearl corsage ornament on her hat and her 1911 Cartier pear-shaped-diamond tiara across her bodice. Cartier Archives.

Jacques, the youngest son, was both artistically gifted and adept at navigating social and cultural complexity. In 1899 Cartier signaled its ambition by moving to prestigious rue de la Paix, adjacent to the world-famous couturier Worth (long a mecca for fashionable European and American women). In 1902 a second boutique was opened in London (led by Pierre and Jacques until 1906, when Jacques alone took charge); a third store was inaugurated in New York in 1909, under Pierre's supervision.

As all the leading Paris jewelry firms at this time worked with the city's superbly skilled independent manufacturing ateliers, reputation and design were crucial to ensuring that Cartier's creations stood out from the competition. At the turn of the century Cartier counted highly influential individuals among its clientele, including Princess Mathilde (niece of Napoleon Bonaparte) and England's Edward, Prince of Wales, and his wife, Alexandra. Edward, a confirmed Francophile, reputedly bestowed on Cartier the sobriquet "king of jewelers and jeweler of kings." His patronage earned Cartier orders from among those invited to the coronation celebrations following Queen Victoria's death in 1901. In 1904 Edward bestowed a royal warrant on Cartier, an honor repeated by seventeen other royal courts in subsequent decades.

Cartier invitation with the French, American, and British flags symbolizing the house's three historical locations: Paris, New York, and London. Cartier New York, 1919. Cartier Archives.

CARTIER JEWELRY

Garland-style jewelry was initially Cartier's signature product. It perfectly complemented the high-fashion gowns of the day, which featured sumptuous fabrics and close-fitting bodices with low, square necklines. The garland style was in some ways conservative, inspired by the diamond-encrusted jewelry of Louis XVI's eighteenth-century French court. Flowers, leafy branches, and baskets (fig. 1) were popular elements (hence the "garland" descriptor), as were bows (fig. 3), stars, scrolls, and meander patterns. Inspiration was also derived from architectural ornamentation, such as metal balustrades and stone relief carving. References to classical antiquity were popular as well; olive and laurel leaves and berries (fig. 4), wheat sheaves, wreaths, arrows, and the head of Medusa (fig. 2) all appear in Cartier's early twentieth-century jewelry. Even the shape of many tiaras derives from the Roman diadem (a smoothly arched form set in the hair, above the brow), transmitted by way of the French Napoleonic court (fig. 7). The

CLOCKWISE FROM TOP LEFT

1. ***Flower basket* corsage ornament** Cartier New York, 1918. Platinum; hexagonal, half-moon, square-, round old-, and single-cut diamonds; natural pearls. Millegrain setting for the basket, 9.5 × 7.4 × 1.6 cm. Cartier Collection CL 256 A18.

2. ***Head of Medusa* pendant** Cartier Paris, 1906. Platinum, gold, round old- and rose-cut diamonds, natural pearls, "angel skin" coral head and tear-shaped drop, enamel. Millegrain setting, length 39.5 cm. Cartier Collection NE 22 A06.

According to Greek mythology, gazing at the snake-haired Medusa turned a viewer to stone. The goddess Athena carried the image of Medusa's severed head on her shield.

3. ***Lace ribbon* brooch** Cartier Paris, 1906. Platinum; gold; cushion-shaped, marquise-cut, round old-, and rose-cut diamonds. Millegrain and collet settings, 17.1 × 6.5 cm. Cartier Collection CL 144 A06. Sold to Sir Ernest Cassel (1852–1921), a friend and private financial adviser to King Edward VII of England.

4. **Tiara** Cartier Paris, special order, 1907. Platinum, round old-cut diamonds, natural pearls. Millegrain setting, 13.4 × 3.4 cm. Cartier Collection HO 26 A07. Provenance: Princess Marie Bonaparte.

Great-granddaughter of Lucien Bonaparte (one of Napoleon's brothers), Marie Bonaparte (1882–1962) married Prince George of Greece and Denmark before becoming a patient, disciple, friend, and patron of Sigmund Freud. A comb decorated with sprays of flowers was among the jewels made for her wedding. It was later transformed into a tiara.

kokoshnik, or *diadème russe*, also popular at this time, has a slightly different shape, typically rising to a low point in the center (see page 29). It derives its name from a Russian folk headdress originally made of cloth.[2] In addition to tiaras, popular jewelry forms included choker necklaces, large *devant de corsage*, or "stomacher," brooches (fig. 5) worn on the bodice, and pendant watches.

Characterized by exquisite detail and decoration that was lavish without being excessive, Cartier's jewelry from this era was in no way a trite revival of earlier traditions. New materials contributed to its appeal, including an abundance of high-quality diamonds from South Africa (mined since the 1870s) and a newly adequate supply of platinum, a nontarnishing white metal that is both strong and ductile. Its use was a rather daring choice for Cartier, for at the time the metal was more associated with science and industry than with jewelry.[3] It was not officially designated as a precious metal in France until 1912. And working with platinum required special skills. Its payoff, however, lay in jewel settings of unparalleled lightness and transparency

Back view of stomacher brooch shown on facing page.

Tiara design drawing. Cartier Paris, 1908. Cartier Archives.

OPPOSITE 5. **Stomacher brooch** Cartier Paris, special order, 1907. Platinum, sapphires, round old- and rose-cut diamonds. Millegrain setting, 21 × 12.9 cm. Cartier Collection CL 292 A07.

The central elements are hinged for flexibility, while the hanging components at the sides can be detached and worn independently of the brooch.

(fig. 9) that contrasted with the slightly heavier look of jewels made of gold topped with silver (fig. 6). Cartier jewels frequently incorporated older gemstones in a variety of historic cuts, but the firm also supplied new stones—improved faceting techniques in the early 1900s enhanced diamonds' brilliance and fire, characteristics intensified by open-backed platinum millegrain settings (in which a band of metal encircles the stone, held in place by a series of tool indentations that resemble fine beads). The effect, especially in the bright electric lighting then becoming popular, was scintillating (see figs. 14–16, page 33).

Although normally hidden from view, the back of a Cartier jewel can be almost as impressive as the front (see page 23 top). The setting's skeletal platinum armature may be constructed from dozens of individually built elements, meticulously hinged together to create a supple ornament that conforms to the body of the wearer. Many jewels were designed with separable components to provide the client with maximum versatility: removal of a tiara's frame allowed it to be worn as a necklace or bodice ornament; pendants could be converted to brooches; and necklace sections could sometimes be removed for wear as bracelets.

OPPOSITE, TOP 6. ***Scroll* tiara** Cartier Paris, special order, 1902. Silver; gold; cushion-shaped, round old-, and rose-cut diamonds. Millegrain setting, height at center 8.1 cm. Cartier Collection HO 08 A02. Sold to the Countess of Essex.

Unlike much Cartier jewelry of the early twentieth century, this tiara is made of gold topped with silver, the whiteness of which enhances the diamonds.

OPPOSITE, BOTTOM 7. **Tiara** Cartier Paris, 1908. Platinum, pear-shaped and round old-cut diamonds, natural pearls. "Muguet" setting for the swinging pear-shaped diamonds, height at center 5 cm. Cartier Collection HO 03 A08.

The hanging diamonds represent one of the earliest examples of the "muguet" (lily of the valley) setting, in which a delicate rim of platinum holds a large brilliant surrounded by several tightly packed diamonds to create the impression of a single stone.

ABOVE LEFT 8. ***Bow* brooch** Cartier Paris, 1913. Platinum, rose-cut and old European-cut diamonds, carved rock crystal. Millegrain and collet settings, 10.8 × 10.8 cm. Private collection.

ABOVE RIGHT Design drawing of a bow brooch. Cartier Archives.

Pearls were another favorite gem in garland-style jewelry, appearing in necklace chains (fig. 10) and bands for the neck or wrist, and incorporated into tiaras, pendants, and brooches (see fig. 1, page 21). The pearls of this era were natural and extremely valuable: according to renowned gemologist G. F. Kunz, in 1908 pearls were four times more valuable than diamonds by weight.[4] A high-quality, well-matched strand of pearls could take years to assemble. American car manufacturer Horace Dodge paid $825,000 for a magnificent strand in 1920,[5] a sum worth perhaps $18,000,000 today. In 1917, Pierre and Louis Cartier exchanged two fabulous pearl necklaces (along with $100) for a Fifth Avenue mansion owned by Mr. and Mrs. Morton Plant, then turned it into Cartier's New York headquarters.[6] Famous historic pearls once owned by European queens and empresses were especially prized: a pearl necklace that had belonged to Marie de Médicis was among the jewels presented to Anna Gould (daughter of robber baron Jay Gould) as a wedding present when she married French count Paul Ernest Boniface (Boni) de Castellane in 1895. Alva Vanderbilt owned pearl necklaces that reputedly once graced the necks of Russia's Catherine the Great and France's Marie Antoinette and Empress Eugénie.[7]

Drawing for a marble plaque for the front of Cartier's New York boutique. Cartier Archives.

Cartier also made innovative use of rock crystal in its jewelry. Carved and engraved, it could accept platinum mounts set with diamonds (fig. 8),

ABOVE 9. **Hair ornament** Cartier Paris, 1902. Platinum, old- and rose-cut diamonds. Millegrain setting, height at center 7 cm. Cartier Collection HO 25 A02. Provenance: Mrs. William Field.

Lila Vanderbilt Field (born Sloane, 1878–1934) was the great-granddaughter of Cornelius Vanderbilt and a cousin of William K. Vanderbilt II and Consuelo Vanderbilt, Duchess of Marlborough. The piece is articulated to achieve an exact fit.

OPPOSITE 10. **Necklace** Cartier Paris, special order, 1911. Platinum, round old- and rose-cut diamonds, natural pearls. Millegrain setting, length 45 cm. Cartier Collection NE 05 A11.

The largest pearl weighs 107.60 grains.

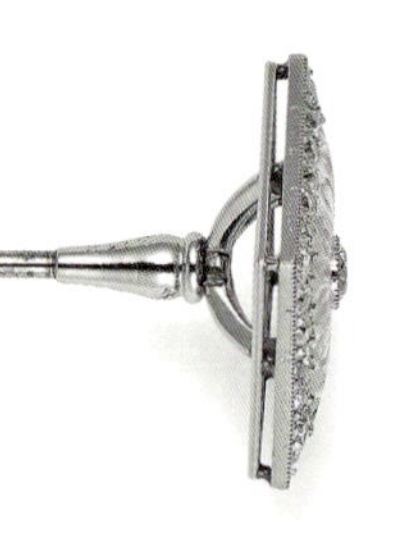

CLOCKWISE FROM TOP LEFT

11. **Gentleman's dress set: cuff links, waistcoat buttons, shirt studs** Cartier, about 1920. Platinum, carved rock crystal, diamonds. Diameter of buttons and cuff links, 1.3 cm. Private collection.

12. **Pendant** Cartier Paris, 1912. Platinum, round old- and rose-cut diamonds, two star sapphire cabochons, round and drop-shaped natural pearls, carved rock crystal. Millegrain setting, 11.5 × 4.5 cm. Cartier Collection NE 11 A12.

This is one of Cartier's first works in rock crystal. Two profile faun heads carved in rock crystal can be seen on either side of the pendant. The central section can be unscrewed and worn as a brooch.

13. **Hat pin** Cartier Paris, 1912. Platinum, carved rock crystal, round old-cut diamond, single-cut diamonds. Length 12 cm. Cartier Collection JA 18 A12.

Rock crystal, diamond, and platinum tiara made by Cartier Paris for Baron Pierre de Gunzburg in 1912. Private collection. Courtesy Sotheby's, London.

emeralds, or sapphires (fig. 12). It was used for simple items such as hat pins (fig. 13) or cuff links and studs (fig. 11), but was also incorporated into brooches, pendants, and even tiaras, including the famous example owned by Russian princess Irina Youssoupova—which was hidden during the Russian Revolution but later discovered, confiscated, and perhaps destroyed[8]—and another even more elaborate tiara made for Baron Pierre de Gunzburg in 1912 (above).

CARTIER'S CLIENTS

Cartier's elegant designs and its expansion to London and New York positioned the firm to take advantage of a market for precious jewelry and other luxury goods that was also in a process of transformation. Nineteenth-century industrialization, growing international trade, and the large-scale, widespread construction of public infrastructure (for transportation, shipping, communications, and the like) generated global economic growth and concentrated vast new wealth in the hands of businessmen and financiers throughout the world. In Europe this phenomenon threatened to undermine aristocratic power and privilege, founded as they were on hereditary rank and land ownership. Some wealthy individuals were granted knighthoods or other titles—German-born English merchant banker Sir Ernest Cassel and Dutch oil executive Sir Henri Deterding among them.[9]

The traditional rulers of India, whose territories had by then been incorporated into the British Empire and who had been relieved of many of their responsibilities of governance, retained their rank and much of their wealth well into the 1900s. Improved transportation allowed them to travel regularly to London and Paris and absorb the latest

Mrs. Cornelius (Grace) Vanderbilt III, about 1909, wearing a Cartier diamond necklace and tiara. Her nineteenth-century Rose brooch, once owned by Princess Mathilde, was bought at Cartier in 1904. Cartier Archives.

fashion trends. Jacques Cartier traveled to India on several occasions to sell directly to the Indian courts. The relationships he formed there stood the firm in good stead, resulting in lavish commissions. In addition, Indian gem dealers became an important source of precious stones and pearls for Cartier. The newly affluent in America cast about for appropriate means of spending and displaying their riches—both to demonstrate their status aspirations and (at least ostensibly) to elevate the cultural level of American society. The homes, possessions, and lifestyle of Europe's aristocracy (observed during socially obligatory European travel) provided the preferred model for emulation. Splendid jewelry, once the prerogative of kings and courtiers, was now flaunted by the world's newly rich, especially Americans. Tiaras,

Plaster cast for Grace Vanderbilt's necklace, 1908. Cartier Archives.

necklaces, and stomachers were ordered by the likes of Gertrude Vanderbilt Whitney, Grace Vanderbilt (opposite), and Nancy Leeds, wife of a tin-mining industrialist (see fig. 21, page 38). Though most of this sumptuous jewelry has not survived (when fashions changed, jewels were commonly disassembled so that the stones could be remounted), exquisite survivors include several pieces once owned by Mary Scott Townsend, whose father made a fortune in coal and railroads. Mrs. Townsend, a prominent hostess, entertained in a stately Louis XVI–style home in Washington, D.C. In 1905 and 1906, she purchased a dazzling tiara with delicate floral scrolls and large, vertically mounted pear-shaped diamonds (fig. 14); an exquisite choker necklace composed of delicate curves of diamond flowers, leaves, and beads (fig. 15); and a ravishing floral corsage ornament (fig. 16). Designed as two crossed sprays of lilies intertwined with a garland of eglantines, the ornament is completely articulated and flexible, so that it could be manipulated to conform to the outline of the bodice.

To the dismay of some, many of the nouveaux riches were not content merely to emulate Europe's aristocracy—they aspired to join its ranks. Consuelo Vanderbilt's marriage to the Duke of Marlborough in 1895 is today the most famous example of a transatlantic marital alliance between American wealth and European rank, but she was far from the first or the last. By 1900, some fifty American women were included in the British peerage.[10] King Edward VII facilitated the integration process, even before taking the crown in 1902. As the court's social leader during the later years of his mother, Victoria, the sociable prince welcomed wealthy Americans to court, personally befriending several. Though not a snob with regard to nationality or inherited rank, Edward was a stickler for some aspects of protocol. Formal presentation at court followed strict rules, among them the wearing of trains and ostrich-feather head ornaments. Formal dress, including a tiara, was obligatory at dinners. According to Consuelo Vanderbilt,

Archive photograph of a *résille* necklace made for Queen Alexandra in platinum and diamonds, with detachable ruby and emerald cabochon drops. She wears it in a 1908 formal portrait (see page 226). Cartier Paris, 1904. Cartier Archives.

Edward once chastised her for wearing a diamond crescent rather than a tiara. She excused herself by saying that because of a travel delay she could not reach her bank, where the tiara was stored, before its closing time.[11] In 1904 Queen Alexandra purchased a spectacular necklace. Called a *résille* (hairnet) necklace, it consisted of a supple network of diamonds with a large central stone and a removable fringe of cabochon rubies and emeralds (above and see page 226).

The Russian imperial court (and its exiled or vacationing members in Paris) was another important source of business. Grand Duchess Maria Pavlovna and her husband, Grand Duke Vladimir Alexandrovich (one of Tsar Nicholas II's uncles), were especially influential. Vladimir headed Russia's Imperial Academy of Arts and later became a patron of Sergei Diaghilev; his wife's salons were

ABOVE LEFT AND RIGHT Drawing and archive photograph of a stomacher brooch made for Maria Pavlovna, Grand Duchess Vladimir, in platinum, diamonds, and sapphires. Cartier Paris, 1910. Cartier Archives.

St. Petersburg's leading social events. Maria Pavlovna ordered numerous jewels from Cartier, including a diamond-and-pearl choker necklace with double-headed imperial eagles and a dazzling *kokoshnik*-style diamond tiara for her daughter Elena's marriage to Prince Nicholas of Greece and Denmark. A 1913 painting of Maria Pavlovna depicts her wearing magnificent sapphire-and-diamond jewelry, including a *kokoshnik* tiara and a stomacher brooch by Cartier (above).[12] She reportedly urged Cartier to set up a permanent boutique in St. Petersburg. Financial commitments to the new branch in New York, as well as Russia's precarious political climate (signaled by the 1911 assassination of Prime Minister Stolypin) and the murder of two Boucheron representatives on their way to Moscow, dissuaded Cartier from this venture.[13]

Astute businessmen with a flair for tasteful publicity, the Cartier brothers made a point of honoring the rank (and vanity) of their clients. The firm publicly displayed the jewels ordered for Princess Marie Bonaparte's marriage to Prince George of Greece and Denmark in 1907 (fig. 17 and page 35 left), and, later, Grand Duchess Maria Pavlovna's pearl necklace with double-headed eagles. When establishing the New

OPPOSITE, TOP TO BOTTOM

14. **Tiara** Cartier Paris, special order, 1905. Platinum, pear-shaped diamonds weighing approximately 17 carats in total, old- and rose-cut diamonds. Millegrain setting, height at center 6.6 cm. Cartier Collection HO 09 A05. Provenance: Mary Scott Townsend and Mrs. Donald McElroy.

The original owner of this tiara, Mary Scott Townsend, was an eminent member of Washington's high society at the turn of the twentieth century. Thora Ronalds McElroy (1907–1990) was her great-niece.

15. **Choker necklace** Cartier Paris, special order, 1906. Platinum, round old-cut diamonds. Millegrain setting, 33 × 5.4 cm. Cartier Collection NE 39 A06. Provenance: Mary Scott Townsend and Mrs. Donald McElroy.

16. ***Lily* stomacher brooch** Cartier Paris, special order, 1906. Platinum, round old- and rose-cut diamonds. Millegrain setting, each branch 27 cm. Cartier Collection CL 134 A06. Provenance: Mary Scott Townsend and Mrs. Donald McElroy.

The setting of curved surfaces gives the brooch a three-dimensional feel. The pistils of the flowers are adorned with tiny diamonds.

Princess Marie Bonaparte's jewels (ordered for her wedding) on display at Cartier Paris in 1907. The laurel leaf tiara opposite is shown at the top of the case. Cartier Archives.

Evalyn Walsh McLean wearing the Hope diamond and the Star of the East diamond, which she had mounted as an aigrette in 1908. According to McLean, she wore both jewels at a dinner for forty-eight that she hosted in Washington, D.C., in 1912. The cost of the event was $40,000, much of it for imported orchids and lilies. Harry & Ewing, Cartier Archives.

York branch, Louis sought the support of J. P. Morgan (one of America's wealthiest and most powerful men), already a Paris customer. They formed a personal friendship, and Morgan guided and encouraged Louis in collecting art.[14] In 1911 the London branch mounted an extremely popular exhibition of tiaras in conjunction with King George V's coronation as a fund-raiser for the Middlesex Hospital (a charity supported by Queen Mary).[15] In addition, the firm gained worldwide renown as a purveyor of great, historic gems such as the 94.8-carat Star of the East diamond and the legendary 45.52-carat blue Hope diamond, both of which were sold to Evalyn Walsh McLean (in 1908 and 1912, respectively). Evalyn (above right) was the daughter of a wealthy Colorado gold miner; her husband's family owned the *Washington Post*. She purchased the Star of the East mounted in a necklace for about $120,000 while on her honeymoon in Paris. "'After all,' I said to Ned, 'this is really an investment. Besides... I can tell my father it's a double gift to cover both my wedding and Christmas.'"[16] The Hope diamond is reputed to have cost McLean $154,000 or more.[17]

Considerable attention was paid to the "customer experience" at Cartier as well, from the tasteful decor of each branch, with private rooms for special clients, to the custom-made stamped-leather cases in which Cartier items were delivered. Customers could choose from a wide array of stock items at all price points; these sometimes included Cartier's most daring designs. Or they could work with the firm's in-house designers to create a special order, frequently incorporating the client's own jewels. Such pieces were often

OPPOSITE 17. ***Laurel leaf* tiara** Cartier Paris, 1907. Platinum, diamonds. Millegrain setting, 19 × 6 cm. Qatar Museums Authority.

This tiara was among the jewels ordered by Marie Bonaparte for her wedding and publicly displayed by Cartier.

The famous dancer and courtesan Carolina "La Belle" Otero.
RMN—Grand Palais/Art Resource, NY.

rather conservative in style, reflecting clients' taste. Cartier salesmen were polished, knowledgeable, and discreet (highly important in an era when wealthy men were accustomed to bestowing valuable gifts on female entertainers, such as performers Lillie Langtry, Lina Cavalieri, and Carolina "La Belle" Otero, opposite). Some of the senior salesmen, including Alfred Buisson in Paris and Jules Glaenzer in New York, were well-known social fixtures, driven about town by chauffeurs and invited to exclusive parties.

CARTIER'S DECORATIVE OBJECTS AND TIMEPIECES

Since its founding, Cartier's repertoire has extended beyond jewelry: they retailed pocket and pendant watches, chatelaines (a lady's accessory designed to hold objects such as keys, a watch, scissors, and the like on chains suspended from a hook or clasp), cane tops, umbrella handles, and even silver services. In the early twentieth century, some of Cartier's accessories and decorative objects were designed to compete directly with those of Fabergé, which was renowned for its intricate, exquisitely detailed enameled Easter egg presentation pieces made for the Russian imperial family. Cartier began to produce gold, enamel, and hardstone cigarette cases, as well as carved hardstone animal figurines (figs. 18, 19, and 20). J. P. Morgan purchased several hardstone plants, likely similar to the hydrangea seen on page 38 (fig. 22). Other popular desk and tabletop items produced by Cartier included ornate picture frames, lorgnettes, bell pushes, writing sets, perfume burners (fig. 24), barometers (fig. 23), calendars, and other devices. Queen Alexandra of Great Britain bought a baroque-style gold picture frame with red and blue enameling around 1905, reputedly as a gift for a goddaughter. J. P. Morgan acquired an elegant neoclassical enameled desk clock (fig. 26) in 1905 and a similarly colored picture frame two years later.[18] A very imposing gold frame (fig. 21) was purchased by Nancy Leeds in 1910. A decade later (after her husband's death and the inheritance of a huge fortune) Nancy married Prince Christopher of Greece and Denmark, thus achieving authentic royal status; she took the name Princess Anastasia of Greece and Denmark.

LEFT TO RIGHT

18. Pig Cartier, about 1905. Carved rhodonite, gold, rose-cut diamonds. 4.1 × 3.1 × 7.1 cm. Cartier Collection AN 16 C05.

19. Rabbit Cartier, about 1904. Carved amethyst, ruby cabochons, silver, rose-cut diamonds. 3.6 × 2.1 × 3.9 cm. Cartier Collection AN 12 C04.

20. Chick Cartier, about 1906. Carved gray agate, white chalcedony, chased gold, rose-cut diamonds. 5 × 4.6 × 3.8 cm. Cartier Collection AN 06 C06.

22. **Hydrangea** Cartier Paris, 1910. Gold, stainless metal, mauve enameled glass paste (flowers), aventurine (leaves), moonstone cabochons (dewdrops), agate (pot), rose-cut diamonds, wood, ivory, glass. 18.2 × 13.7 × 13.7 cm. Cartier Collection FL 05 A10. Sold to Pierre Cartier.

21. **Frame** Cartier Paris, 1910. Pink and green gold, silver, buff-top *calibré*-cut sapphires, carved rock crystal, natural pearls. Monogram *WBL*. 32 × 24 cm. Cartier Collection PF 15 A10. Sold to Mrs. W. B. Leeds.

The frame holds a photograph of Nancy Leeds (modern print). She wears a tiara surmounted by seven diamonds created by Cartier in 1913. Born May Stewart (1878–1923), she first married banker George Worthington. Divorced five years later, she remarried tin magnate William Bateman Leeds. Widowed in 1908, Nancy Leeds became an important Cartier jewelry client. In 1910 she made the news by buying a Cartier necklace of pearls and diamond rondelles for $570,000. Her third marriage, in 1920, was to Prince Christopher of Greece and Denmark.

LEFT 23. **Barometer** Cartier, 1908. Silver, gold, silver-gilt, enamel. Diameter 7.8 cm. Cartier Collection IO 35 A08. Originally with ivory at the back.

CENTER 24. **Perfume burner** Cartier Paris, 1907. Aventurine (urn and stopper), silver-gilt, enamel, sapphire cabochons. 13.1 × 5.6 cm. Cartier Collection FK 16 A07.

RIGHT 25. **Desk clock with minute repeater** Cartier Paris, 1909. Platinum, gold, silver, agate, enamel, sapphire cabochons, moonstone, rose-cut diamonds. Rectangular 8-day movement, minute repeater, gold-plated, Swiss lever escapement, bimetallic balance, Breguet balance spring; hand-setting and winding mechanism, 13.5 × 8.8 × 6.1 cm. Cartier Collection CR 11 A09.

Minute repeaters are mechanically sophisticated. When the moonstone button is depressed, the clock chimes the hour, quarter hour, and minutes.

In the 1890s Cartier also sold pocket watches by a number of makers, including Vacheron Constantin. Louis Cartier was reportedly the prime mover in the Cartier firm's decision at the end of the decade to create a new specialty in fine clock- and watchmaking, a deliberate effort to revive France's earlier greatness in this field.[19] Working with numerous specialized or exclusive Paris workshops that produced the movements, faces, cases, and other decorative elements, Cartier began designing inventive and colorful desk clocks (fig. 25). Special features included indications of the days of the week and the months, rotating dials, and diamond motifs such as stars to mark the hours and minutes. Eye-catching materials included engine-turned metal covered with colored enamel, agate, onyx, nephrite, and rock crystal. The first of Cartier's famous "mystery clocks" was produced in 1912; one was sold to J. P. Morgan Jr. in December 1913.[20] These clocks have transparent dials in which the hands appear to be suspended and move without any visible mechanism. The early examples had rock crystal dials and cases and restrained neoclassical decoration. (The design remained popular for decades: an example with mother-of-pearl inlay was sold to Evalyn Walsh McLean in 1927; see fig. 63, page 68).

Cartier's early twentieth-century ladies' watches were produced in flat, ball-shaped, or egg-shaped models with lovely colored-enamel cases (fig. 27) that hung from a black cord, a ribbon (fig. 30), or a chain

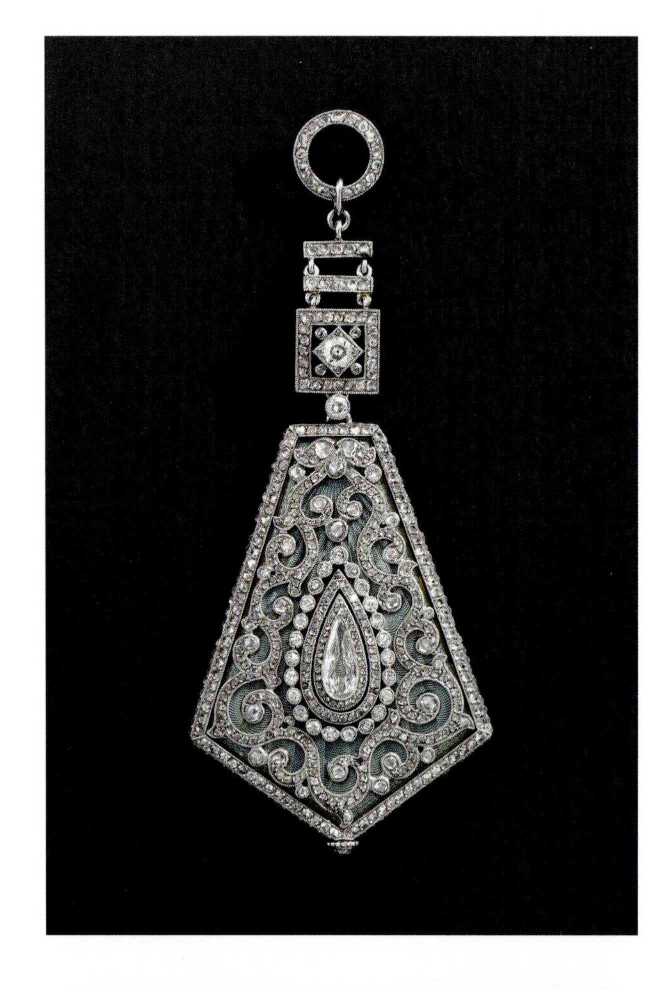

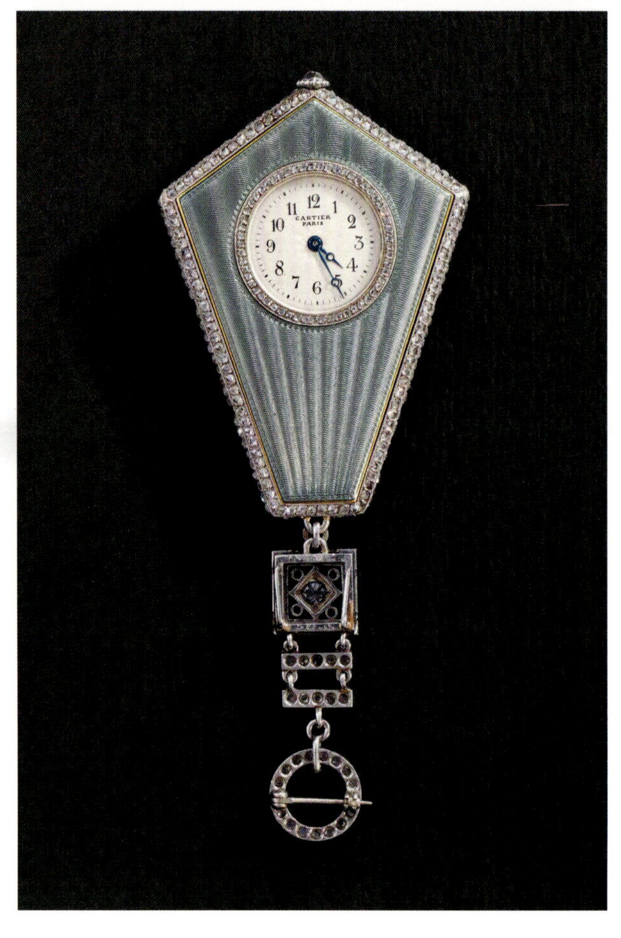

ABOVE 26. **Clock with strut (in the style of a Louis XVI wall clock)** Cartier Paris, 1904. Chased gold, platinum, silver-gilt, ivory plaque, rose-cut diamonds, enamel. Round 8-day movement, gold-plated, 15 jewels, Swiss lever escapement, bimetallic balance, Breguet balance spring. 18.5 × 2.5 × 7.3 cm. Cartier Collection, CO 16 A04. Sold to John Pierpont Morgan.

J. P. Morgan (1837–1913) was one of America's wealthiest and most powerful financiers and a discerning collector of art, books and manuscripts, and gems.

RIGHT 27. **Pendant/Lapel watch** Cartier Paris, 1911. Platinum; gold; translucent steel-gray enamel over guilloche gold ground; pear-shaped, round old-, and rose-cut diamonds. Millegrain setting. Breguet hands in blued steel. Length 9 cm. Chas Schwartz & Son.

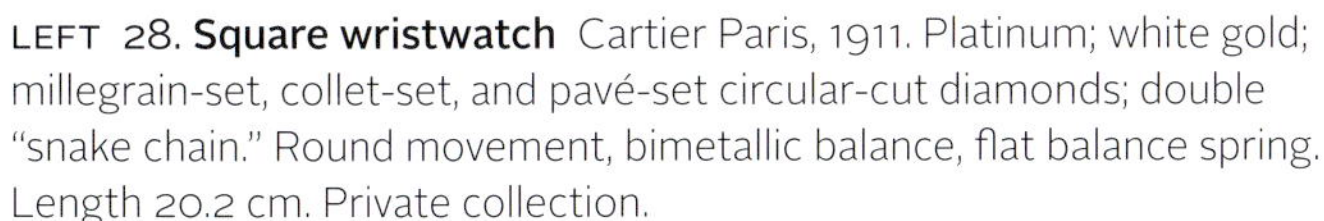

LEFT 28. **Square wristwatch** Cartier Paris, 1911. Platinum; white gold; millegrain-set, collet-set, and pavé-set circular-cut diamonds; double "snake chain." Round movement, bimetallic balance, flat balance spring. Length 20.2 cm. Private collection.

CENTER 29. **Bracelet-watch** Cartier Paris, 1911. Platinum, rose-cut and collet-set single-cut diamonds. Round LeCoultre movement, *fausses* Côtes de Genève decoration, rhodium-plated, 8 adjustments, 18 jewels, Swiss lever escapement, bimetallic balance, Breguet balance spring. Length 16.1 cm. Cartier Collection WWL 48 A11.

RIGHT 30. **Lapel watch** Cartier Paris, 1913. Platinum case with matte gold back ornamented with rose-cut diamonds set in platinum, platinum and diamond brooch, sliding belt-buckle motif, suspension loops, moiré ribbon. Rectangular with cut corners Jaeger-LeCoultre 113 movement, Côtes de Genève decoration, rhodium-plated, 8 adjustments, 19 jewels, Swiss lever escapement, bimetallic balance. Pendant length 4.5 cm. Private collection.

of enamel, diamonds, and pearls. Bracelet watches had cases framed with diamonds (fig. 28) and straps of black ribbon, woven seed pearls, or platinum mesh trimmed with diamonds (fig. 29). Men's pocket watches were made in numerous styles, including novel models with rock crystal cases or ultraflat movements hidden inside a gold coin. Cartier also pioneered the modern man's wristwatch, made for the convenience of active individuals such as aviator Alberto Santos-Dumont (see fig. 178, page 168). Featuring simple gold or platinum cases and plain leather straps, these models transformed watch aesthetics and heralded a new lifestyle.

THE BALLETS RUSSES ERA

The year 1909 witnessed the first Paris performances of the Ballets Russes, landmark cultural events with far-reaching repercussions for dance, music, and set design, as well as interior decoration, fashion, and jewelry. Produced by the magnetic Russian impresario Sergei Diaghilev, the ballets were an intoxicating mix of avant-garde music and dance, vivid color, exoticism, and eroticism. Story lines of some of the 1909 productions (*Armida's Pavilion*, *Polovtsian Dances*, and *Cleopatra*) refer back to fantastic imagined versions of seventeenth-century France, medieval Central Asia, and ancient Egypt. Attended by Paris's cultural elite (Marcel Proust, Auguste Rodin, and Odilon Redon, among others),[21] the performances were received with rapturous enthusiasm. Equally sensational were *The Blue God* and *Afternoon of a Faun* in 1912 and *The Rite of Spring* in 1913.

Perhaps the most influential work, at least with regard to popular culture, was *Scheherazade*, performed in 1910 with music by Nikolai Rimsky-Korsakov

Léon Bakst stage design for the Ballets Russes production of *Scheherazade*. Gouache and watercolor with gold highlights on paper, 1910. Musée des arts décoratifs, Paris.

Aquamarine aigrette belonging to Olga, Countess Hohenfelsen (later Princess Paley). Olga and her husband, Grand Duke Paul Alexandrovich, supplied the aquamarines for the aigrette and the matching necklace and *devant de corsage*. Courtesy Sotheby's.

and choreography by Michel Fokine and featuring dancers Ida Rubinstein, Vaslav Nijinsky, and Tamara Karsavina. The erotic, luridly violent story involves a jealous Persian ruler who discovers that his favorite wife is unfaithful and orders the slaughter of the entire court, including his wife. Léon Bakst's set (opposite) depicted an oriental seraglio with billowing green curtains, huge hanging lanterns, and tiled walls and floors. The dancers wore pantaloons of brilliantly colored patterned fabrics, midriff-baring tops, and multiple strands of pearls.

The effect of the *Scheherazade* performances was amplified by publicity in fashionable magazines such as *Comœdia illustré* and quickly inspired new trends in interior design, fashion, and jewelry. Couturier Paul Poiret responded by designing clothing with rich, colorful fabrics, tapered skirts, flaring "lampshade" blouses, and turbans. Cartier created new colored-stone jewelry, including a staggering 478-carat vivid blue sapphire that was set as a pendant, with a delicate diamond-and-platinum mounting (fig. 31). Cartier also created stunning aigrettes (head ornaments made to hold feather plumes) set with huge diamonds[22] to be worn with the era's exotic ensembles. In June 1911, Poiret and his wife, Denise, hosted a lavish "Thousand and Second Night" party for some three hundred guests, who were encouraged to attend in Persian costumes. The event's success, chronicled in the press, triggered a spate of costume parties.

The era's height of extravagance was likely the Thousand and One Nights Ball, a costume party and dinner for twelve hundred people at the Paris residence of Countess Aynard de Chabrillan on May 29, 1912. The spectacular event was reported in the *New York Times* and lived on in the ecstatic memories of Gabriel-Louis Pringué.[23] Léon Bakst painted the house's tented entrance court with frescoes of a Persian palace, and one of the guests, Spanish prince Luís Fernando de Orleans y Borbón, wore the Blue God costume from the Ballets Russes production of the same name. Guests arrived in an array of exotic costumes and extravagant jewels. "The most striking entrance was that of the Princess d'Arenberg, who was on an elephant richly bedecked with Indian trappings."[24] Other noblewomen arrived in golden cages or dressed as ancient Egyptians.

Costumed guests at the Thousand and One Nights Ball in Paris, May 1912. *L'Illustration*, July 27, 1912, pages 60–61. Prince Luís Fernando de Orleans y Borbón appears at upper left. The hostess, Countess Aynard de Chabrillan, is second from right, upper row. Mary Evans Picture Library.

Some of the guests (reportedly "nearly everyone prominent in Paris society," including Cartier clients such as the Aga Khan and the Maharaja of Kapurthala) had their photographs taken in costume; an assortment was published in both *Femina* and *L'Illustration* magazines (opposite).

About a month after this event, Russian grand duke Paul Alexandrovich (an uncle of Tsar Nicholas II) and his wife, Olga (see page 18), took possession of a magnificent, specially commissioned Cartier diamond, aquamarine, and platinum jewelry suite that is strongly evocative of the era (the couple supplied the aquamarines). Most spectacular is the oriental-style aigrette with intertwined diamond flowers and vines and two huge aquamarines (see page 43).

The opulent, heady world inhabited by Cartier's clients was brought to an abrupt end by the outbreak of World War I and the unfolding of the Russian Revolution. Sons of the English and European nobility were among those who fought and died in the ruinous war that engulfed the Continent. National boundaries were redefined, royal and imperial families were deposed, and the aristocracy lost much of its wealth and privilege. Consuelo Vanderbilt and other society ladies devoted energy (and funding) to causes such as medical care for the wounded and refugee relief. A successful charity campaign initiated by Vanderbilt and headquartered at Cartier's in London in 1917 solicited the donation of jewels to be sold for the benefit of children.[25] In Russia, Grand Duke Paul's palace was commandeered by the Bolsheviks, and the family's jewels, placed in a bank for safekeeping, were confiscated (as were the Russian crown jewels). Both the grand duke and his son Vladimir were executed by the revolutionaries in 1919. Paul's wife, Olga (now Princess Paley), and her two daughters escaped from Russia; the Cartier aquamarine and diamond suite are the only important jewels of hers known to have survived.

31. **Pendant** Cartier Paris, 1913. Platinum, 478-carat sapphire, diamonds. Qatar Museums Authority. Purchased by King Ferdinand of Romania in 1921.

The Cartier firm's business was drastically affected by both the war and the Russian Revolution. The enormous sapphire pendant made by the house in 1913 (fig. 31) did not find a buyer in the years of turmoil. It was finally purchased in 1921 by King Ferdinand of Romania for his wife, Marie (see page 71 left), who had lost many of her jewels to the Bolsheviks. More personally, brothers Pierre and Jacques Cartier both served in the French military; Louis was appointed to a position in the Red Cross.[26] All three survived the war, and Cartier went on to thrive in the 1920s. But the world that emerged from the trauma and devastation of the Great War was profoundly altered—its class structure shaken, its technology and economy in transition, and its social norms (especially for women) very much in flux.

MARTIN CHAPMAN

NEW OUTLOOK

ART DECO 1918–1939

THE PERIOD BETWEEN THE TWO WORLD WARS proved to be one of Cartier's greatest moments. Having already established its reputation internationally through its stores in London and New York, Cartier became the byword for "jewelry" in the 1920s and 1930s and *the* place for the rich and famous to shop. In the popular novel *Gentlemen Prefer Blondes*, published in 1925, Cartier was the only jeweler for the gold-digging flapper heroine, Lorelei Lee. She mentions it—and no other jeweler—ten times in her "diary" (see page 48). On a different level, the leading status of the jeweler was borne out by its impressive clientele. Eminent Americans were devoted customers during these years. Figures from high society ranged from actress Gloria Swanson (see page 51) and decorator Elsie de Wolfe to the more stately Marjorie Merriweather Post (see page 228)—all of whom, incidentally, were independent women with their own fortunes. Americans dominated the new order of society between the two wars, and for Cartier they almost eclipsed the crowned heads of Europe and the Edwardian newly rich who had been the firm's principal customers before World War 1.

In 1919, the House of Cartier restructured its organizational model, making the New York and London branches legally independent of Paris (although cooperation was extensive). Each branch was directed by a different brother (Louis in Paris, Pierre in New York, and Jacques in London), with designs that responded to local tastes.[1] As business volume expanded and the pace of modern life quickened, Cartier needed the capacity to fill orders quickly and cater to local preferences. Cartier New York enlarged its previously small local workshop in 1917 and again in 1925; Cartier London opened an in-house workshop in 1922; Cartier Paris founded its own workshop in 1929.[2] Some of the craftsmen and designers in New York and London came from Paris, however, enabling all three branches to maintain uniformly high standards of both workmanship and design.

OPPOSITE Actress and model Alden Gay wearing Cartier jewels, photographed by Edward Steichen. Condé Nast Archive.

Lorelei Lee and an admirer shopping for jewelry on the rue de la Paix, Paris. Illustration by Ralph Barton from Anita Loos's serialized novel *Gentlemen Prefer Blondes*, 1925.

Cartier adapted its designs to suit a changing society in the 1920s. Abandoning the line of white diamond jewelry in the delicate Louis XVI style so popular on both sides of the Atlantic before the war, the jewelry firm looked to fashion for its new direction. This in a way was nothing new for Cartier, which since the turn of the century had been closely associated with the couture house of Worth by marriage[3] and proximity—Worth's premises were next door on rue de la Paix (see page 66). But in this new era, under the direction of Louis Cartier the firm took a fresher approach, bringing in abstract geometric forms, stylized ornamentation (often in the form of flowers and fruit), and brilliant color (opposite, top). Striking and unusual color combinations of blue sapphires, green emeralds, orange coral, and black onyx (figs. 32 and 33) started to appear at Cartier and were the keynotes of the period.

The fashions of the 1920s, which included tubular silhouettes, short skirts, and cropped hair, demanded new forms of jewelry. Designer Charles Jacqueau took the lead in evolving these more modern designs, which appeared at Cartier in the form of buckle brooches to accentuate low-waisted dresses (fig. 40), long *sautoirs* (fig. 34) hanging down the décolletage, brooches for the bodice (figs. 35, 36, and 37), and hat pins to secure cloches (fig. 38). Novel elements of these jewels include graduated-pearl tassels and rock crystal or onyx geometric shapes (see page 52 top and bottom right). Sapphires, rubies, and emeralds provided colorful accents. Sleeveless frocks demanded bracelets (often worn in multiples); Cartier produced geometrically patterned examples in cabochon and faceted colored stones as well as diamonds (figs. 43 and 44). One bracelet features a rock crystal bowl filled with ruby-bead fruit (fig. 42). Long pendant earrings (fig. 41) complemented short hairstyles, and the bandeau generally replaced the grandest form of jewelry, the tiara. The bandeau was worn low on the brow rather than on top of the head and was often decorated with geometric patterns rather than leaves and scrolls (fig. 45 and see page 55 top). The overall characteristics of Cartier's designs, however, were—as always—restraint and a lightness of touch, with delicate forms and mounts with pavé-set diamonds.

As fashions changed in the 1930s, Cartier's jewelry forms adapted as well. Couture's slim, slinky silhouette called for short necklaces (fig. 49) rather than dangling *sautoirs* and for clip brooches that

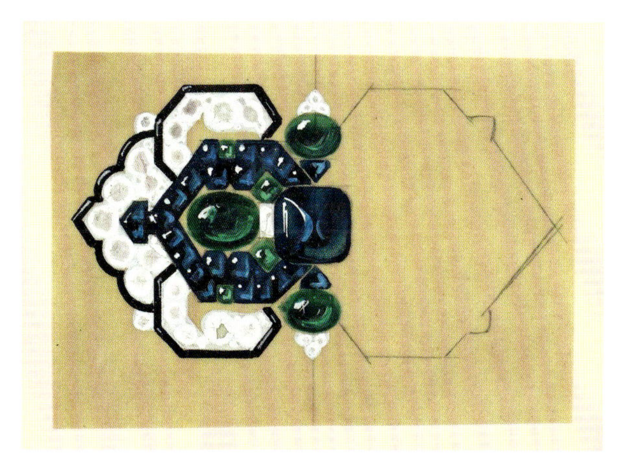

Design drawing of brooch with diamonds, sapphires, and emeralds. Cartier Paris, 1924. Cartier Archives.

TOP 32. **Bracelet** Cartier Paris, 1922. Platinum, coral, cushion-shaped emerald, collet-set emerald and onyx cabochons, pavé-set circular-cut diamonds. Length about 20.5 cm. Private collection.

ABOVE 33. **Bracelet** Cartier Paris, 1924. Platinum, pentagonal and round old- and single-cut diamonds, onyx plaques. 18.5 × 1.4 cm. Cartier Collection BT 29 A24.

LEFT 34. **Diamond *sautoir*** Cartier Paris, 1928 (pendant) 1929 (chain). Platinum, diamonds. Length 79 cm. Cartier Collection NE 14 A29.

OPPOSITE Movie star Gloria Swanson in a cut-steel spangled gown, 1922.

Design drawing of brooch. Cartier Paris, 1923. Cartier Archives.

Design drawing of brooch (fig. 40). Cartier Paris, 1923. Cartier Archives.

CLOCKWISE FROM LEFT

35. **Brooch** Cartier New York, special order, 1928. Platinum, round old-cut diamonds. 15 × 4.3 cm. Cartier Collection CL 178 A28. Provenance: Collection of Sir Elton John.

36. **Brooch** Cartier Paris, special order, 1926. Platinum, round old-cut diamonds. Diameter 4 cm. Cartier Collection CL 240 A26.

The slightly curved body has an entirely openwork setting.

37. **Brooch** Cartier New York, special order, 1927. Platinum, round old-cut diamonds, square faceted emerald, onyx cabochons, enamel. 7.6 × 2.4 × 0.5 cm. Cartier Collection CL 190 A27.

38. **Cliquet pin** Cartier New York, special order, 1927. Platinum; round old-, single-, and rose-cut diamonds; briolette-cut emeralds; enamel. 4.9 × 1.7 × 1.1 cm. Cartier Collection CL 83 A27.

The shaft attached to the upper component of a cliquet pin is thrust through the fabric of a hat or other garment. The lower element "clicks" into place, securing the jewel.

OPPOSITE, TOP TO BOTTOM

39. **Brooch** Cartier Paris, special order, 1924. Platinum, cushion-shaped and round old- and single-cut diamonds, cultured pearl, rock crystal, *calibré*-cut onyx and onyx beads. 11.6 × 10.3 × 1.1 cm. Cartier Collection CL 235 A24.

The upper part of this brooch was made to order to receive the client's trefoil pendant with pearl drop. The motif composed of the pearl, its socket, and the onyx beads is a recent reconstruction based on archive documents.

40. **Brooch** Cartier Paris, 1924. Platinum, gold, approximately 57.60-carat Sri Lankan sapphire cabochon, round old- and single-cut diamonds, frosted rock crystal, pearls, mother-of-pearl, enamel. 9.3 × 3.7 cm. Cartier Collection CL 02 A24.

This brooch was originally made with a carved emerald in the place of the sapphire cabochon.

41. **Pair of ear pendants** Cartier Paris, 1923. Platinum, round old-cut diamonds. 6.4 × 1.3 cm. Cartier Collection EG 38 A23. Sold to the queen of Spain.

TOP TO BOTTOM

42. **Bracelet** Cartier New York, 1926. Platinum, gold, round old- and single-cut diamonds, ruby beads studded with collet-set diamonds, rock crystal, onyx, enamel. Length 18.6 cm. Cartier Collection BT 54 A26.

43. **Strap bracelet** Cartier Paris, special order, 1926. Platinum; baguette-, French-, round old-, and single-cut diamonds; step-cut emeralds. 19 × 2 × 0.5 cm. Cartier Collection BT 118 A26.

44. **Strap bracelet** Cartier Paris, special order, 1928. Platinum; baguette-, round old-, and single-cut diamonds; buff-top and *calibré*-cut sapphires. Length 17 cm. Cartier Collection BT 93 A28.

In the 1920s, bandeaus were worn low on the brow, as shown in this 1921 photograph of film actress Marion Davies.

could be worn in pairs instead of buckle brooches. Many of these jewels were made of platinum, densely encrusted with white diamonds and sometimes incorporating rock crystal elements (figs. 46, 47, and 48). The more sculptural and uncompromising mode of international modernism of the late 1920s and early 1930s—as seen in pieces made by the jeweler Fouquet—went largely ignored by Cartier. However, Cartier increased the scale of its jewelry during the thirties—especially those pieces made in London. Substantial necklaces, bracelets (see fig. 212, page 198), and clip brooches with large, rectilinear step-cut or emerald-cut gemstones were the signature jewelry of the day. The popularity of the tiara surged in preparation for the 1937 coronation in London of George VI, for which Cartier made many examples (see figs. 206, page 194, and 213, page 198).[4] American-born Lady Granard, whose massive necklace and vanity case are included in this volume (figs. 50 and 51), had three enormous tiaras made during this era.[5] By the late 1930s, the art deco style faded away as fashions changed.

45. **Bandeau** Cartier New York, 1924. Platinum, approximately 51-grain natural pearl, pear-shaped and round old-cut diamonds. Height at center 5.3 cm. Cartier Collection HO 28 A24. Provenance: Estate of Doris Duke.

Daughter and only heiress of James Buchanan Duke—the founder of the American Tobacco Company and the Duke Power company—Doris Duke (1912–1993) was a prominent philanthropist, with interests in gardening, historic preservation, and art. She inherited this bandeau from her mother, Nanaline Duke.

TOP 46. **Pair of ear clips** Cartier Paris, 1934. Platinum, white gold, round old- and single-cut diamonds, carved rock crystal. 2 × 1 cm. Cartier Collection EG 19 A34.

ABOVE LEFT 47. **Bracelet** Cartier Paris, 1930. Platinum, baguette- and round old- and single-cut diamonds, rock crystal half-disks and beads. Diameter 7.9 cm. Cartier Collection BT 27 A30. Sold to Gloria Swanson.

ABOVE RIGHT 48. **Bracelet** Cartier Paris, 1930. Platinum, round old- and single-cut diamonds, rock crystal half-disks. Diameter 7.1 cm. Cartier Collection BT 28 A30. Sold to Gloria Swanson.

In the 1930s Gloria Swanson (1899–1983) was at the height of her fame, following her success in silent film and the early "talkies," and had just married Michael Farmer, the third of her six husbands. Swanson wore the bracelets in at least two films: *Perfect Understanding* (1932) and *Sunset Boulevard* (1950).

OPPOSITE 49. **Necklace** Cartier London, 1928. Platinum, diamonds, natural pearls. Department of Mineral Sciences, National Museum of Natural History, Smithsonian Institution, G6757. Gift of Mrs. Arthur Wallace Dunn.

The necklace, which initially included four strands of pearls, was purchased by Alice Whitacre Croll, wife of William Luther Croll, a prominent American dental surgeon who practiced in London. Virginia McKenney Dunn (Mrs. Arthur Dunn) was Mrs. Croll's niece.

OPPOSITE 50. **Necklace** Cartier London, special order, 1932. Platinum, round old- and rose-cut diamonds, cushion-shaped polished 143.23-carat emerald. Height at center 8.8 cm. Cartier Collection NE 25 A32. Sold to Lady Granard.

Lady Granard (born Beatrice Mills) was the daughter of the American financier and philanthropist Ogden Mills. She married the eighth Earl of Granard in 1909 and later inherited a successful horse-racing stable in France. Lady Granard was a regular client of Cartier London, where she purchased lavish jewelry. This necklace was made using stones belonging to the client.

ABOVE 51. **Large vanity case** Cartier London, special order, 1935. Gold, platinum, round old-cut diamonds, enamel. Interior has mirror and four compartments, including a covered compartment for cigarettes. 15.2 × 8.5 × 2.3 cm. Cartier Collection VC 44 A35. Ordered by the Countess of Granard.

ART DECO

The roots of Cartier's art deco style and its use of stylized, geometric forms go back to the early 1900s. Three brooches from that era, made of platinum with diamonds, sapphires, and pearls, feature simple geometric shapes with small stones arranged in intricate decorative patterns (figs. 53, 54, and 55). A groundbreaking example of one of these new types of jewelry is a brooch-pendant (fig. 56); its geometric form encloses a large cabochon sapphire that is set into a rectangular frame outlined in *calibré*-cut sapphires and mounted with complementary diamonds. It is a daringly conceived piece without any historical precedent. Another geometric and brilliantly colored brooch is set with emeralds in the form of a stylized bowl of fruit (fig. 57). A delicate *sautoir* features sapphires, diamonds, and tassels of small, graduated pearls (fig. 52). A prewar tiara of conventional *kokoshnik* shape but decorated with stylized tendrils of foliage set under a line of black squares shows the modern influence of the Vienna Secession (fig. 58). Another important influence was the brilliant color and exoticism of the Ballets Russes, which hit Paris like a storm in 1909 (see pages 42–45). Charles Jacqueau was very much involved in the circle of artists and designers inspired by the Ballets Russes, and his jewelry reflected this fresh approach.[6]

The Exposition internationale des arts décoratifs et industriels modernes, held in Paris in 1925, crystallized the character of modern design and confirmed Paris as the world center of the luxury trades. Like the architecture and interior design shown at the fair, the jewelry was largely abstract and geometric, relieved by stylized ornamentation and rendered in brilliant color. The aesthetic of the exposition was so strong that it gave its name to what we now know as the art deco style. Louis Cartier chose to show both with the jewelers in the Grand Palais and with the couture houses in the Pavillon de l'Élégance. The interior of the Pavillon de l'Élégance, which was designed by Armand-Albert Rateau, housed Lanvin, Callot Soeurs, and Worth along with Cartier, some of whose jewelry was shown on clothed mannequins. These displays enabled visitors to see how Cartier jewelry would interact with the new fashions (see page 63 left).

The firm showed about 150 pieces made over the three previous years, the most remarkable and original of which was a set consisting of a bandeau and necklace-cum-shoulder ornament. The set was named

52. **Necklace** Cartier Paris, 1910. Platinum; single-, round old-, and rose-cut diamonds; faceted and *calibré*-cut sapphires; natural pearls. Millegrain setting; total length 44.3 cm, length of pendant 13 cm. Cartier Collection NE 16 A10. Provenance: Mary Scott Townsend and Mrs. Donald McElroy.

The carefully graduated size of the pearls lends great dynamism to this pendant.

OPPOSITE, TOP TO BOTTOM

53. ***Lozenge* brooch** Cartier Paris, 1912. Platinum; round old-cut diamonds; rectangular, triangular, and square faceted sapphires; natural pearls. 4.6 × 3.8 cm. Cartier Collection CL 249 A12. Sold to a member of the Rothschild family.

54. **Brooch** Cartier Paris, special order, 1910. Platinum, faceted and *calibré*-cut sapphires, round old-cut diamonds. Millegrain setting, diameter 4.2 cm. Cartier Collection CL 202 A10. Sold to Grace Vanderbilt (Mrs. Cornelius Vanderbilt III).

Originally a hat pin made for the Rothschild family, this was later transformed by Cartier into a brooch.

55. **Brooch** Cartier Paris, 1907. Platinum, round old- and rose-cut diamonds. Millegrain setting, 3.8 × 3.8 cm. Cartier Collection CL 99 A07.

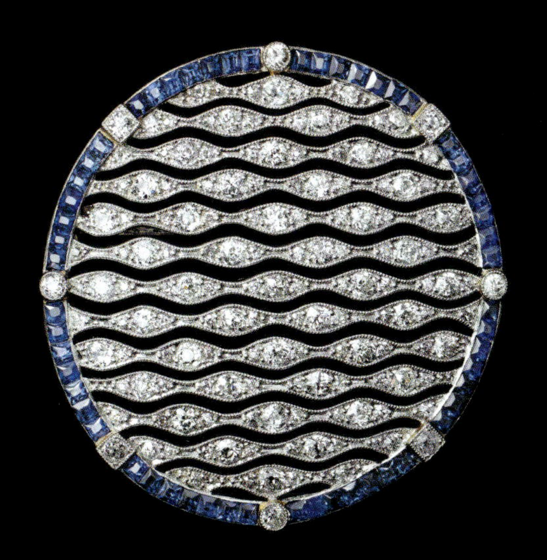

Design drawing of brooch (fig. 57). Cartier Paris, 1913. Cartier Archives.

TOP LEFT 56. **Brooch-pendant** Cartier Paris, 1912. Platinum, gold, round old- and single-cut diamonds, three sapphire cabochons, faceted and *calibré*-cut sapphires. 7.4 × 4 cm. Cartier Collection CL 197 A12.

TOP RIGHT 57. **Brooch** Cartier Paris, 1913. Platinum; round old-cut diamonds; triangular beveled, cabochon, and drop-shaped emeralds; natural pearls; onyx. 9.7 × 3.6 cm. Cartier Collection CL 183 A13.

This brooch was exhibited in the *Collection of Jewels Created by Messrs Cartier from the Hindoo, Persian, Arab, Russian and Chinese* at Cartier New York in November 1913.

ABOVE 58. **Tiara** Cartier Paris, 1914. Platinum, round old-cut diamonds, natural pearls, *calibré*- and fancy-cut onyx, enamel. Height at center 4.3 cm. Cartier Collection HO 27 A14.

Cartier display at the 1925 Paris exposition. Bérénice, a suite of emerald jewelry, was featured prominently. Cartier Archives.

An illustration of the Bérénice suite in *La Gazette du Bon Ton,* a leading fashion magazine of the time. Cartier Archives.

Bérénice by *La Gazette du Bon Ton*, the leading fashion magazine of the day (above right). The bandeau was made of rows of melon-cut Indian emeralds; the necklace draped across the collarbone and over the shoulder, its stylized tasseled ends attached to the back of the dress. It was designed to show off three large carved Mughal emeralds set within a band of diaperwork ornamentation made of pearls and black enamel. This use of carved Indian stones heralded an era of exotic jewelry for the firm. Designs embracing Indian, ancient Egyptian, Persian, and Chinese influences would become an important part of Cartier's production during these years and ran parallel with mainstream art deco designs. Sadly, the daringly striking Bérénice necklace did not find a buyer and was eventually broken up.[7]

LUXURY ACCESSORIES

The 1920s and 1930s were also the era of the luxury accessory. Vanity cases provide some of the most typical examples of the time. Made of gold and decorated with enamel, onyx, and sometimes gemstones, they could be vehicles for lavish decoration, often designed in brilliant color, resulting in exotic fantasies of various types (fig. 59). Their gold interiors were carefully fitted with compartments to hold powder, lipstick, and rouge—and, of course, mirrors. They were intentionally eye-catching—part of the new ritual of women putting on makeup in public—but they also reflected Louis Cartier's interest

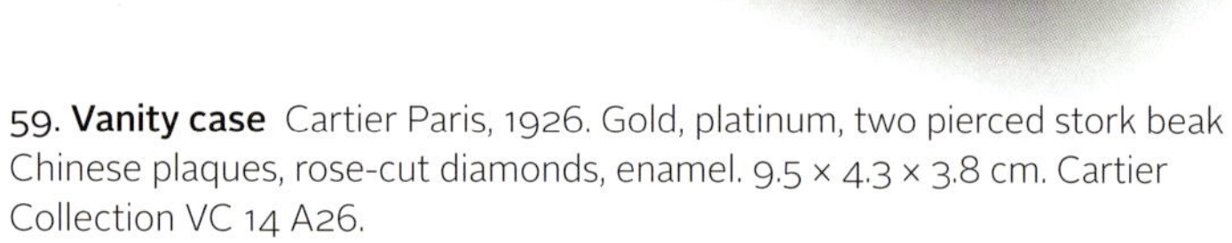

59. **Vanity case** Cartier Paris, 1926. Gold, platinum, two pierced stork beak Chinese plaques, rose-cut diamonds, enamel. 9.5 × 4.3 × 3.8 cm. Cartier Collection VC 14 A26.

The interior is fitted with a cigarette compartment placed behind a mirror, a lipstick holder, and a covered powder compartment. The swastika, an ancient and widely used motif in Hinduism, is a religious symbol of good luck in the form of a cross with ends turned toward the left or right.

in producing elaborate works of art in miniature. Cartier's handbags of the 1920s, constructed of gold frames decorated with enamel, mother-of-pearl, rock crystal, diamonds, and colored stones, are also exquisite. The pouches were generally made of solid-colored cloth (see fig. 108, page 112) or suede but sometimes were fashioned of richly patterned silk brocade (fig. 60). A handbag with a jeweled frame made for Mrs. Condé Nast has her address engraved inside so someone could return it to her if she lost it (fig. 61).

In an era when smoking was near universal for men and women, Cartier responded with singular designs for those who indulged. Cigarette cases were the most prominent. In 1936 King Edward VIII admitted to Lady Honor Channon that he had

60. **Evening bag** Cartier Paris, about 1930. Platinum, diamonds, mother-of-pearl, rock crystal, onyx, fabric. Height of bag 15.2 cm, width of frame 14 cm. Private collection.

61. **Evening bag** Cartier Paris, 1929. Gold; platinum; carved emeralds and rubies; onyx; baguette-, single-, and square-cut diamonds; enamel; suede. The interior of the mount engraved: *Mrs. Conde Nast 1040 Park Avenue New York City.* 15.5 × 16 cm. Cartier Collection EB 05 A29.

American publisher Condé Nast owned *Vogue*, *House & Garden*, *Vanity Fair*, and *Glamour* magazines.

taken a great liking to her cigarette case, which was engraved with her honeymoon destinations, and had one made at Cartier London and given to him by Mrs. Simpson for Christmas in 1935.[8] Cases for men were usually flat and could be slightly rounded in order to fit in men's pockets (see figs. 140, page 138, and 200, page 184), but women's cases were more solid and rectilinear for the handbag. Geometrically patterned cases were made with hardstones, such as lapis lazuli and turquoise (see fig. 160, page 154). Some of the cases featured ingenious mechanisms. A cigarette case made for Virginia Graham Fair Vanderbilt, crafted of gold enameled with the Persian motifs popular for smoking accessories (vaguely alluding to Turkish tobacco), has a spring-loaded base; when the user slides back the top, a cigarette pops up (fig. 62). Cartier also made other smoking accessories, such as tabletop smokers' sets (see fig. 152, page 146), lighters (see fig. 141, page 138), holders (see fig. 155, page 148), and even ashtrays (see fig. 156, page 148). The extensive range of accessories sold in New York included special orders such as a silver traveling cocktail set complete with shaker, lemon press, and tumblers (see fig. 194, pages 176–77).

Invitation for an exhibition of holiday gifts at the rue de la Paix boutique. Cartier Paris, 1920. Cartier Archives.

Watches were an important part of Cartier's business. They could be incorporated into fine jewelry, such as pendants for women (see fig. 111, page 114); mounted for display on a desk; or combined with a leather strap for everyday use as a wristwatch or with a diamond bracelet for evening wear. Some were even incorporated into lighters (see fig. 153, page 147) and pencils (see fig. 189, page 173). The Cartier watch became a status symbol worn by generations of famous men, such as Rudolph Valentino, Clark Gable, Argentine president Juan Perón (see fig. 181, page 169), and many others. Cartier's clocks were incorporated into sleek writing sets and handsome multipurpose instruments that could also include a calendar, barometer, thermometer, and compass (see fig. 166, page 162).

The most elaborate objects sold by the jeweler during this era were its so-called mystery clocks (fig. 63). With their platinum-and-diamond hands that appear to float around the dial with no apparent mechanism, these clocks were truly works of art. Constructed out of a host of precious and semiprecious materials, including rock crystal, onyx,

OPPOSITE 62. ***Persian* cigarette case** Cartier Paris, special order, 1932. Gold, platinum, enamel, single-cut diamonds. 9 × 8.5 × 1.7 cm. Cartier Collection CC 88 A32. Ordered by Mrs. W. K. Vanderbilt II.

Virginia Graham Fair (1875–1935) was the daughter of millionaire Irishman James Graham Fair, who made his fortune from the discovery of the Comstock silver lode in Nevada and was elected United States senator in 1881. Virginia married William K. Vanderbilt II (1878–1944) in 1899.

When the sliding cover of this case is pulled back, the cigarettes pop up thanks to a spring-driven mechanism (*système élévateur*).

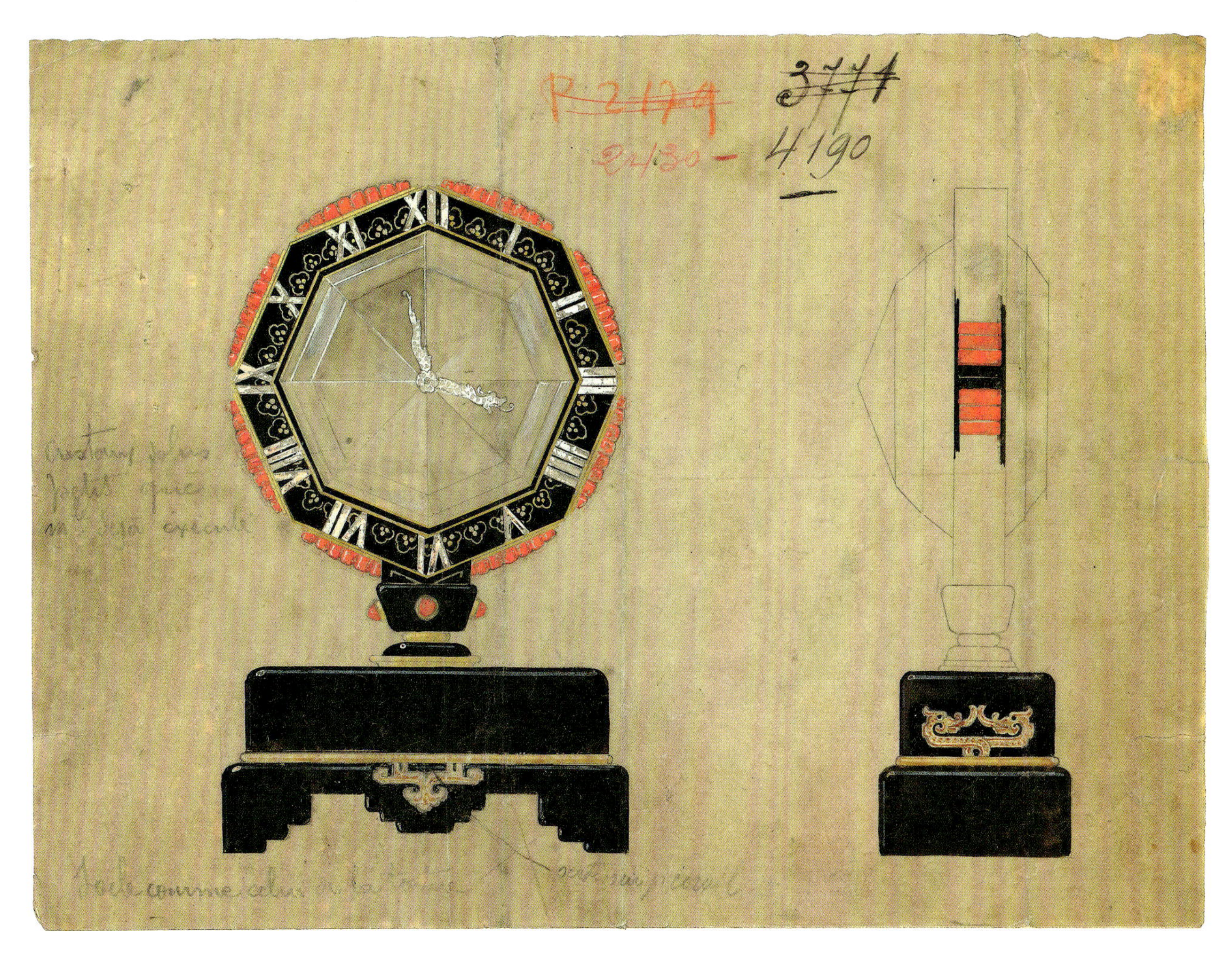

Design drawing for a single-axle mystery clock. Cartier Paris, 1929. Cartier Archives.

gold, platinum, and diamonds, they were to Cartier what the Easter eggs were to Fabergé.[9] Composed of myriad components and decorative finishes, the objects were so complex that they could take up to a year to make. The earliest examples, from around 1912, were of modest proportions and had rectangular cases made of rock crystal, but in the 1920s they became larger and more sculptural, and some were embellished with jade figures. The clocks' "mystery," which Cartier never intended to reveal, was that each hand was fixed onto a flat disk of glass with a concealed, notched edge that was driven by gears running from a movement hidden in the base. The clocks were conceived by the ingenious clockmaker Maurice Couët, and many were designed by Cartier designers Charles Jacqueau and George Rémy.[10] They varied from typical art deco forms to the bizarrely exotic. Six magnificent mystery clocks (all made between 1923 and 1925) take the form of an Asian gate, or portico, of rock crystal or rose quartz, with the transparent dial suspended from the crossbar (in which the mechanism was concealed).[11] One model made between 1920 and 1931 had a single central axle and a dial that was octagonal in shape (above). The most elaborate and dramatic were the clocks mounted on Chinese hardstones (see pages 122–27).

OPPOSITE 63. ***Model A* mystery clock** Cartier New York, 1927. Gold, platinum, rock crystal, rose-cut diamonds, mother-of-pearl, onyx. Rectangular 8-day movement, gilded, 13 jewels, Swiss lever escapement, bimetallic balance, Breguet balance spring. Hand-setting and winding mechanism underneath the base. Height 13.6 cm. Cartier Collection CM 28 A27. Sold to Evalyn Walsh McLean.

Daisy Fellowes, photographed by Wladimir Rehbinder in *Vogue*,
Sept. 15, 1923 . Condé Nast Archive.

CELEBRITIES AND HIGH SOCIETY

Celebrities and high society figures were among Cartier's principal clients in the 1920s and 1930s. Although the firm has always been very discreet about its clientele, it was through these people that Cartier's reputation was enhanced. In New York, Cartier's principal salesman, Jules Glaenzer, gave parties at which celebrities from stage and screen, such as George Gershwin and Charlie Chaplin, would mix with high society to spread word of Cartier. Even when she was well into her seventies, and voted one of the world's best-dressed women by Parisian couturiers, the socially savvy American decorator Elsie de Wolfe was happy to promote Cartier's jewelry in *Vogue*.[12] A good customer, she purchased both jewelry and a clock.[13] Marjorie Merriweather Post (of the Post cereal fortune) was a faithful customer starting in the 1920s. Her massive emerald brooch is one of the most remarkable pieces Cartier ever made (below right). Fashioned from large Indian emeralds and suspended from a buckle of diamonds and emeralds, it was originally made in London in 1923 before it was transformed for Mrs. Post in New York in 1928. She also bought a large, Indian-style

ABOVE Queen Marie of Romania wearing a Cartier diamond-and-pearl bandeau and a Cartier *sautoir* with 478-carat sapphire pendant bought in 1921 (see fig. 31, page 45). Cartier Archives.

RIGHT Emerald, diamond, platinum, and enamel brooch owned by Marjorie Merriweather Post, made by Cartier London in 1923 and transformed in 1928. Hillwood Estate, Museum & Gardens, bequest of Marjorie Merriweather Post, 1973.17.75.

LEFT 64. **Cigarette case** Cartier London, about 1932. Silver, silver-gilt. Lid engraved in May 1936 with the royal cipher *ER VIII* (King Edward VIII). 7.2 × 8.2 × 1.1 cm. Cartier Collection CC 101 C32.

Edward ruled Great Britain for less than a year before abdicating to marry American divorcée Wallis Simpson.

ABOVE 65. **Clip-brooch** Cartier London, special order, 1937. Gold. Pierced monogram with the initials *W E* (for Wallis and Edward) topped by the ducal crown. 3 × 2 × 0.5 cm. Cartier Collection CL 86 A37. Made as a special order for the Duke and Duchess of Windsor soon after their marriage.

emerald necklace in 1929 and is known to have worn the two together (see page 228), but, as often happened with Mrs. Post's pieces, the necklace was later transformed.

According to Jean Cocteau, Daisy Fellowes (see page 70) launched "more fashions than any other woman in the world."[14] She was regularly on the best-dressed lists compiled by Parisian couturiers in the 1930s. Truly international, she was the epitome of café society: the daughter of a French duke, the American heiress to the Singer sewing machine fortune, and the wife of an Englishman. Her relationship with Cartier is one of the longest of any of its patrons, stretching from the 1910s to the 1960s (see pages 242–45).

Although to a lesser extent than during the Edwardian age, royalty continued to be patrons of Cartier between the wars. Indeed, royal arms representing the royal warrants were emblazoned on the exterior of the rue de la Paix store.[15] In about 1920, after her jewels were seized by the Bolsheviks during the Russian Revolution, Queen Marie of Romania commissioned new jewelry from Cartier, including her famous diamond-and-pearl bandeau (see page 71 left).[16] Queen Ena of Spain also had a very large diamond-and-pearl tiara, fashioned with scroll motifs, made by Cartier Paris in 1920.

Cartier supplied jewelry for the London coronations of 1902, 1911, and 1937. In this period various members of the British royal family patronized Cartier despite the fact that there were also British official jewelers to the Crown. The Duchess of York was presented with a halo tiara from Cartier by her husband just before she became queen late in 1936. Although these tiaras were intended to be worn vertically, that is, perpendicular to the head like Southeast Asian headdresses, it seems to have been worn horizontally like a conventional tiara. It has since become

The Duke and Duchess of Windsor at a dinner at the Hôtel Lambert, 1957. The duke's cigarette case rests on the table in front of him, and the duchess's gold egg-shaped vanity case by Cartier is in front of her.

world famous as the tiara lent by Queen Elizabeth to Catherine Middleton to wear at her 2011 wedding to Prince William.

King Edward VIII engraved a silver cigarette case (fig. 64) from Cartier during his short reign as king and bought many jewels there during his courtship and marriage to Wallis Warfield Simpson. He set the abdication crisis in motion on October 27, 1936, when he presented Mrs. Simpson with an engagement ring of a fine, 19.77-carat Colombian emerald bought at Cartier London. As Duke of Windsor he continued to patronize Cartier in London, Paris, and New York. The gold clip-brooch bearing the duke and duchess's combined first initials, *WE* (fig. 65), was one of many small tokens Cartier London made for the former king to give as presents to his dwindling band of supporters.

MARGARET YOUNG-SÁNCHEZ
WITH A CONTRIBUTION BY YVONNE MARKOWITZ

FOREIGN FASCINATION

CARTIER IS JUSTLY FAMED AS A PIONEER OF ART deco jewelry before World War I and as one of its greatest practitioners during the 1920s and early 1930s. Among the house's most dazzling and distinctive creations are jewels, timepieces, and accessories designed in exotic styles—everything from necklaces and tiaras to vanity cases, cigarette cases, and clocks were produced in seemingly limitless variety. Ancient Egypt, China and Japan, and India and the Islamic world were the principal sources of stylistic inspiration, but Cartier's designers were rarely literally faithful to a specific foreign artistic tradition, and they often combined an assortment of patterns and motifs into fantastic mélanges that can only be termed exotic fantasies.

The seeds of this later florescence are evident well before the war, in jewelry that is usually called garland style. Scattered among the familiar flowers and scrolls of Cartier's Louis XVI–inspired diamond jewelry and the laurel leaves and columns of its neoclassical items are many harder-to-categorize pieces, such as a choker patterned with lozenges and undulations that recall Turkish brocade fabric; Grace Vanderbilt's "Byzantine" necklace with hexagonal pendants (see page 30); and Virginia Graham Fair Vanderbilt's grand *écharpe* bodice ornament, composed of diamond chains and openwork roundels from which hang pendants with huge, pear-shaped diamond drops. Cartier's restless and occasionally incoherent eclecticism in the early twentieth century was furthered by trends in design education that emphasized books and museum objects, rather than foreign travel and study, as design sources.[1] Louis Cartier was a connoisseur of Islamic art and collected Persian metalwork, carpets, manuscripts, and jewelry;[2] he encouraged his designers to visit and sketch at museums such as the Louvre and made an extensive library of world art history and design volumes available to them. Nonetheless, their creativity was constrained by the conventions of high jewelry and

OPPOSITE Sir Yadavindra Singh, Maharaja of Patiala, photographed in 1941 wearing the necklace set with the De Beers diamond created by Cartier for his father, Sir Bhupinder Singh, in 1928 (see fig. 78, page 89). Cartier Archives.

the sometimes conservative taste of Cartier's wealthy clientele. These dictated the predominance of white diamonds supplemented by a narrow selection of precious stones: emeralds, blue sapphires, and rubies.

As noted on pages 42–43, Sergei Diaghilev's opera and ballet performances created a sensation in the first decades of the twentieth century, sweeping away existing conventions in fashion, jewelry, and interior design and generating a vogue for overtly exotic cultures and styles. The prewar productions of the Ballets Russes evoked ancient Egypt (*Cleopatra*, 1909; opposite), Central Asia (*Prince Igor*, 1909), the Islamic world (*Scheherazade*, 1910), India and Southeast Asia (*The Blue God*, 1912), and China (*The Nightingale*, 1914). Evocative rather than historically accurate, the Ballets Russes inspired Charles Jacqueau and other Cartier designers to experiment with new materials and bold designs. Jacques Cartier's travels to the Middle East and India in 1911, during which he met with sheikhs and maharajas and purchased pearls and gems, undoubtedly stimulated his imagination. In 1912 and 1913, after Jacques's return, Cartier issued beautifully decorated invitations to exhibitions of "Indian" and "Hindoo, Persian, Arab, Russian and Chinese" jewels and objets d'art in its London and New York shops (left). World War I interrupted the designers' processes of experimentation and development, but they burst forth with vigor in the 1920s.

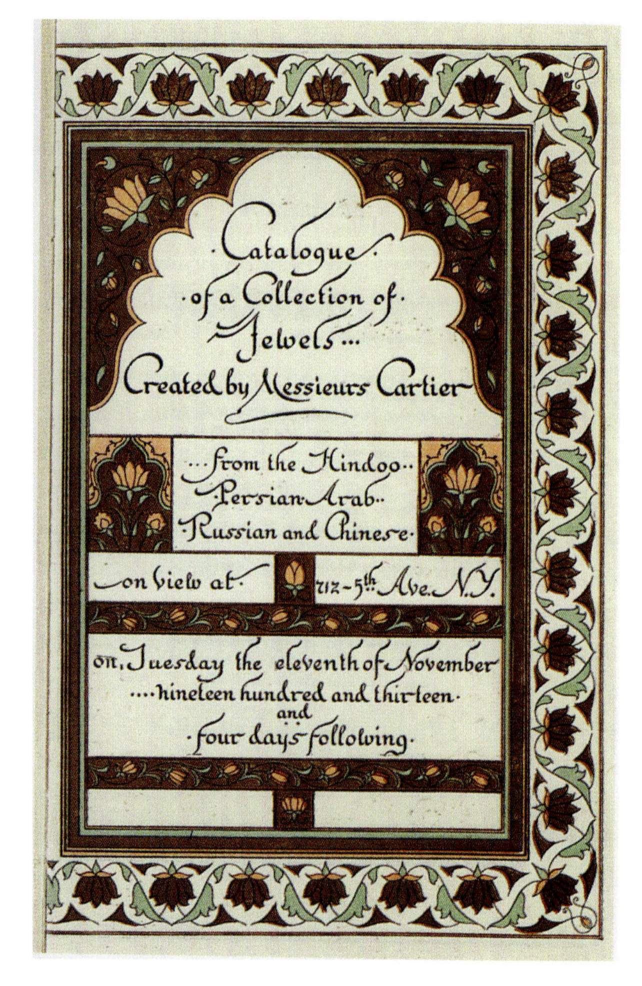

Catalogue of a Collection of Jewels... Created by Messieurs Cartier

...from the Hindoo.. Persian Arab.. Russian and Chinese.

on view at 712-5th Ave. N.Y.

on Tuesday the eleventh of November ....nineteen hundred and thirteen. and four days following.

First page of the catalog for a jewelry exhibition held in November 1913 at Cartier New York. Cartier Archives.

The strong colors of oriental carpets, Islamic manuscript paintings, ancient Egyptian wall paintings, and ceramics and textiles from eastern Asia inspired the use of richly hued semiprecious materials: lapis lazuli, coral, onyx, nephrite, jadeite, turquoise, and mother-of-pearl. These materials, added to the traditional fine jewelry repertoire of diamonds, pearls, emeralds, rubies, and sapphires, gave Cartier the means to satisfy tastes both conservative and daring and to produce objects suitable for formal and informal occasions.

Economically, the decade of the 1920s was a time of expansion, as countries rebuilt after the war's great destruction and the stock market encouraged a broad segment of the population to invest. Men were returning to the civilian workforce, while women sought to expand the social and economic freedoms they gained during the war years. Culturally there was a hunger for novelty, luxury, and even frivolity. Luxury spending in the United States was fueled by a drastic postwar cut in the income tax rate on wealthy individuals.[3] Jewels owned by royal and aristocratic Russians then in exile were sold to generate income; Cartier brokered some sales and also purchased jewels to provide gemstones for new works.

With branches in the world's leading political, cultural, and economic centers, Cartier was in a position to supply its clients with innovative jewelry, precious accessories, and luxurious objects.

EGYPT

Europe's fascination with ancient Egypt, stimulated by the accounts of travelers and artists, extends back to the eighteenth century. Napoleon's 1798 Egyptian expedition resulted in the multivolume *Description de l'Égypte*, a copy of which was owned by Louis Cartier. Egyptian-inspired jewelry decorated with pharaoh, sphinx, cobra, and lotus-blossom motifs was produced in Italy, France, England, and America throughout the second half of the 1800s. Yellow gold, micromosaics, and multicolored enamels were common materials; many jewels incorporated ancient faience scarabs—the ancient Egyptian symbol of birth and regeneration.[4] Excavations of Egyptian tombs in 1895 and 1914 revealed caches of ancient jewelry that were extensively described by the international press.

The discovery of Tutankhamun's tomb in 1922 generated even greater popular excitement. Jewels in the tomb included earrings, necklaces, collars, bracelets, and pectorals. In Paris, couturiers produced dresses and accessories of Egyptian inspiration. Jewelry with Egyptian themes appeared in fashion magazines and quickly hit the markets. Many of the ornaments fell into the costume jewelry category, although several leading high-style jewelry houses also took advantage of the public fascination with the boy king.

Cartier's jewels sometimes incorporated fragments of Egyptian antiquities into contemporary bejeweled settings. The artifacts were purchased from a number of dealers operating in Paris during the early decades of the twentieth century. Among them were the Kalebdjian brothers, at 12, rue de la Paix, and Dikran Kelekian, who had a shop at 2, place Vendôme.[5] The scarab remained fashionable through the 1920s. Several brooch–belt buckle hybrids designed by Cartier utilized a specific form of the scarab—the three-part funerary beetle with outstretched wings (see page 78 bottom). Each segment of this amulet has multiple piercings along the perimeter to facilitate attachment to the linen wrappings of a mummy (see page 78 top). In one Cartier brooch, the feathered wings of bright blue faience are ancient, while the carved smoky quartz body is contemporary (fig. 66). Following the decorative pattern on the antiquity, the wings are embellished by two bands of glittering pavé-set diamonds. Small bezel-set emerald cabochons were cleverly employed to disguise the stringing holes in the faience, and similar stones serve as three-dimensional eyes. Another brooch features an ancient scarab body with elaborate curved wings composed of platinum, gold, diamond, ruby, citrine, emerald, and onyx (fig. 67). A third example (owned by Linda Lee Porter, wife of Cole Porter) has

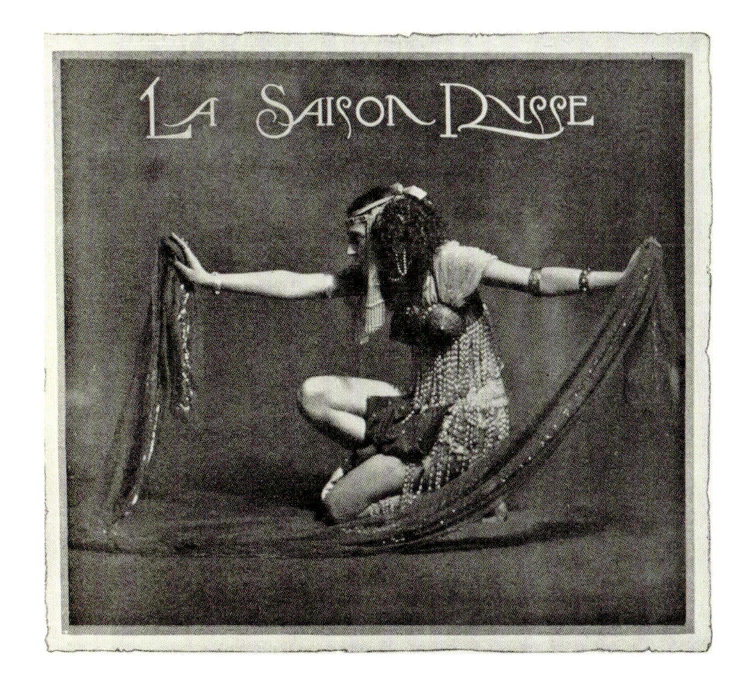

Photograph of Russian dancer Ida Rubinstein costumed as Cleopatra. *Comœdia illustré*, June 15, 1909. Bibliothèque nationale de France.

Winged scarab, Egyptian, Late Period, Dynasty 25, 760–660 BC or later. Faience; scarab body: 7.3 x 5 cm; wings: 6.3 x 4.1 cm (each). Museum of Fine Arts, Boston; Hay Collection—Gift of C. Granville Way, 72.3019a–c.

an antique scarab body with modern faience wings of a slightly paler color (fig. 68 left).

Three Cartier ornaments incorporate rarer antiquities. One features the profile head of Horus, the falcon-headed god who was the personification of kingship (fig. 69). This artifact once served as one of two decorative terminals at the back of a Middle Kingdom broad collar, an ornament typically composed of multiple rows of strung beads. Cartier designers embellished the terminal along the base by adding a delicate row of coral-and-onyx lotus blossoms, Egyptian symbols of creation and rebirth. The flowers emerge from a bed of white diamonds, a reference, perhaps, to the life-giving Nile. A second brooch incorporates a faience pendant of Sekhmet, a fearsome warrior goddess often depicted as a lion-headed woman wearing a sun disk fronted by a rearing cobra (fig. 71). Here, the goddess rises from a thicket of lotus blossoms made of precious stones set in platinum with onyx and black-enamel highlights. It is an unusual composition that may have its source in an object from Tutankhamun's tomb: a sculpture showing the head of the young king as it emerges from an open lotus. The third brooch was illustrated by Cartier London in a 1924 advertisement published in the *Illustrated London News* (see page 80 bottom).[6] At the center of the imposing jewel, atop a ram's head, is Sekhmet's profile head wearing her sun disk headdress. Behind her is the arc of the night sky, a semicircle of vivid blue lapis studded with diamond stars and edged by diamonds (fig. 70).

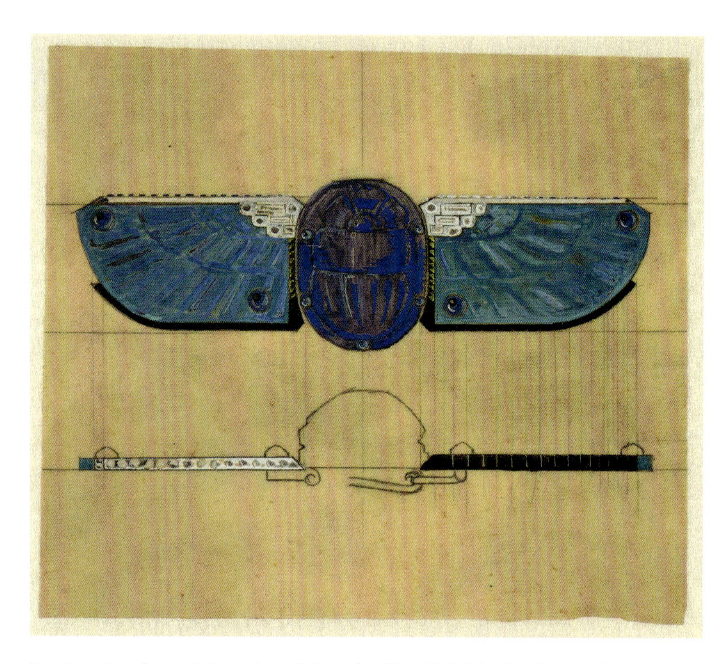

Design drawing of *Scarab* belt buckle (fig. 68 left). Cartier Paris, 1926. Cartier Archives.

TOP 66. ***Scarab* brooch** Cartier London, 1924. Gold, platinum, blue Egyptian faience, round old-cut diamonds, emerald cabochons, smoky quartz (scarab), enamel. 13 × 5 × 2 cm. Cartier Collection CL 32 A24.

The term *apprêts* at Cartier referred to a stock of fragments from disassembled jewelry, watches, and other objects, including ancient items from Persian, Indian, Chinese, and Egyptian art.

CENTER 67. ***Scarab* brooch** Cartier London, 1925. Gold; platinum; round old- and single-cut diamonds; ruby, emerald, citrine, and onyx cabochons; blue Egyptian faience. 12.4 × 5.5 × 1.9 cm. Cartier Collection CL 264 A25.

Originally, this brooch could also be worn as a belt buckle.

BOTTOM LEFT AND RIGHT 68. ***Scarab* brooch and bracelet** Cartier Paris, 1926. Brooch: Gold, platinum, diamonds, cabochon sapphires, ancient Egyptian faience scarab, faience wings. 12.7 × 3.8 cm. Bracelet: Platinum, faience, enamel, lapis lazuli, turquoise, onyx, diamonds. Length 16.5 cm. Private collection. Provenance: Linda Lee Porter; Princess Natalie Paley (daughter of Olga, Princess Paley, and Grand Duke Paul Alexandrovich).

Design drawing of *Horus* brooch (fig. 69). Cartier Paris, 1925. Cartier Archives.

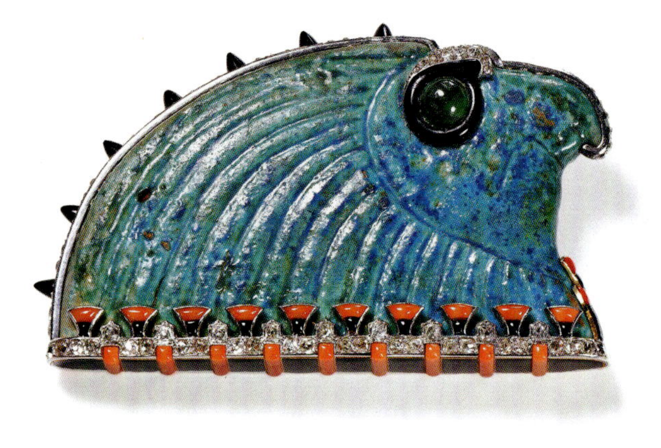

69. ***Horus* brooch** Cartier Paris, 1925. Platinum, gold, blue Egyptian faience, round old- and single-cut diamonds, emerald cabochon, coral, onyx studs and cabochons, enamel. 4.5 × 7.1 cm. Cartier Collection CL 263 A25.

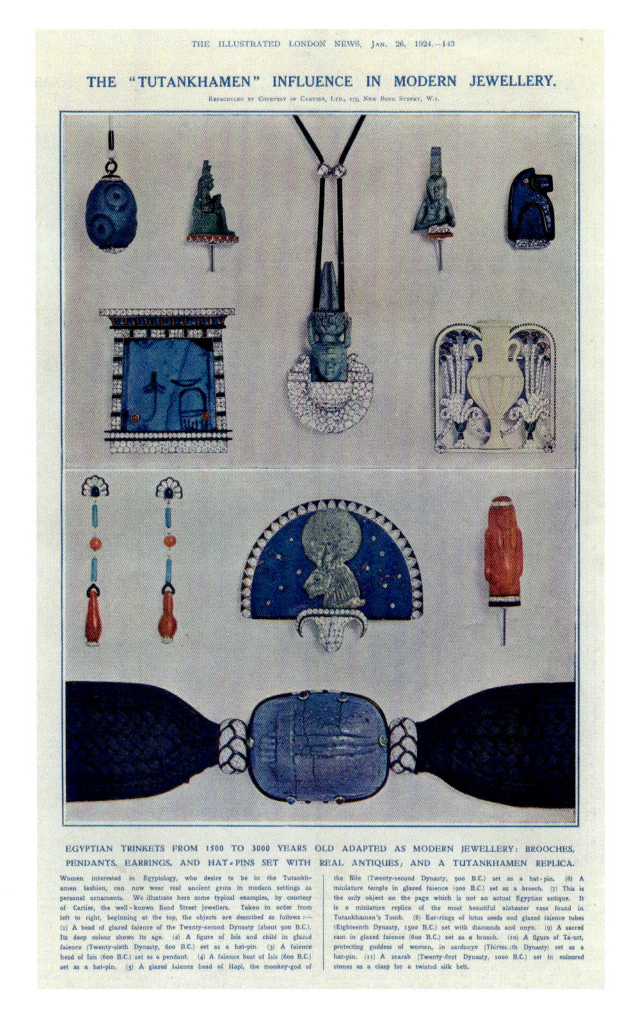

THE ILLUSTRATED LONDON NEWS, JAN. 26, 1924.—143

THE "TUTANKHAMEN" INFLUENCE IN MODERN JEWELLERY.

REPRODUCED BY COURTESY OF CARTIER, LTD., 175, NEW BOND STREET, W.1.

EGYPTIAN TRINKETS FROM 1500 TO 3000 YEARS OLD ADAPTED AS MODERN JEWELLERY: BROOCHES, PENDANTS, EARRINGS, AND HAT-PINS SET WITH REAL ANTIQUES, AND A TUTANKHAMEN REPLICA.

Women interested in Egyptology, who desire to be in the Tutankhamen fashion, can now wear real ancient gems in modern settings as personal ornaments. We illustrate here some typical examples, by courtesy of Cartier, the well-known Bond Street jewellers. Taken in order from left to right, beginning at the top, the objects are described as follows:—(1) A bead of glazed faience of the Twenty-second Dynasty (about 900 B.C.). Its deep colour shows its age. (2) A figure of Isis and child in glazed faience (Twenty-sixth Dynasty, 600 B.C.) set as a hat-pin. (3) A faience head of Isis (600 B.C.) set as a pendant. (4) A faience bust of Isis (600 B.C.) set as a hat-pin. (5) A glazed faience head of Hapi, the monkey-god of the Nile (Twenty-second Dynasty, 900 B.C.) set as a hat-pin. (6) A miniature temple in glazed faience (900 B.C.) set as a brooch. (7) This is the only object on the page which is not an actual Egyptian antique. It is a miniature replica of the most beautiful alabaster vase found in Tutankhamen's Tomb. (8) Ear-rings of lotus seeds and glazed faience tubes (Eighteenth Dynasty, 1500 B.C.) set with diamonds and onyx. (9) A sacred ram in glazed faience (600 B.C.) set as a brooch. (10) A figure of Ta-urt, protecting goddess of women, in sardonyx (Thirteenth Dynasty) set as a hat-pin. (11) A scarab (Twenty-first Dynasty, 1000 B.C.) set in coloured stones as a clasp for a twisted silk belt.

Page in the *Illustrated London News*, Jan. 26, 1924, showing "The 'Tutankhamen' Influence in Modern Jewellery." All jewelry is by Cartier. Mary Evans Picture Library.

Cartier made several vanity cases in the Egyptian style that incorporated small antiquities. One rectangular container follows the same color scheme—green, deep blue, and orange-red—found in Egyptian decorative arts (fig. 72). Adorning its front and back are the fragments of a small calcite stele (split in half) known as a cippus. It depicts Horus as a child holding a scorpion and a lion while standing on a pair of crocodiles (missing). To either side of the deity are magical hieroglyphic inscriptions believed to heal and protect against snakebites and scorpion stings. The case was owned by diplomat and author Ira Nelson Morris, the husband of Constance Lily Rothschild.[7]

A shrine-shaped vanity case also demonstrates an awareness of Egyptian color symbolism and materials (fig. 73). The box was designed around a blue faience figure of the household god Bes, who is often depicted with musical instruments. Above the figure is a gem-set open lotus, and along the sides are freely rendered hieroglyphs giving the names and titles of the New Kingdom pharaoh Thutmose III.

During the 1920s, Cartier created a variety of smoking-related accessories, some with Egyptian

OPPOSITE, TOP 70. **Brooch** Cartier London, 1923. Gold, platinum, blue Egyptian faience, round old- and single-cut diamonds, lapis lazuli, enamel. 5.8 × 7.2 cm. Cartier Collection CL 321 A23.

OPPOSITE, BOTTOM 71. ***Sekhmet* brooch** Cartier Paris, special order, 1925. Gold, platinum, blue Egyptian faience, ruby and emerald cabochons, round old- and single-cut diamonds, onyx cabochons, enamel. 8.3 × 3.7 cm. Cartier Collection CL 278 A25.

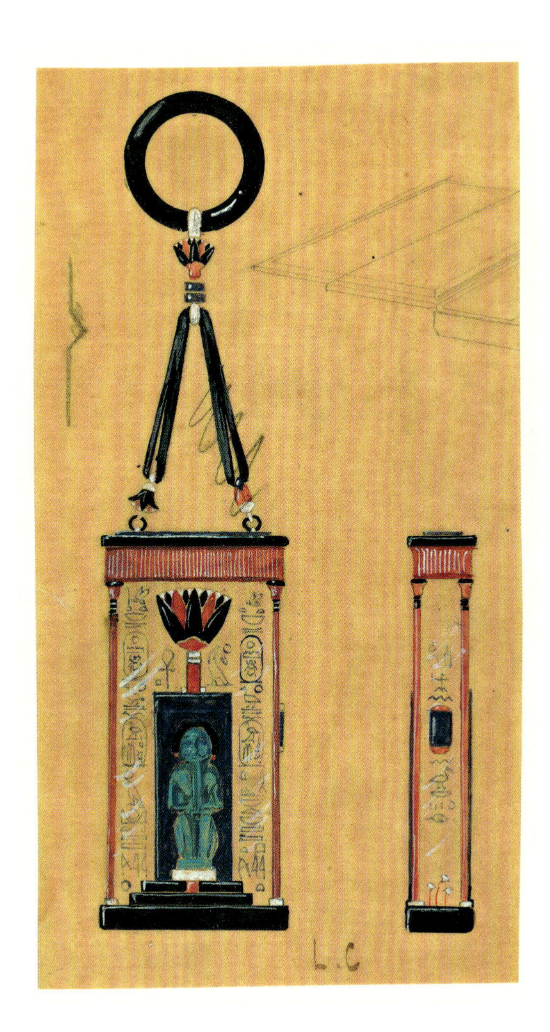

Design drawing of *Egyptian* vanity case (fig. 73). Cartier Archives.

OPPOSITE 72. ***Egyptian* vanity case** Cartier Paris, 1927. Gold, platinum, Egyptian calcite plaque (sawn in half), rose-cut diamonds, *calibré*-cut and carved buff-top emeralds and emerald matrix cabochons, coral, lapis lazuli, enamel. 9.9 × 5.2 × 2.1 cm. Cartier Collection VC 65 A27. Sold to Ira Nelson Morris.

After inheriting and expanding a prosperous company, Ira Nelson Morris (1875–1942) sold his holdings and devoted himself to politics and writing. As the American ambassador to Sweden he served as mediator in secret negotiations between Washington and Lenin's revolutionary government in Moscow.

ABOVE 73. ***Egyptian* vanity case** Cartier Paris, 1924. Gold, platinum, mother-of-pearl, Egyptian blue faience, coral, onyx, lapis lazuli, rose-cut diamonds, enamel, leather double strap. 9.3 × 4.5 × 2 cm. Cartier Collection VC 64 A24. Sold to Mr. François Coty.

Known as the father of modern perfume, the French politician and industrialist François Coty (1874–1934) expanded the perfume market by making scents for the general public that combined natural essences with synthetic fragrances.

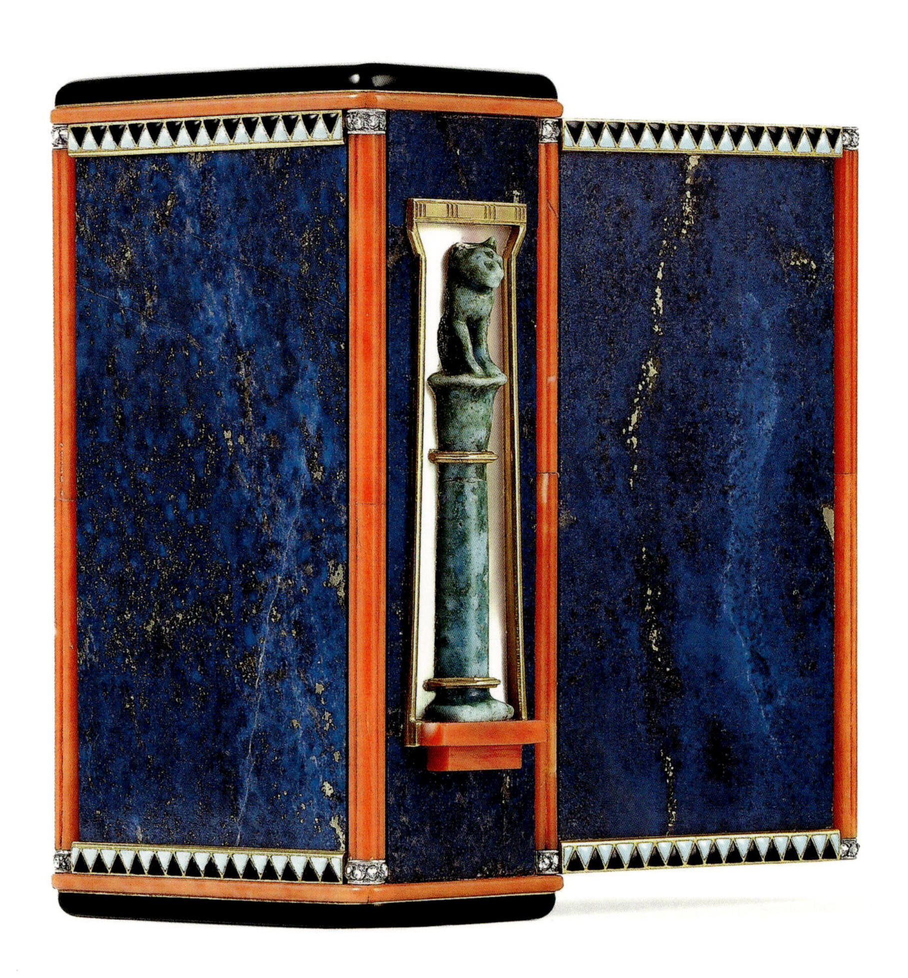

TOP 74. ***Egyptian* cigarette case** Cartier Paris, special order, 1929. Gold, platinum, lapis lazuli, coral, blue faience (statuettes), mother-of-pearl, rose-cut diamonds, enamel. 8.3 × 5.2 × 2.8 cm. Cartier Collection CC 89 A29. Ordered by Ira Nelson Morris.

The two Egyptian figures (late period, 4th–3rd century BC), which came from the firm's stock of oriental *apprêts*, represent the goddess Bastet sitting on a column.

ABOVE 75. **Cigarette holder** Cartier Paris, about 1925. Platinum, lapis lazuli (bowl and rings), coral (shaft and mouthpiece), emerald cabochons, rose-cut diamonds. Length 11.4 cm. Cartier Collection CH 02 C25.

OPPOSITE 76. ***Egyptian* striking clock** Cartier Paris, 1927. Gold; silver-gilt; mother-of-pearl; coral; Egyptian deity set with emerald, cornelian, and enamel; lapis lazuli; enamel. Rectangular 8-day movement, striking mechanism (hour and quarter-hours), gold-plated, beaded decoration, 3 adjustments, 15 jewels, platform escapement, bimetallic balance, Breguet balance spring. 24 × 15.7 × 12.7 cm. Cartier Collection CDB 21 A27. Sold to Florence Blumenthal.

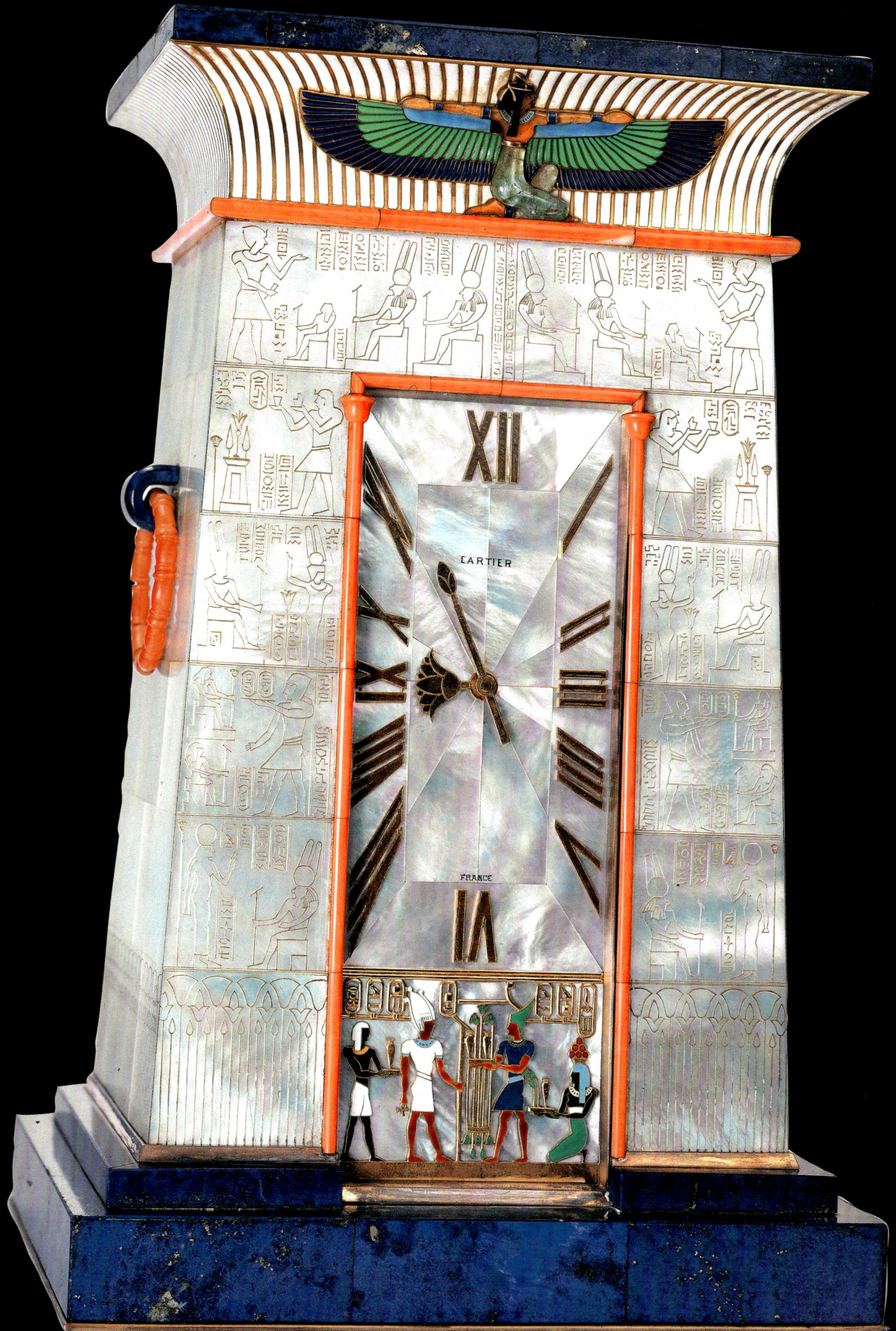
CARTIER
FRANCE

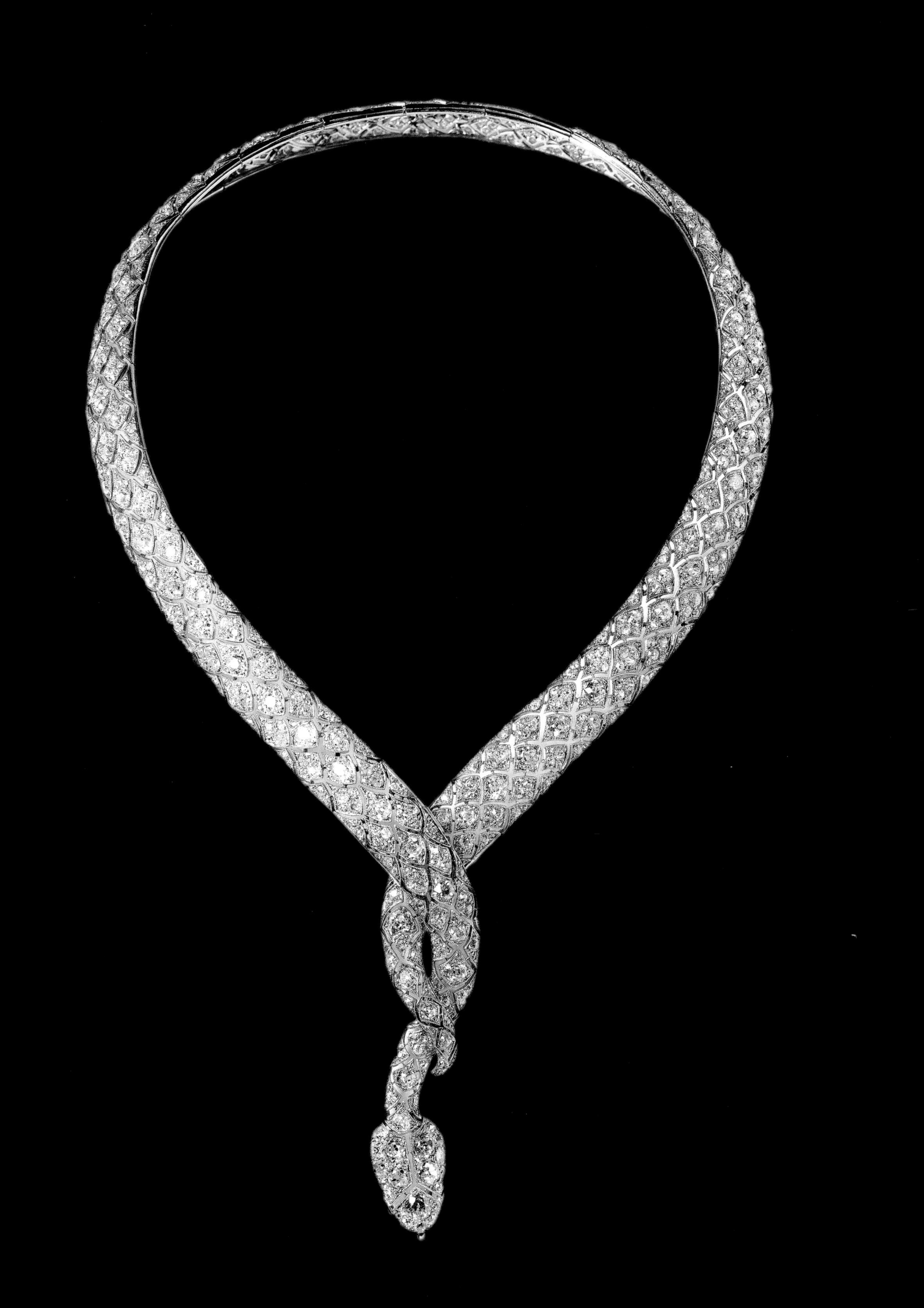

themes. One such cigarette case features an enshrined faience cat goddess seated on a papyrus column, which is mounted in a rectangular box composed of lapis lazuli plaques (fig. 74). Lapis lazuli was prized by the Egyptians, who imported it from Afghanistan and used it sparingly for their most precious ornaments. Coral and lapis lazuli were also used to create an elegant cigarette holder that resembles an Egyptian column (fig. 75).

One of the most extraordinary Egyptian-inspired objects fashioned by Cartier designers is a clock made in 1927 (fig. 76). It resembles the gateway to the Khonsu Temple at Karnak, although the clock's cornice is ornamented with a winged goddess rather than the winged sun disk seen on the original monument. The open and closed lotus-blossom hands on the mother-of-pearl dial are based on the observation that during the night the lotus closes its bloom and sinks into the water, reemerging in the morning. As such it was a highly suitable image for a modern device that tracked the hours. Below the dial is a colorful scene depicting two images of the king and the kneeling Nile god Hapi. The markings that accompany the figures on the pylons are fanciful renderings of ancient hieroglyphs.

Possibly inspired by ancient Egyptian art (but not based directly on an ancient prototype) is a necklace in the form of a supple diamond-and-platinum snake that loops around the wearer's neck (fig. 77).

INDIA AND THE ISLAMIC WORLD

Since the time of Aristotle, India was known as a source of diamonds.[8] Approximately two thousand years later, in the mid-seventeenth century, India's alluvial deposits in the Golconda region continued to yield diamonds, a supply controlled by the Mughal emperor. Merchant and geographer Jean-Baptiste Tavernier visited the court of Emperor Aurangzeb in 1665 and acquired many large diamonds, including the Tavernier Blue (later known as the Hope diamond).[9] In addition to diamonds, Indian royal treasuries were filled with rubies and sapphires from Ceylon and Burma (as Sri Lanka and Myanmar were then known), emeralds from Colombia, and pearls from the Persian Gulf. As a center of the international gem trade, India was long associated in European popular imagination with fabulous wealth (for example, in Frances Hodgson Burnett's 1905 novel *A Little Princess*, Captain Crewe, an Englishman, discovered a hugely valuable diamond mine in India; his daughter, Sara, was left penniless in England when he died of a fever).

Jewelry made of gold and precious gems was an essential attribute of traditional Indian kingship. Each material was thought (by both Hindus and Muslims) to embody spiritual qualities; the ownership and display of precious jewelry was essential to rulers' legitimacy. From the eighteenth century onward, Indian rulers offered valuable gems to English monarchs as tokens of fealty, including the famous Koh-i-noor diamond. Cartier's first Indian-style commission came from Queen Alexandra (a necklace made of Indian pearls, rubies, and cabochon emeralds) in her new role as empress of India following the death of Queen Victoria in 1901.[10] Alexandra and Edward VII's visit to India in 1906 stimulated even greater popular interest in the region and its culture.

Under British rule, Indian princes became frequent visitors to London and Paris for both official business and pleasure. The Aga Khan (spiritual leader of the far-flung Isma'ili Muslim community) and the Maharaja of Kapurthala were among the guests in attendance at Countess Aynard de Chabrillan's 1912 Paris costume party (see pages 44–45). They and other cosmopolitan Indian princes

OPPOSITE 77. ***Snake* necklace** Cartier Paris, 1919. Platinum, round old-cut diamonds. Millegrain setting, length 22 cm. Cartier Collection NE 20 A19.

The clasp on this completely open-backed necklace is placed at the point where the tail entwines. Although rigid when in place, the body of the snake is sufficiently flexible to be opened and slipped around the neck. The use of the scale motif on a curved surface is exceptional.

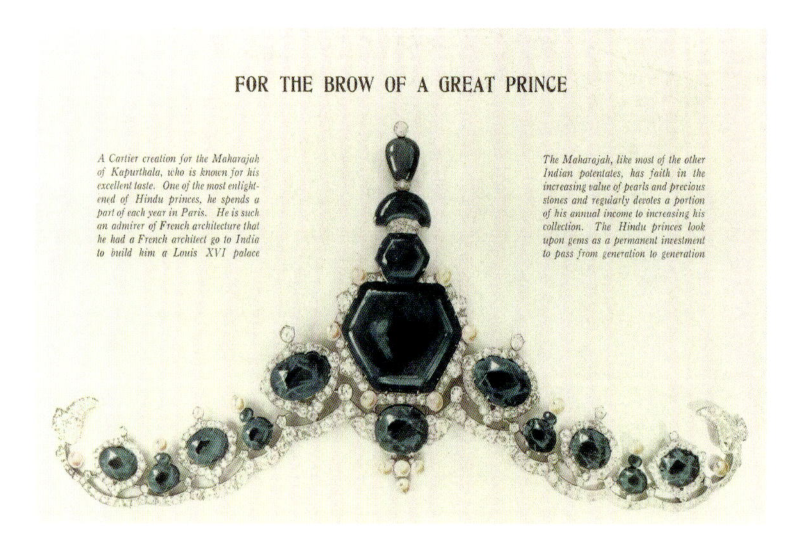

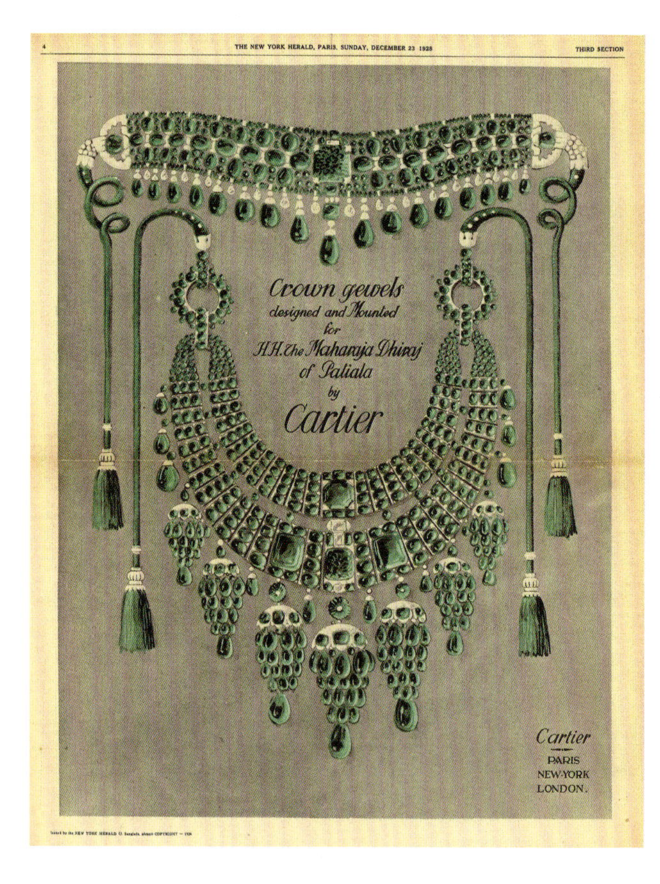

ABOVE Advertisement in *Spur* magazine, 1927, featuring the emerald, pearl, and diamond turban ornament commissioned from Cartier by the Maharaja of Kapurthala in 1926. Cartier Archives.

RIGHT Advertisement for Maharaja of Patiala jewels designed by Cartier, *New York Herald Paris*, Dec. 23, 1928. Cartier Archives.

indulged a taste for European goods, including furniture, automobiles, clothing, watches, and jewelry.[11] They patronized an array of Parisian jewelers, purchasing everything from conventional gentlemen's pocket watches and garland-style diamond-and-platinum jewelry to traditional Indian jewelry forms updated with platinum settings. In celebration of his fiftieth anniversary of rule, the Maharaja of Kapurthala commissioned a remarkable diamond-and-emerald turban ornament from Cartier in 1926 (above left), which the firm proudly advertised the following year. Cartier's largest commission, from Maharaja Bhupinder Singh of Patiala, was to fashion thousands of pearls and precious stones from the royal treasury into an array of new jewels. The commission took three years to complete and was publicized with a 1928 exhibition and large-format brochure (above right). Perhaps the most spectacular single item was a huge, multistrand platinum necklace (fig. 78) set with hundreds of white and colored diamonds, including the light yellow 234.65-carat De Beers diamond (from South Africa; by this time India's diamond sources were largely exhausted). This necklace, which covered the entire chest, is worn with a diamond collar, jeweled belt, strands of pearls and large diamonds, and a tiaralike turban ornament in a 1941 photograph of the maharaja's son and successor, Yadavindra Singh (see page 74). Another Indian jewelry form made by Cartier is a *bazuband* bracelet (worn on the upper arm) fashioned of platinum and densely set with diamonds supplied by Indian businessman Sir Dhunjibhoy Bomandji in 1922 (fig. 80). The diamond links that once allowed the chain to encircle the arm are no longer present.

Many of Cartier's English, European, and American clients purchased jewels based on Indian forms or jewels that incorporated imported

OPPOSITE 78. **Necklace** Cartier Paris, special order, 1928. Platinum, old- and rose-cut diamonds (chain and links), yellow and white zirconias, white topazes, synthetic rubies, smoky quartz, citrine. Height at center 27 cm. Cartier Collection NE 40 A28. Created for Sir Bhupinder Singh, Maharaja of Patiala.

OPPOSITE 79. **Bandeau** Cartier Paris, special order, 1923. Platinum, cushion-shaped and round old-cut diamonds. Height at center 7.5 cm. Cartier Collection HO 05 A23.

Parts of this bandeau can be detached to form two strap bracelets.

ABOVE 80. ***Bazuband*** **upper arm bracelet** Cartier Paris for Cartier London, special order, 1922. Platinum, old-cut diamonds. 22.3 × 14 × 0.2 cm. Cartier Collection BT 08 A22. Sold to Sir Dhunjibhoy Bomandji.

Sir Bomandji (1862–1937), originally from Bombay, was a shipping magnate who owned many estates in India and England. As a philanthropist, he supported numerous charities in both India and Britain.

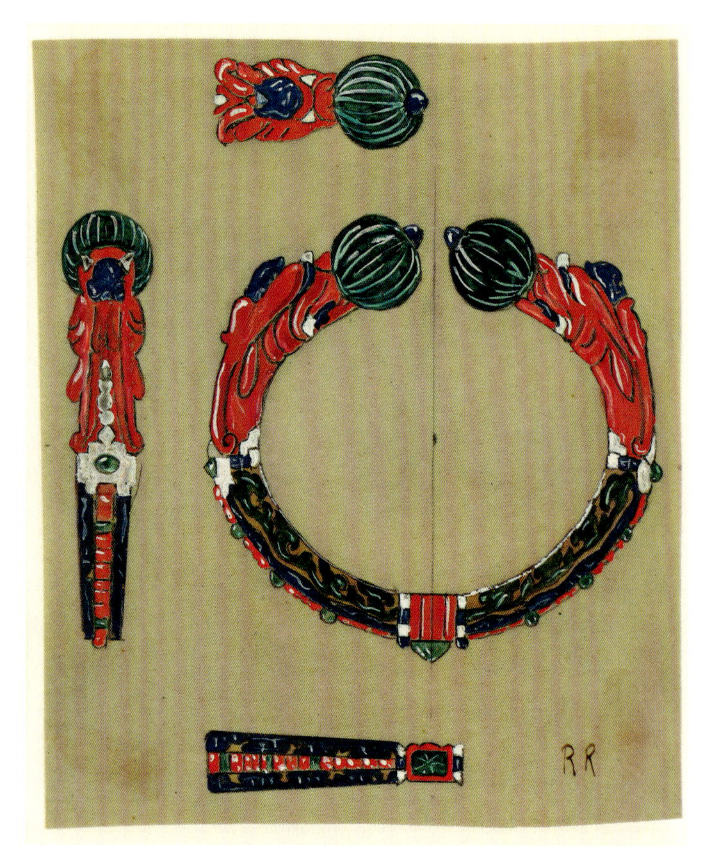

Design drawing of *Chimera* bangle (fig. 81). Cartier Archives.

Indian components. Cartier made a luxurious diamond-encrusted bangle bracelet with mythical serpent-head (makara) terminals (fig. 82). Another bracelet has coral serpent heads that resemble Chinese dragons along with green, blue, and black enameling (fig. 81 and left). More modern in taste is a supple, Indian-inspired diamond bandeau from 1923 (fig. 79).

Traditional Indian gemstones were often polished rather than faceted and set in closed-back mountings, sometimes with enamel-decorated reverse surfaces. Others were drilled as beads or drops. Large flat-cut emeralds were frequently carved with floral designs or engraved with written inscriptions. Cartier

ABOVE 81. ***Chimera* bangle** Cartier Paris, 1928. Gold; platinum; cushion-shaped, single-, pear-, and baguette-cut diamonds; fluted, carved, buff-top, and cabochon emeralds; carved, cabochon, and buff-top sapphires; carved coral; enamel. 7.4 × 8.2 × 1.6 cm. Cartier Collection BT 109 A28. Sold to Ganna Walska.

Of Polish origin, the opera singer Ganna Walska (1887–1984) was married to Alexander Smith Cochran (dubbed "the richest bachelor in the world") and later Harold Fowler McCormick, heir to the McCormick farm machinery fortune.

The bracelet opens by twisting one of the two dragon heads. The eyes are represented by inverted cushion-shaped diamonds.

OPPOSITE 82. ***Chimera* bracelet** Cartier Paris, special order, 1929. Platinum; pear-shaped, round old-, single-, and French-cut diamonds; sapphire cabochons; buff-top sapphires and emeralds; rock crystal. 7.8 × 7.7 × 1.8 cm. Cartier Collection BT 64 A29.

LEFT TO RIGHT

83. **Necklace** Cartier Paris, 1924. Platinum, carved emeralds and sapphire, sapphire and lapis lazuli beads, diamonds. Necklace length 73.5 cm, pendant drop 9.3 cm. Private collection. Provenance: Baron Eugène de Rothschild.

84. **Bracelet** Cartier Paris, 1923. Platinum, gold, round old- and rose-cut diamonds, carved 57.80-carat emerald, fluted emerald beads, onyx rondelles, enamel. 19.4 × 2.6 cm. Cartier Collection BT 40 A23.

Imported from Colombia, the central emerald was carved on both sides in India during the Mughal dynasty, in the late seventeenth or early eighteenth century. The Mughals believed that carving emeralds could enhance their beneficial powers. The bracelet, made for stock, originally had two coral beads instead of two emerald beads, plus two coral rondelles.

85. ***Sautoir*** Cartier New York, special order, 1925. Platinum, single-cut diamonds, carved hexagonal 85.60-carat emerald, fluted emerald beads, natural pearls. Length 75.1 cm, width of pendant 4.4 cm. Cartier Collection NE 42 A25.

purchased many of these colorful gems through agents in India and incorporated them into its own designs. Some of the stones were centuries-old Mughal carvings; others were likely carved at Cartier's behest. A lovely 1924 necklace has large carved emeralds and sapphires that hang from a pale sapphire-bead chain (fig. 83 and below left). It was purchased by Baron Eugène de Rothschild and illustrated in *Vogue* magazine;[12] a similar example was owned by the Aga Khan and worn by his wife for her presentation at the English court in 1930 (below right). A *sautoir* made in 1925 has a strand of gadrooned emerald beads from which hangs a floral-carved hexagonal emerald with three emerald drops (fig 85). A bracelet features a large, similarly carved emerald (in this case, rectangular) with tapering straps made of onyx discs and diamond rondelles (fig. 84).

Multicolored enamel is a common feature of Mughal jewelry from Jaipur. Cartier imported enamel plaques and applied them to the surface of

ABOVE Design drawing of Rothschild necklace (fig. 83). Cartier Paris, 1924. Cartier Archives.

RIGHT Princess Andrée Carron, wife of the Aga Khan III, wearing her Cartier emerald tiara and emerald-and-sapphire *sautoir*, 1930. Mary Evans Picture Library.

gold accessories such as vanity cases (fig. 88), makeup boxes (fig. 89), cigarette cases, and lighters (fig. 87). An exquisite vanity case owned by Pierre Cartier's wife, Elma, is decorated with an enamel plaque inset with jade, sapphires, and rubies (fig. 86). The vase and flowering plant motif recalls Mughal carpets. A vanity case inlaid with diamonds, pearls, emeralds, turquoise, and mother-of-pearl (fig. 91) is adorned with a nichelike motif reminiscent of carpets or Islamic book bindings. The cover of a charming compact with an attached lipstick holder is ornamented by an eight-pointed star inlaid with an Indian elephant and surrounded by turquoise cabochons (fig. 90).

CLOCKWISE, FROM ABOVE LEFT

87. **Lighter** Cartier Paris, 1928. Gold, platinum, rose-cut diamonds, enamel. Central appliqué, a Persian plaque of polychrome enamel (flowers and birds). 4.5 × 3.3 × 1.3 cm. Cartier Collection LR 09 A28.

88. **Vanity case** Cartier Paris, 1932. Pink and yellow gold, platinum, rose-cut diamonds, enamel. Central appliqué, a Persian plaque of polychrome enamel. "Kodak" system catch operated by pressing the two push-pieces on the sides. 8.7 × 5.8 × 1.6 cm. Cartier Collection VC 29 A32.

The interior is fitted with a mirror, a lipstick holder, and a covered powder compartment.

89. **Makeup box** Cartier Paris, 1929. Ribbed gold, platinum, rose-cut diamonds, enamel. Central appliqué, a Persian plaque of polychrome enamel. 3.2 × 3.1 cm. Cartier Collection PB 34 A29.

OPPOSITE 86. **Vanity case** Cartier London, 1928. Gold, rose-cut diamonds, sapphire and ruby cabochons, jade, onyx, enamel. 11 × 3.8 cm. Pierre Cartier Foundation FPC 10.

The interior is fitted with a mirror, two covered compartments (one with lipstick holder), and a place for a comb.

ABOVE 90. **Powder compact with lipstick holder** Cartier Paris, 1925. Yellow and pink gold, turquoise cabochons and beads, sapphire cabochons, mother-of-pearl, hardstone, enamel. Diameter of compact 6.3 cm. Cartier Collection VC 51 A25.

The interior is fitted with a mirror and a powder compartment with sifter.

OPPOSITE 91. **Vanity case** Cartier Paris, 1924. Gold; platinum; mother-of-pearl and turquoise parquetry; leaf-carved, engraved, and cabochon emeralds; pearls; rose- and old-cut diamonds; enamel. 10.9 × 5.9 × 2 cm. Cartier Collection VC 34 A24.

The design of this item was inspired by fifteenth- to seventeenth-century book bindings (perhaps a volume owned by Louis Cartier, who collected them). Originally, the center featured a Persian miniature taken from the firm's stock of *apprêts*. It was replaced by the carved emerald in 1926. The interior is fitted with a mirror, lipstick holder, tortoiseshell comb, and two covered powder compartments.

EAST AND SOUTHEAST ASIA

In its ongoing search for novelty and innovation, Cartier sought inspiration in the art of China and (to a lesser extent) Japan and Thailand. China, a source of fascination for Europeans since the journeys of Marco Polo in the twelfth century, inspired recurrent fads in European architecture, interior decoration, and furniture making in the seventeenth and eighteenth centuries.[13] In the late nineteenth and early twentieth century, railroad construction, scientific exploration, and the looting of both historic and archaeological treasures brought Chinese art to the international market, including Paris.[14] Japan was forcibly opened to foreign trade in 1854, and Japanese art quickly gained popularity in the United States and Europe, as painters and designers mined Japanese prints, textiles, and decorative arts for novel compositions, motifs, and patterns.

Imported Japanese kimonos were adopted for wear in domestic settings, and by the early 1900s Japanese influence was felt in European women's fashion in the form of loose, rectangular sleeves, V-shaped necklines, and tapering skirts. But by the late 1910s and throughout the 1920s, the influence of Chinese dress (in the form of straight silhouettes, tubular sleeves, and even "coolie" hats) eclipsed that of Japan.[15] Such trends are evident in fashion designer Jeanne Paquin's garments displayed in the Pavillon de l'Élégance at the 1925 Paris art deco exhibition. One dress featured large Chinese dragons on the waist panel.[16] The performing arts also participated in the trend: in 1919 Russian artist Alexandre Jacovleff displayed his sketches of Chinese theatrical performances in Paris; in 1920 the Ballets Russes staged

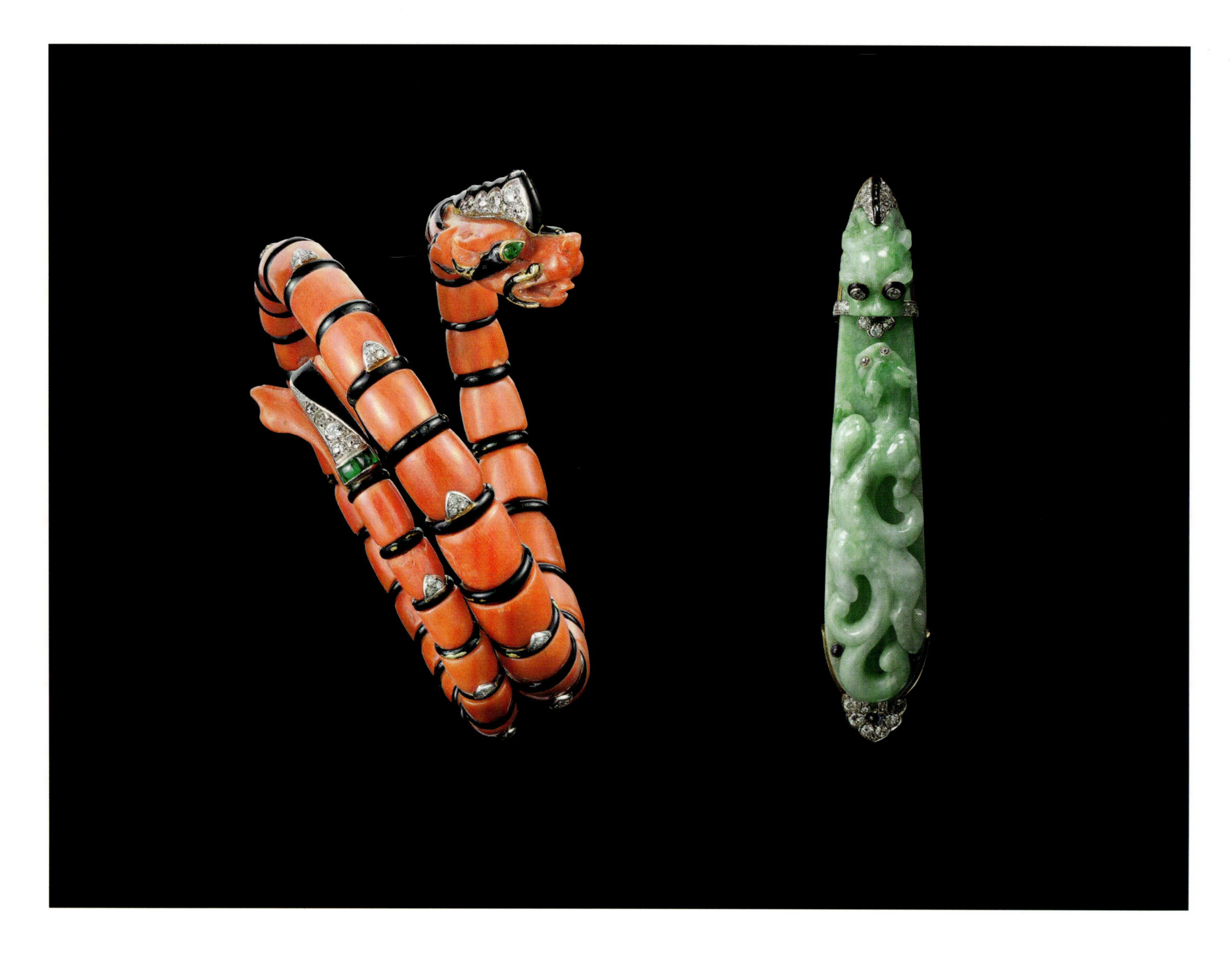

94. **Pair of apple blossom branches** Cartier Paris, about 1925. Agate, stained ivory, moonstone, enamel, gold, wood, glass. 14 × 14.4 × 7 cm each. Private collection.

a production of *The Song of the Nightingale*, with Chinese costumes by Henri Matisse.[17]

Cartier produced a limited quantity of jewelry in response to the popular enthusiasm for China. Some items incorporated imported Chinese components, such as a carved antique jade dragon belt hook mounted in gold and platinum as a brooch, with enamel and inset gems (fig. 93). Other pieces utilized Chinese motifs, such as stylized dragon scrolls on brooches and buckles and a serpent transformed into a coral, diamond, and black enamel bracelet (fig. 92). More numerous than jewels, however, was Cartier's production of Asian-influenced personal accessories and decorative objects for the home. Creation of hardstone plants (like those made in the century's first decade) was revived, including a pair of exquisite apple blossom branches that resemble tiny bonsai (fig. 94).[18] Similar in feeling is a lovely bracelet with hinged panels of pavé diamonds against which appear delicate flowering branches (fig. 95).

OPPOSITE, LEFT 92. **Bracelet** Cartier Paris, 1924. Platinum, gold, rose-cut diamonds, emerald cabochons, coral, enamel. Diameter 7 cm. Pierre Cartier Foundation FPC 12.

OPPOSITE, RIGHT 93. ***Dragon* brooch** Cartier Paris, special order, 1924. Gold, platinum, round old- and single-cut diamonds, sapphire cabochons, carved jade, enamel. 9.5 × 1.9 cm. Cartier Collection CL 80 A24.

This brooch was made from an eighteenth- or nineteenth-century Chinese carved jade belt clasp supplied by the client.

ABOVE 95. **Bracelet** Cartier New York, 1925. Platinum, brilliant- and single-cut diamonds, emerald and ruby cabochons, onyx. Length 19.1 cm. Cartier Collection BT 141 A25.

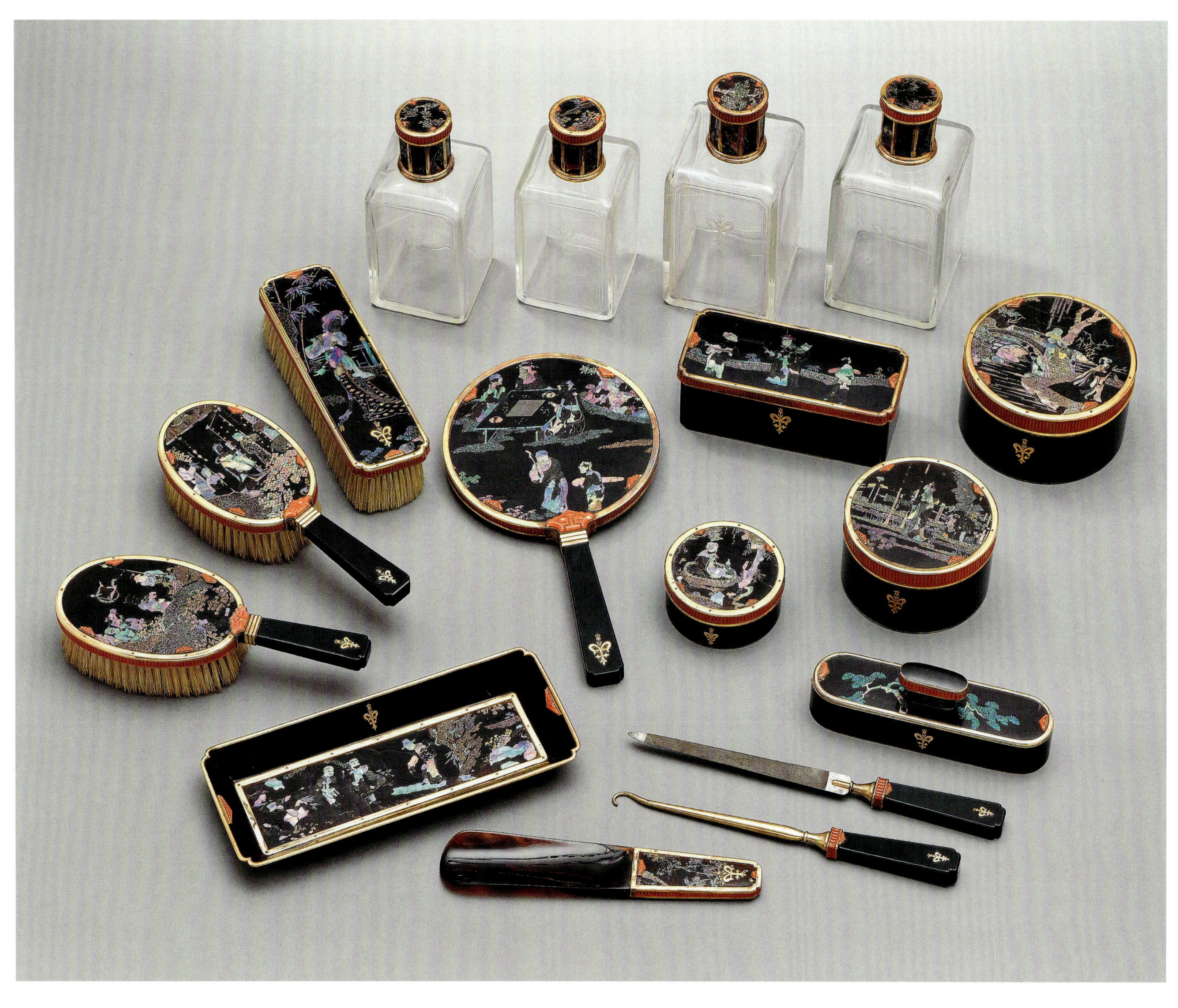

97. **Desk clock with strut** Cartier Paris, 1929. Gilded metal, platinum, ebonite (case), *laque burgauté* plaque, moonstone cabochon, mother-of-pearl, coral cylinders, rose-cut diamonds, enamel. Round 8-day movement, *fausses* Côtes de Genève decoration, rhodium-plated, 3 adjustments, 15 jewels, Swiss lever escapement, bimetallic balance, Breguet balance spring. Retractable winding crown at 3 o'clock. 8.3 × 8.3 × 2.2 cm. Cartier Collection CDS 06 A29.

The case, originally of ivory, was redone in ebonite in 1930, prior to sale.

Panels of imported Chinese *laque burgauté* with figural scenes of inlaid mother-of-pearl (tinted blue, green, and purple) were incorporated into an assortment of objects, from ladies' vanity cases and cigarette cases to vases, toiletry sets (fig. 96), clocks (fig. 97), and table cigarette boxes (see fig. 157, pages 149–51). The dark, subtle lacquer in these items contrasts with platinum, gold, diamonds, and coral. Cartier also used nineteenth-century Chinese wood panels inlaid with mother-of-pearl and hardstones. An exquisite vanity case frames such panels in turquoise and coral, surmounted by a scrolled cornice and diamond-studded dragon (fig. 99). An additional touch of exoticism is an inscribed oval Islamic turquoise plaque below the onyx finger ring. A powder compact suspended by enameled chains from a lipstick case features a Chinese phoenix on a mother-of-pearl ground (fig. 98). Cartier displayed this object at the 1925 exposition, an indication of its high estimation. Yet another vanity case has an enameled black surface inlaid with peony flowers in cabochon emeralds, sapphires, coral, and moonstone (fig. 100).

The effective color combination of jade green and coral orange occurs repeatedly in Cartier accessories from the 1920s, including a 1927 handbag with a mother-of-pearl, coral, and jadeite frame and a lovely green suede pouch (fig. 103). It perfectly complements a vanity case with Chinese carved-jadeite panels framed by coral and black enamel (fig. 101) and a cigarette holder of white and green jade, black onyx, tiny diamonds, and platinum (fig. 102).

Among Cartier's grandest Chinese-style items is a large clock in the form of an Asian table screen (fig. 104). A rectangular Chinese jade panel, carved with a high-relief landscape on both sides, is framed in enamel, coral, and gold. On one face, the dragon and spear-shaped hands indicate the hours and minutes. On the other, a clambering enameled dragon disguises the shadow of the embedded drive shaft connecting the hands to the hidden clock mechanism in the base.[19]

OPPOSITE 96. **Vanity set** Cartier Paris, 1927. Silver, gold, *laque burgauté* panels, enamel, coral, obsidian, glass. Tallest flask 16.5 × 7.6 × 7.6 cm, tray 21.3 × 8. 9 × 2.2 cm, mirror 25.4 × 14 × 1.3 cm. From the collection of Barbra Streisand. Purchased by Florence Blumenthal and subsequently by Count Edmond de Fels, Prince de Heffingen.

OPPOSITE 98. **Powder compact with lipstick holder** Cartier Paris, 1925. Gold, platinum, mother-of-pearl, ivory, lacquer, rose-cut diamonds, emerald cabochons, enamel. Back has monogram of two entwined Cs. Handle-shaped lipstick holder. Interior fitted with a mirror and a gold-stemmed puff. 12.5 × 6.4 cm; diameter of powder compact 4.9 cm. Cartier Collection VC 58 A25.

The inlaid ivory plaque on the lid came from Cartier's *apprêts*. Chinese symbols include the phoenix (which represented the empress) and the *ruyi* motifs on the borders, symbols of abundance and authority.

ABOVE 99. ***Chinese* vanity case** Cartier Paris, 1924. Wood (plaques), mother-of-pearl, malachite, lapis lazuli, turquoise, agate, coral, gold, platinum, rose-cut diamonds, onyx, enamel. 21.5 × 6.3 × 2.1 cm with cord and finger ring. Cartier Collection VC 67 A24.

The inlaid wood plaques (nineteenth century) were supplied by Louis Cartier himself, whereas the turquoise stones came from the firm's stock of *apprêts*. The plaques depict a famous ancient Chinese story about Su Wu, a historical figure who symbolizes loyalty and commitment. The *shou* ideogram on the friezes means "long life." The interior is fitted with a mirror and a cigarette compartment with gold retaining clip.

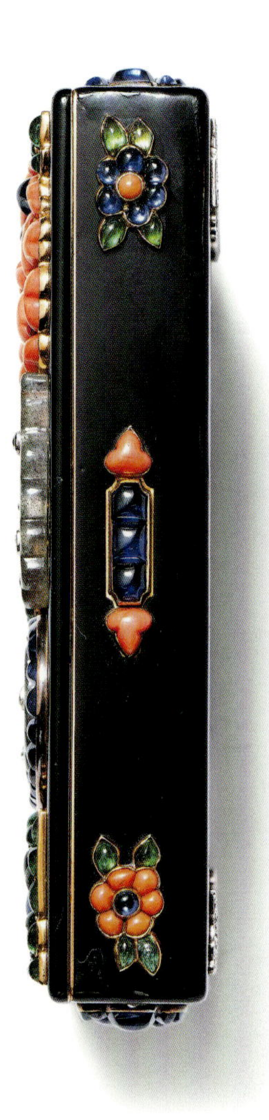

100. **Vanity case** Cartier Paris, 1927. Pink and yellow gold; platinum; enamel; sapphire, emerald, topaz, and coral cabochons; moonstone; old-, rose-, and single-cut diamonds; enamel. 10.4 × 6 × 2.2 cm. Cartier Collection VC 41 A27.

The interior is fitted with a mirror, lipstick holder, and two covered powder compartments with two gold-stemmed puffs.

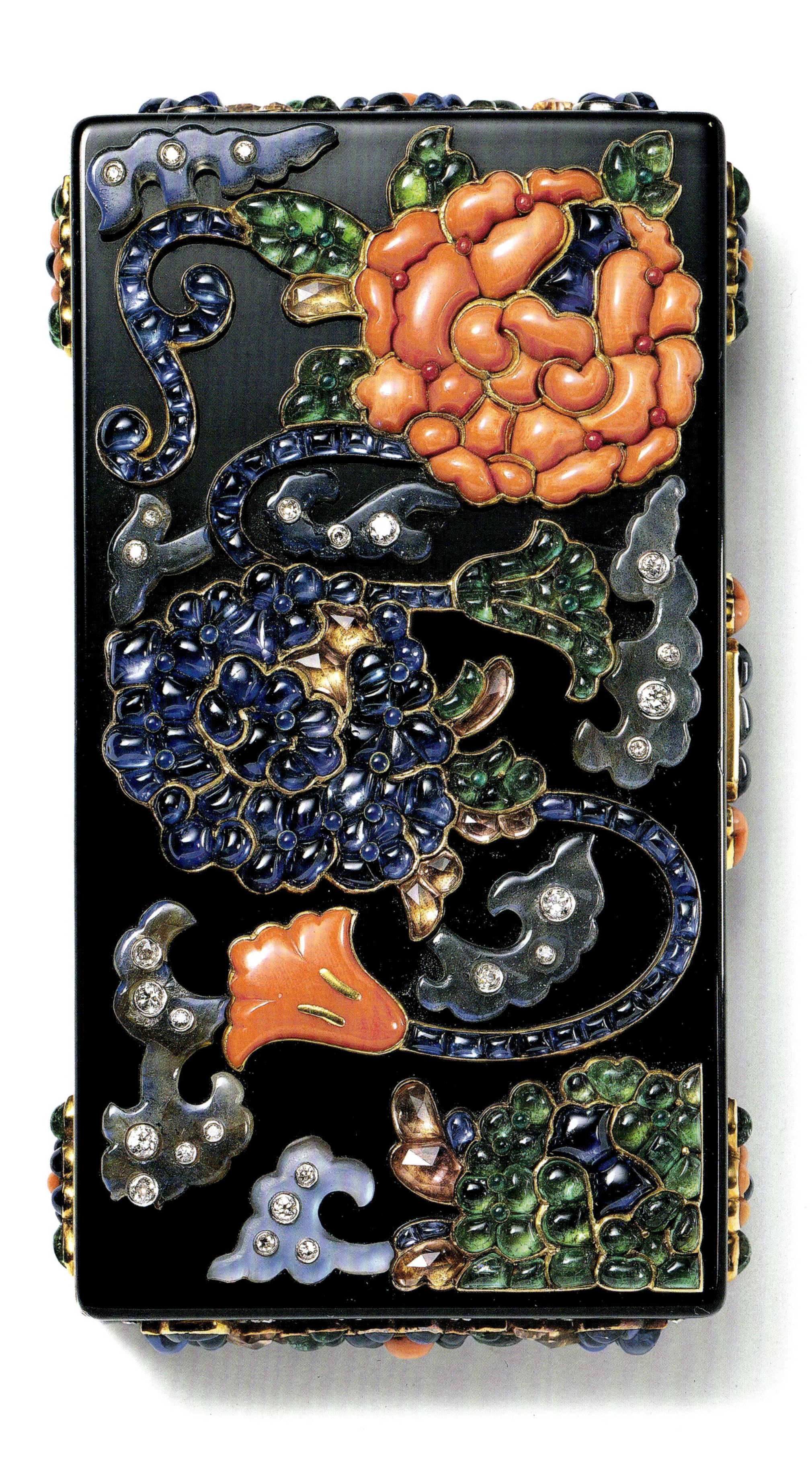

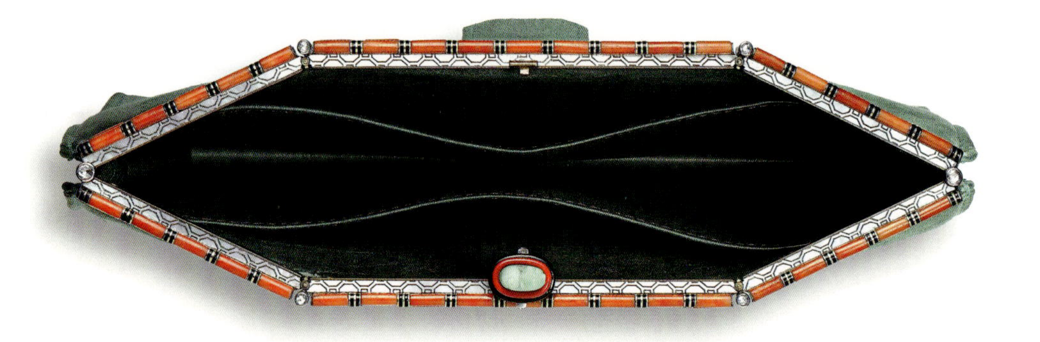

OPPOSITE, CLOCKWISE FROM TOP LEFT

101. **Vanity case** Cartier Paris, 1929. Gold, platinum, two carved-jade plaques (China, nineteenth century), mother-of-pearl, coral, enamel, rose-cut diamonds. 9.1 × 5.9 × 2.2 cm. Cartier Collection VC 73 A29.

The interior is fitted with a mirror, lipstick holder, a place for a comb, and two powder compartments.

102. **Cigarette holder** Cartier Paris, about 1925. Platinum, white and green jade, onyx, rose-cut diamonds. Length 13.6 cm. Cartier Collection CH 06 C25.

103. **Clutch bag** Cartier Paris, 1927. Silver; gold; a jade chimera, onyx, and enamel clasp; mother-of-pearl; coral; rose-cut diamonds; enamel; green suede. 17 × 28 cm. Cartier Collection EB 16 A27.

Side and top views.

ABOVE 104. **Large *Screen* clock** Cartier (manufactured in Paris), 1926. Platinum, gold, carved white jade, onyx, coral, mother-of-pearl, rose-cut diamonds, enamel. Rectangular 8-day movement, gold-plated, Swiss lever escapement, bimetallic balance, Breguet balance spring. Transmission axle masked by the dragon and the carved coral ball beneath the screen. The time is set by manually turning the hands. Winding is done at the back of the base. 32.7 × 29.5 × 12 cm. Cartier Collection CDB 23 A26.

The dial, without glass, is of white jade carved with a Chinese genre scene in front and a landscape in back.

EXOTIC FANTASY

The late 1920s was a time of economic expansion and widespread prosperity that fueled creativity in all the arts, including literature, cinema, architecture, and design. It was also a time of feverish excess in personal behavior, profligate spending, political corruption, and rampant financial speculation. The Wall Street crash of 1929 and the ruinous credit contraction that followed annihilated great fortunes and precipitated the global Great Depression. Those whose wealth survived the crash continued to spend lavishly, however, and escapist fantasy pervades 1930s film

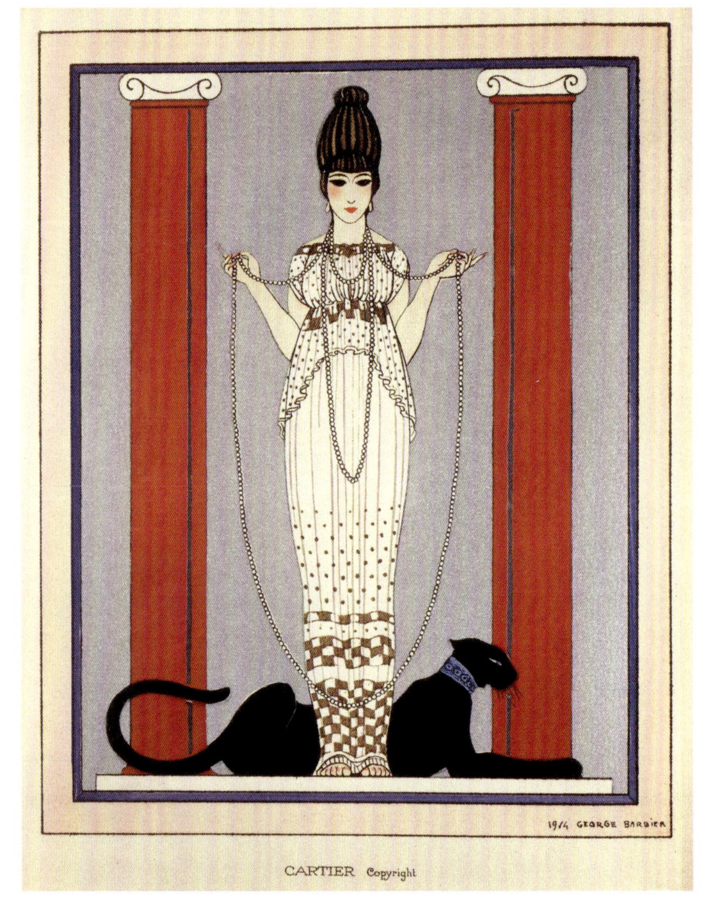

LEFT Mrs. Henry Mond wearing Cartier jewelry for the 1930 Jewels of Empire Ball, held in London. Cartier London Archives.

ABOVE George Barbier, *Woman with a Black Panther,* commissioned by Cartier for a 1914 invitation. Cartier Archives.

and fashion, as well as interior design—especially in entertainment venues such as theaters, restaurants, ocean liners, and hotels. The 1930 Jewels of Empire charity ball, held in London, epitomizes the ethos of this rather uncertain era, when high society strove to maintain its spirits and Cartier sought to encourage new spending on jewelry to complement glamorous dresses. At the ball, prominent women dressed to represent specific jewels, such as ruby, turquoise, jade, and emerald. Cartier supplied Mrs. Henry Mond's lavish jade jewelry, which included a Southeast Asian–style tiara (opposite, left). Mrs. Wilfred Ashley wore a spectacular Cartier emerald-and-diamond tiara (below left and right).

The panther motif, now so closely identified with Cartier, first appeared in a 1914 watercolor, commissioned from George Barbier for an invitation card, in which a woman in ancient Greek garb stands between red columns with a collared black panther crouching behind her (opposite, right). Soon, feline pelt patterns with pavé-set diamond grounds and black onyx spots appeared on Cartier watches (fig. 105). After World War I and throughout the 1920s, the spotted panther pelt and the panther motif recurred on watches, bracelets (fig. 110 and see fig. 32, page 49), hair ornaments, and handbags (fig. 108). Black enamel vanity cases were decorated with panthers (figs. 106 and 107) or gazelles in mysterious landscapes, with trees and flowers rendered in carved multicolored gems.

Carved emeralds, rubies, and sapphires from India were incorporated into new, modern versions of the flower-filled basket motif (fig. 112). They were also combined with diamonds and pearls and used to embellish bracelets (fig. 109) and watch straps (fig. 113), evening bag frames, and necklaces. An unusual pendant watch is adorned with a carved-emerald leaf

ABOVE Cartier emerald-and-diamond tiara worn by Mrs. Wilfred Ashley to the Jewels of Empire Ball in 1930. Cartier London Archives.

RIGHT Mrs. Wilfred Ashley at the Jewels of Empire Ball. Cartier London Archives.

(fig. 111). An exquisite, all-blue bracelet was worn by Mrs. William Randolph Hearst (fig. 114), while a more lavish bracelet chosen by the elegant Mona von Bismarck (then Mrs. Harrison Williams) has a vivid green jade Buddha's hand (a variety of citron) flanked by straps of rock crystal, sapphires, emeralds, and diamonds (fig. 115). The renowned decorator Nancy Lancaster (Mrs. Ronald Tree) owned a lush *sautoir* with strands of pearls and ruby beads and detachable diamond and carved-ruby components that could be worn as bracelets (fig. 116).

True tutti frutti jewelry pieces (a mixture of rubies, emeralds, sapphires, and diamonds) are a riot of color, often organized as undulating vines with carved-gem leaves, flowers, and fruits. Linda Lee Porter owned two such bracelets (fig. 120) as well as a pair of clip brooches (fig. 119). Unusual variants include a bracelet with sapphire, emerald, onyx, and pearl beads studding the central branch and larger carved rubies and emeralds along the edges (fig. 117); another bracelet incorporates diamonds, six star sapphires of lavender color, and carved leaf-shaped sapphires and rubies (fig. 118). A stunning ring in the same taste includes a huge (48.8-carat) carved emerald (fig. 121). The face of an extraordinary bracelet watch with a tutti frutti strap is covered by a crystal of emerald (fig. 122). An evening bag (fig. 123) very similar to one owned by Marjorie Merriweather Post has a jewel-decorated frame and a pouch covered with tiny pearl beads.

One of Cartier's most magnificent jewels from this era is a 1938 necklace (fig. 124) made in Paris.

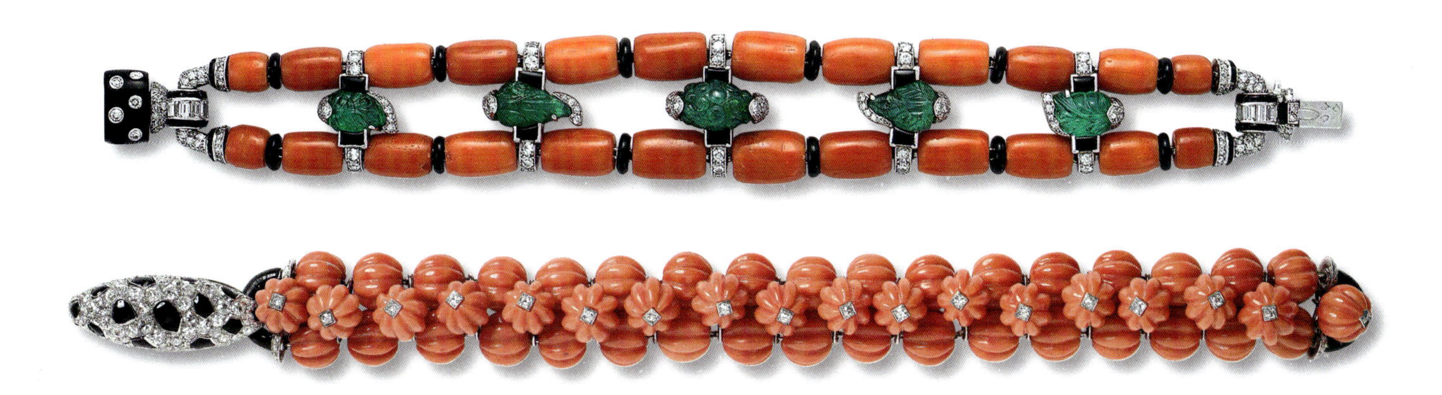

OPPOSITE, FAR LEFT 105. **Panther-pattern watch-brooch** Cartier Paris, 1915. Platinum, pear-shaped and old-cut diamonds, onyx, double black silk cord. Rectangular LeCoultre caliber 111 movement with cut corners, *fausses* Côtes de Genève decoration, silver-plated, 8 adjustments, 19 jewels, Swiss lever escapement, bimetallic balance, flat balance spring. Length 15.5 cm. Cartier Collection WB 33 A15. Sold to Pierre Cartier.

Created in 1914, the panther-skin onyx-and-diamond pavé setting has remained one of Cartier's signature motifs.

OPPOSITE, TOP CENTER 106. ***Panther* vanity case** Cartier Paris, 1925. Enamel, buff-top *calibré*-cut rubies, mother-of-pearl, ruby cabochon sun and turquoise cabochon flowers, onyx, diamonds. Push-piece designed as a gem-set songbird. Interior with fitted mirror, perfume vial, lipstick case, and covered powder compartment; mounted in gold and platinum. 10.2 × 4.3 × 1.5 cm. Private collection. Provenance: Art Deco Treasures: Jeweled Boxes and Clocks, The Prince and Princess Sadruddin Aga Khan Collection.

OPPOSITE, TOP RIGHT 107. ***Panther* vanity case** Cartier Paris, 1928. Gold, platinum, enamel, rose-cut and baguette-cut diamonds, carved and square emeralds, *calibré*-cut and faceted rubies, onyx cabochons. Interior fitted with mirror, lipstick case, covered powder compartment, and cigarette compartment with gold openwork retaining clip. 10.9 × 5.5 × 1.8 cm. Cartier Collection VC 08 A28.

This item is part of a series of cases inspired by Georges Barbier's drawings of panthers, dogs, and gazelles. Another case decorated with greyhounds (see fig. 143, page 140) belonged to Elma Rumsey, Pierre Cartier's wife.

OPPOSITE, BOTTOM RIGHT 108. **Evening bag** Cartier Paris for Cartier New York, special order, 1924. Platinum; round old-, rose-, and single-cut diamonds; onyx; enamel; black satin; black cord. 19 × 7.6 cm. Cartier Collection EB 03 A24.

TOP 109. **Bracelet** Cartier Paris, 1930. Platinum, coral, carved emeralds, onyx, single-cut and baguette-cut diamonds. Length 19 cm. Private collection.

ABOVE 110. **Bracelet** Cartier Paris, 1930. Platinum, gold, round old- and single-cut diamonds, fluted coral beads, onyx (spots), enamel. Length 20.5 cm. Cartier Collection BT 13 A30.

Each bead of coral in the central strand is studded with a collet-set diamond.

TOP LEFT 111. **Pendant watch** Cartier Paris, about 1925. Necklace: Platinum, onyx beads, emeralds, enamel, diamonds. Pendant watch: Platinum; carved, baguette, and cabochon emeralds; *calibré*-cut sapphires; rose-cut and baguette diamonds; onyx; enamel bezel; black and red enamel case. Watch: 2.3 × 2.5 × 3.5 cm. Private collection. Provenance: Art Deco Treasures: Jeweled Boxes and Clocks, The Prince and Princess Sadruddin Aga Khan Collection.

TOP CENTER 112. ***Flower basket* pendant** Cartier London, 1924. Platinum; gold; enamel; onyx; diamonds; carved emeralds, rubies, and sapphires. Height 9 cm. Private collection.

TOP RIGHT 113. **Bracelet-watch** Cartier New York, 1927. Platinum; carved, baton-shaped, and cabochon rubies; baguette-, rose-, square-, and circular-shaped old-cut diamonds. Oval LeCoultre caliber 103 movement, *fausses* Côtes de Genève decoration, rhodium-plated, 8 adjustments, 19 jewels, Swiss lever escapement, bimetallic balance, Breguet balance spring. Length 16 cm. Cartier Collection WWL 23 A27.

CENTER 114. **Bracelet** Cartier New York, 1927. Platinum; round old-, brilliant-, and single-cut diamonds; engraved hexagonal 59.39-carat sapphire; carved, buff-top, *calibré*-cut, and cabochon sapphires; cabochon, buff-top, and *calibré*-cut emeralds. 18.5 × 2.8 cm. Cartier Collection BT 77 A27. Sold to Mrs. William Randolph Hearst.

In 1903, Millicent Veronica Wilson (1882–1974) married American press baron William Randolph Hearst. Mrs. Hearst did much charitable work during and after World War I.

ABOVE 115. **Bracelet** Cartier New York, 1927. Platinum, rock crystal, carved jadeite and sapphires, emerald cabochons, pavé-set diamonds. Length about 18 cm. Private collection. Provenance: Owned by Mrs. Harrison Williams (later Mona von Bismarck).

OPPOSITE 116. ***Sautoir*** Cartier London, special order, 1930. Platinum; square brilliant-, round old-, single-, and rose-cut diamonds; carved rubies; ruby cabochons and beads; natural pearls. Total length 62.1 cm. Cartier Collection NE 27 A30. Sold to Mrs. Ronald Tree.

American Nancy Perkins (1897–1994) married Ronald Tree, and later the British Member of Parliament C. G. Lancaster. After purchasing the famous decorating firm Colefax & Fowler, she became a well-known interior decorator under the name of Nancy Lancaster.

TOP 117. **Bracelet** Cartier Paris, about 1932. Platinum, old European- and single-cut diamonds, engraved ruby beads, fluted emerald beads, emerald cabochon, sapphire cabochons, onyx beads, natural pearls. 17.7 × 3.5 cm. Private collection.

ABOVE 118. **Bracelet** Cartier Paris, special order, 1927. Platinum; gold; brilliant- and French-cut diamonds; lavender-colored star sapphires; square, cabochon, and carved sapphires; carved rubies; rectangular-cut and cabochon emeralds; *calibré*-cut onyx. 18.7 × 3.5 cm. Private collection.

OPPOSITE, TOP 119. ***Tutti Frutti* double clip brooch** Cartier Paris, special order, 1935. Platinum; osmior; brilliant-, round old-, baguette-, and single-cut diamonds; carved sapphires, rubies, and emeralds; emerald, ruby, and sapphire cabochons; buff-top and *calibré*-cut rubies and sapphires; faceted sapphires. 9.8 × 4.5 × 1.7 cm. Cartier Collection CL 266 A35. Sold to Mrs. Cole Porter.

Mrs. Porter supplied most of the stones for these clips; she may have obtained them by dismantling another tutti frutti item. The two clip brooches can be snapped together or taken apart and worn separately. Osmior is a platinum-like alloy of gold, copper, nickel, and zinc.

OPPOSITE, BOTTOM 120. ***Tutti Frutti* strap bracelet** Cartier Paris, 1929. Platinum; brilliant- and single-cut diamonds; carved sapphires, emeralds, and rubies; sapphire and emerald cabochons; ruby beads studded with collet-set diamonds. 18 × 4.1 × 0.8 cm. Cartier Collection BT 111 A29. Sold to Mrs. Cole Porter.

Linda Lee (1883–1954) was born in Louisville, Kentucky, and married the wealthy Edward Thomas. After her divorce, she married the famous American composer Cole Porter in 1919. Considered one of the most beautiful women in the world, Mrs. Porter purchased Cartier jewelry for herself and cigarette boxes by Cartier as gifts for her husband.

ABOVE 121. **Ring** Cartier London, 1928. Platinum, carved 48.8-carat emerald, onyx, rubies, sapphires, diamonds. Height 3.5 cm. Private collection.

RIGHT 122. ***Tutti Frutti* bracelet-watch** Cartier Paris, 1929. Platinum, table-cut emerald (over watch face), baguette-cut and collet-set diamonds, carved emeralds, carved sapphires and rubies, emerald and sapphire cabochons. Rectangular LeCoultre caliber 118 movement, rhodium-plated, 8 adjustments, 17 jewels, Swiss lever escapement, bimetallic balance, flat balance spring. Length 17.5 cm. Cartier Collection WWL 99 A29.

123. ***Tutti Frutti* evening bag** Cartier New York, 1930. Gold; platinum; carved rubies, emeralds, and sapphires; ruby, emerald, and sapphire beads and rondelles; emerald cabochons; brilliant-, old round-, and single-cut diamonds; natural pearls and seed pearl fabric; enamel; silk cord. 16.7 × 13.9 cm. Cartier Collection EB 27 A30.

Although its form and materials seem to evoke traditional Indian jewelry, it is a quintessentially Cartier creation, fusing traditional and nontraditional elements into a vividly colored and uniquely opulent design. Massive in scale, the necklace is fastened with long cords, like a traditional Indian necklace. But the cords are made of braided gold, rather than silk, with a jeweled slide to adjust the length. A row of diamond-and-ruby flowers mounted in gold appears to be of Indian manufacture, but most of the necklace's faceted diamonds and engraved rubies, sapphires, and emeralds are in collet or claw settings. The brilliant tutti frutti color palette is itself European, rather than authentically Indian: sapphires are generally considered inauspicious in India and were not commonly incorporated into traditional jewelry.[20]

OPPOSITE 124. **Necklace** Cartier Paris, special order, 1938. Gold; platinum; old European-cut diamonds; carved pear-shaped and square emeralds; fluted emerald beads; *calibré*-cut rubies; ruby beads and cabochons; carved sapphires, rubies, and emeralds; half pearls; enamel. Height at center 11 cm. Private collection.

ABOVE 125. ***Le Ciel* clock** Cartier Paris, 1928. Platinum, rock crystal, jade, obsidian, onyx, coral, moonstones, diamonds, divided axle movement with 13-jewel platform escapement. 21.9 × 7.6 × 1.6 cm. Private collection.

OPPOSITE 126. **Clock with Fō dogs** Cartier Paris, 1926. Platinum; gold; ebony; rock crystal; lapis lazuli; carved rubies, emeralds, and sapphires; pearls; mother-of-pearl; onyx; coral; rose-cut diamonds; enamel. Round Longines 8-day caliber 1941 movement, gold-plated, 19 jewels, Swiss lever escapement, bimetallic balance, Breguet balance spring. 22 × 18 × 6 cm. Cartier Collection CDB 12 A26.

The ebony base was added later to support a protective glass display case (not shown).

Cartier's clocks from this era are endlessly inventive in both form and function; each is a work of art in its own right (see page 126). A 1926 model has a mother-of-pearl mosaic face (framed in coral) between two rock crystal pillars surmounted by Chinese Fō dogs. Affixed to each pillar is a coral flower pot from which sprouts a tutti frutti flowering plant (fig. 126). Another clock features two carved-jade carp swimming through pink quartz water with mother-of-pearl waves. Above them, rising out of mother-of-pearl spray, is a fanlike rock crystal face on which the hours are marked off in Roman numerals (fig. 127). The dragon-shaped diamond hand sweeps forward, then snaps back every twelve hours. Below is a smaller pearl-rimmed dial with Arabic numerals that rotates; the minutes are indicated by a fixed pointer. A fourth clock has a vivid blue dial supported by the raised tails of two green jade fish with coral fins. They in turn rest upon the rock crystal waters of a fountain (fig. 125).

Most fascinating of all are the mystery clocks, several of which incorporate Chinese hardstone sculptures from the 1700s or 1800s (see page 125 right). One has a lionlike Chinese agate chimera wearing a jeweled saddle that supports a citrine, diamond, and enamel

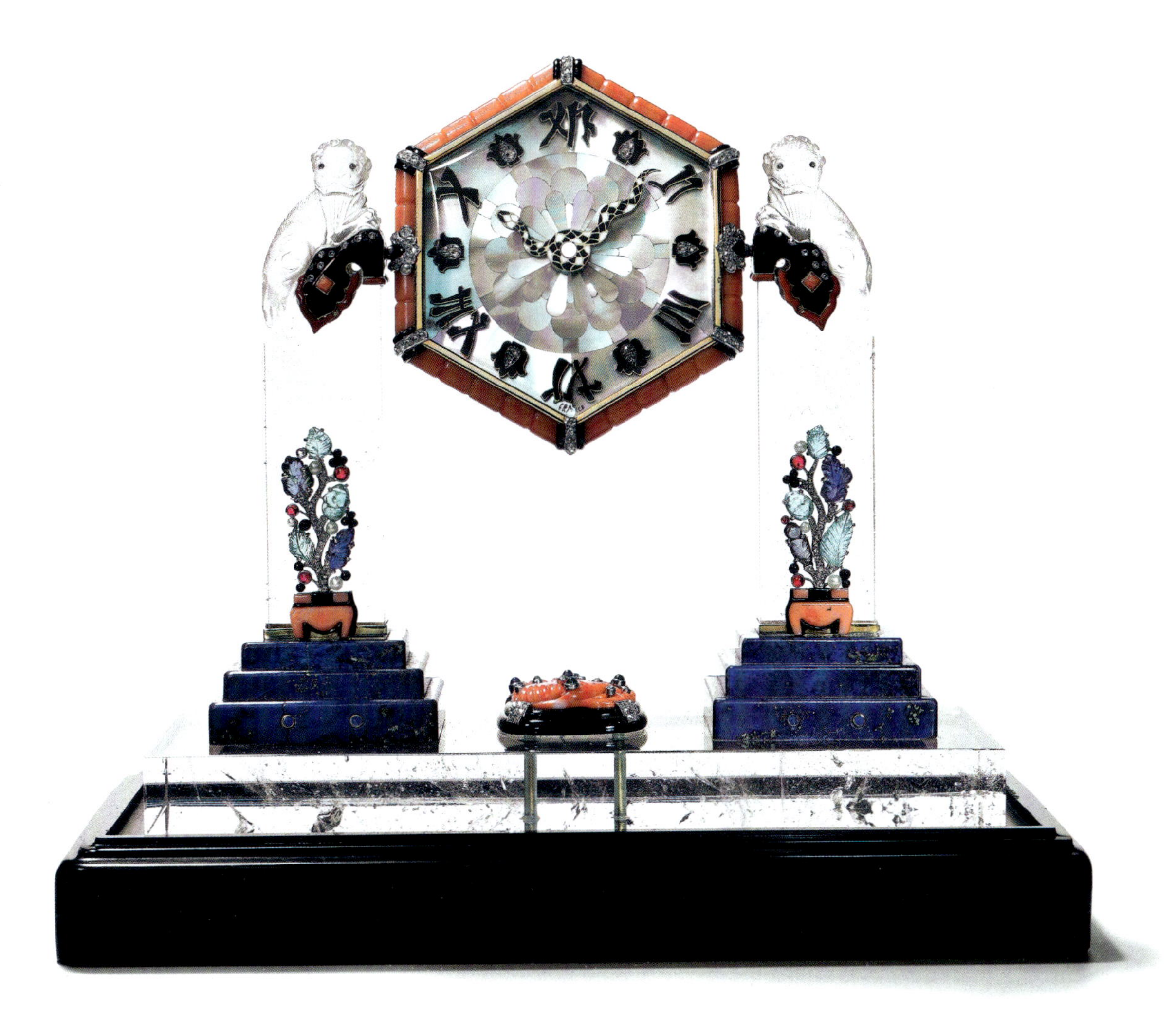

OVERLEAF, LEFT 127. ***Carp* clock with retrograde hand** Cartier Paris, 1925. Platinum, gold, gray jade, obsidian, rock crystal, mother-of-pearl, pearls, coral, emerald cabochons, rose-cut diamonds, mauve lacquer, enamel. Rectangular 8-day movement, gilded, retrograde hour hand, platform escapement, bimetallic balance, flat balance spring. 23 × 23 × 11 cm. Cartier Collection CS 11 A25.

The jade carps are Chinese in origin, dating from the eighteenth century. Although this clock is not, strictly speaking, a mystery clock, it is the third in a series of twelve clocks featuring animals or figurines made between 1922 and 1931. Since the hour hand cannot make a complete rotation, when it reaches the VI on the right it springs back to the start, hence the name "retrograde hand."

OVERLEAF, RIGHT 128. ***Chimera* mystery clock** Cartier New York, 1926. Gold, platinum, citrine, agate, nephrite, onyx, coral, rose-cut diamonds, pearls, emerald cabochons, enamel. Rectangular 8-day movement, gold-plated, 15 jewels, bimetallic balance, Breguet balance spring. Transmission axle masked by a carved piece of coral beneath the chimera. Hand-setting and winding mechanism underneath the base. 17 × 13.8 × 7.5 cm. Cartier Collection CM 23 A26.

This was the sixth in Cartier's series of animal/figurine mystery clocks. It incorporates a nineteenth-century Chinese carving.

25 30 35 40 45

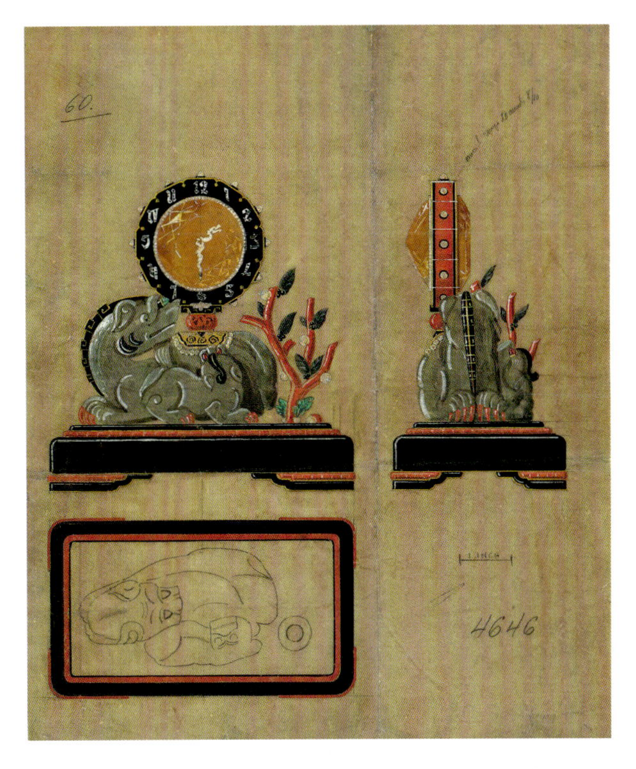

Design drawing of a *Chimera* mystery clock. Cartier Paris, 1929. Cartier Archives.

OPPOSITE 129. **Striking mystery clock with deity** Cartier Paris, 1931. Platinum, gold, white jade, rock crystal, onyx, nephrite, rose-cut diamonds, pearls, turquoise cabochons, coral, enamel. Rectangular 8-day movement, striking mechanism (hours and quarter-hours), gold-plated, Swiss lever escapement, bimetallic balance, Breguet balance spring. Hand-setting and winding mechanism on back of base. 35 × 28 × 14 cm. Cartier Collection CM 04 A31. Sold to Paul-Louis Weiller.

This mystery clock was the last in Cartier's series of twelve animal/figurine clocks. The jades, of Chinese origin, date from the nineteenth century. The clock's first owner, Paul-Louis Weiller (1893–1993), was an engineer and pilot during World War I. A pioneer of the aeronautic industry, he was also a great art patron. In 1937 Weiller notably bought the 245.35-carat Jubilee diamond, the world's fourth largest at the time.

ABOVE 130. **Seal watch-brooch** Cartier Paris, 1929. Gold; platinum; round old-, baguette-, single-, and rose-cut diamonds; buff-top ruby cabochons; ruby beads; carved jade; onyx; enamel. Oval LeCoultre caliber 103 movement, Côtes de Genève decoration, rhodium-plated, 2 adjustments, 19 jewels, bimetallic balance, Swiss lever escapement, flat balance spring. 11.2 × 2.8 × 1.6 cm. Cartier Collection WB 34 A29.

The watch is set in a nineteenth-century Chinese jade seal featuring a Buddhist lion figure.

OVERLEAF, LEFT Turtle desk clock made by Cartier Paris in 1928. Gold, platinum, nephrite, frosted glass, onyx, mother-of-pearl, lapis lazuli, turquoise, rubies, emeralds, sapphires, diamonds, enamel, eight-day gilt lever movement, 19 jewels. 6 closed (14 open) × 10.8 × 9 cm. Private collection.

OVERLEAF, RIGHT 131. ***Elephant* mystery clock** Cartier Paris, 1928. Platinum, gold, jade, coral, onyx, crystal, mother-of-pearl, pearls, rose-cut diamonds, enamel. Rectangular 8-day movement, gold-plated, 13 jewels, Swiss lever escapement, bimetallic balance, Breguet balance spring. Movement set in a gilded metal case attached to the base of the pagoda and seated within the elephant's back. Hand-setting and winding mechanism accessed by lifting the pagoda to reach the movement. 20 × 15.5 × 9.2 cm. Cartier Collection CM 20 A28. Provenance: the Maharaja of Nawanagar.

dial (fig. 128). Another, purchased by the Maharaja of Nawanagar, is a Chinese jade elephant wearing a carved saddlecloth surmounted by a bead-fringed, mother-of-pearl-and-enamel saddle (fig. 131). The clock is tucked into a pagoda-roofed howdah atop the saddle. Still another spectacular example has a carved nephrite base and a turquoise enameled frame with diamond-and-platinum numerals around the crystal clock face. Behind the clock stands a Chinese jade statue of a goddess holding a basket or jar. Flanking it are a crouching Chinese lion (with a coral rose in its mouth) and a jade flower pot from which grows a branching coral "plant" with pearl flower buds (fig. 129). A tiny watch-brooch that incorporates a carved Chinese jade seal into a setting of platinum, diamonds, and rubies (fig. 130) shares the same aesthetic.

The color, novelty, and sheer exuberance of Cartier's exotic jewelry, accessories, and timepieces make them instantly recognizable. Unequaled in both daring design and impeccable craftsmanship, they epitomize art deco's most creative period.

MARGARET YOUNG-SÁNCHEZ

THE ART OF SMOKING

In 1900, tobacco consumption in Western Europe and North America was undergoing a rapid transformation. Chewing was the most popular way for Americans to consume tobacco throughout the nineteenth century (to the disgust of foreign observers such as Charles Dickens). Upper-class men often smoked tobacco in the form of cigars. This was a ritualized masculine activity, usually savored in the dining room (after the ladies' departure) or in other exclusively male venues. Carefully graded by quality and origin, cigars were sold in decorative boxes and tins, stored in humidors of figured wood or silver, and trimmed before smoking with finely decorated cutters and guillotines (figs. 132 and 133). Pipe smoking, a nineteenth-century symbol of middle-class respectability (especially in England), was also an activity confined to men. Cigarettes, little more than a niche product at the turn of the century, were about to explode in popularity, spawning a huge international industry devoted to the growing and processing of tobacco and to the manufacture, packaging, advertising, and distribution of the finished product. Over the course of the next fifty years, cigarette smoking would be enthusiastically embraced by both men and women—a trend that both responded to and influenced changing social norms. The social interactions and physical gestures associated with cigarette smoking were used to communicate class identity, social status, and wealth; to enhance personal style; and to convey erotic messages. Cartier, always keenly attuned to popular trends, both served and shaped the evolving culture of smoking, providing the world's style leaders with a fabulous variety of chic, luxurious tobacco accoutrements.[1]

OPPOSITE Actress Marlene Dietrich, wearing top hat and tails, smokes a cigarette, about 1935.

THE MODERN HISTORY OF SMOKING

An indigenous American plant, tobacco was first encountered by Columbus's men during his first voyage of exploration in 1492. The crew received tobacco leaves as a gift in the Bahamas and observed tobacco being smoked in Cuba—several sailors tried smoking it themselves. In succeeding centuries, tobacco was cultivated for medicinal purposes in Europe and was also smoked and snuffed for pleasure. It became an extremely profitable commercial crop in North America, which supplied both domestic and foreign consumers. But despite tobacco's long international history, by the late 1800s cigarettes were particularly associated with Spain, Turkey, and the Crimean Peninsula. In the popular imagination, they evoked languid, Turkish scenes (opposite) and images of sultry, dangerous beauties (such as Carmen, the cigar-factory worker and heroine of Prosper Mérimée's 1845 novella of the same name, later adapted into an 1875

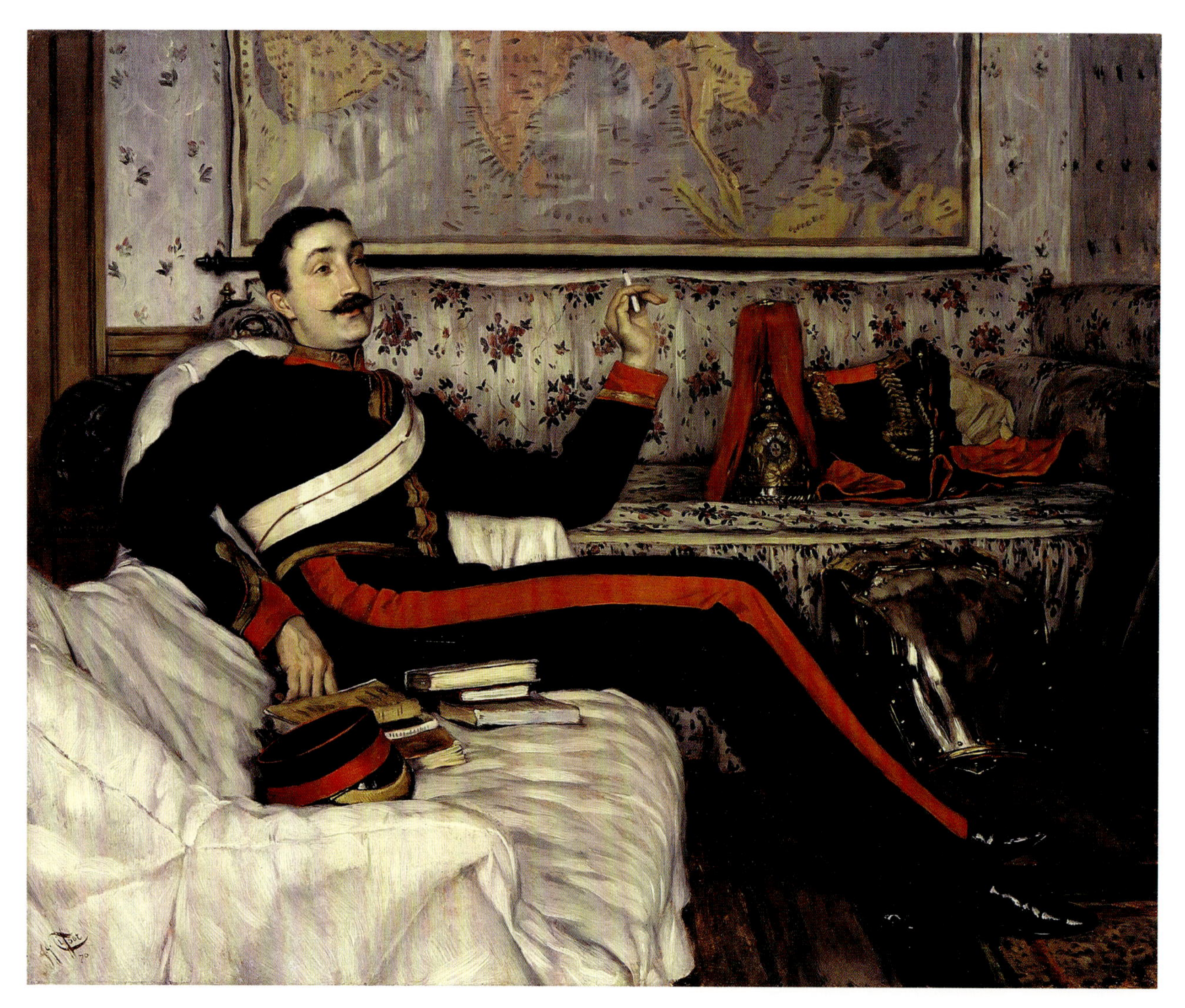

James Jacques Tissot (1836–1902), *Frederick Burnaby*, 1870. Oil on canvas. National Portrait Gallery, London.

Rudolf Ernst (1854–1932), *Le Fumeur*, 1888. Oil on canvas. Private collection. Courtesy of Artcurial Briest Poulain F. Tajan, Paris, France.

opera by Georges Bizet) who smoked paper-wrapped, shredded-tobacco *papelotes* (cigarettes). English and European soldiers picked up the cigarette-smoking habit during foreign tours of duty and popularized it at home. James Tissot's 1870 portrait of the debonair young Frederick Burnaby conveys the appeal perfectly: the handsome, uniformed Royal Horse Guards officer lounges in his quarters, a cigarette held casually between two fingers (opposite). Aside from their adventurous associations, cigarettes were lighter, easier to smoke, and more elegant than either cigars or pipes.

While cigarettes grew in popularity among men during the 1800s, they were still socially unacceptable for respectable women, a taboo enhanced by fear of damage to women's delicate constitutions. Nonetheless, images of women (from demure, fully clothed maidens to saucy, scantily clad actresses and romanticized Turkish damsels) commonly appeared on packaging for cigarettes and other forms of tobacco. In 1880 a technological breakthrough cleared the way for mass production (and mass consumption) of cigarettes. The mechanical rolling machine, invented by American James Bonsack and immediately adopted by cigarette manufacturer James Duke, boosted production from the maximum three hundred cigarettes per hour that a skillful hand roller could make to as many as twelve

TOP 132. **Cigar cutter** Cartier Paris, 1923. Gold, sapphire cabochons. 5.5 × 3.9 × 0.4 cm. Cartier Collection SA 15 A23.

ABOVE 133. ***Guillotine* cigar cutter** Cartier Paris, about 1907. Gold, enamel, button pearls. Diameter 3.3 cm. Cartier Collection SA 16 C07.

Originally, sapphire cabochons were set in place of the pearls.

thousand per hour.[2] The cost advantage allowed Duke to bring retail prices down and simultaneously invest huge sums on advertising (cigarette companies were pioneers of many advertising strategies still used today). The machine-made cigarettes were also uniform in size and regular in shape, enhancing their aesthetic appeal. Cigarette companies began marketing light, "healthful" blends as part of a deliberate effort to expand their market and attract female buyers.

The social (and sexual) dynamics of smoking at the turn of the twentieth century are illuminated in an early chapter of Edith Wharton's 1905 novel *The House of Mirth*. The well-bred but impecunious heroine, Lily Bart, takes her first step down the path to ruin when she visits (unchaperoned) the private apartment of Lawrence Selden. There she accepts the cigarette he offers, leaning forward flirtatiously to light it from the tip of his cigarette. Later the same day, in the company of a proper potential suitor, she pretends that she is not a smoker (to the amusement of a married friend, who is more open about her smoking habit).[3] At this time, women who smoked in public places such as hotels and restaurants were sometimes asked to leave,[4] and in 1910 Theodore Roosevelt's daughter Alice (Mrs. Nicholas Longworth) was admonished for smoking by *The Woman's Daily*.[5]

134. **Cigarette holder** Cartier Paris, 1912. Platinum, rose-cut diamonds, faceted and *calibré*-cut sapphires, amber, albatross bone. Length 24.7 cm. Cartier Collection CH 20 A12. Sold to Jacques Cartier.

The custom-made curved case (above the cigarette holder) conforms to the shape of the holder.

Russian attitudes toward cigarette smoking were more accepting—Russian aristocrats and members of the imperial family smoked regularly, and cigarette cases of silver, gold, and fine wood, decorated with enamel, engraving, and gold mounts, were favorite gifts. Grand Duchess Maria Pavlovna, one of Cartier's greatest jewelry customers (see pages 31–32), was an avid smoker; among the jewels and precious objects she smuggled out of Russia during the Russian Revolution were numerous ornate cigarette cases.[6] Wealthy Russian travelers to Paris likely helped stimulate the popularity of cigarettes; certainly they influenced the form, materials, and decorations of cigarette cases made by Cartier and other Parisian firms in the early twentieth century.

In 1907 Cartier manufactured an exquisite engine-turned gold case with blue, white, and green enamel and diamond-set thumbpieces (fig. 135). It has separate compartments for cigarettes and matches and a rough striking surface on one end. Its delicacy and ornamentation might suggest a ladies' accessory, but the slightly curved shape (for carrying in a pocket) is more typical of men's cases and likely reflects Russian taste. Fabergé and other Russian firms were famed for their use of hardstone; in the same vein is a lovely Cartier case made in 1912 of hollowed agate with a diamond-and-sapphire clasp and hinges. It bears the initials of Lady Henriette Acton-Mitchell (fig. 137). A 1914 Cartier case was carved from a block of nephrite. The form, typical of Russian cases made in the late 1800s, has match and cigarette compartments as well as a wick, or tinder cord, that can be pulled through one side (fig. 136). Men's cases were often simpler, with rectangular shapes, rounded corners, and a slightly curved form for comfortable carrying. These were often made of silver and sparely decorated with engraving or colored-gold inlay (see fig. 198, page 182). An extraordinarily elegant cigarette holder from the same era (fig. 134) was bought by Jacques Cartier. The long, curved tube is made of albatross bone; the cup is of amber with diamond and sapphire mounts.[7] It is easy to imagine it being used by a lady wearing a Poiret dress, turban, and jeweled aigrette.

135. **Cigarette case** Cartier Paris, 1907. Gold, silver, enamel, rose-cut diamonds. 9.8 × 5.9 × 1.3 cm. Cartier Collection CC 41 A07.

On the left side is a compartment for matches with an external striking surface.

ABOVE 136. ***Russian*** **cigarette case** Cartier Paris, 1914. Nephrite, gold, *calibré*-cut onyx, enamel, silk cord. 11 × 6.5 cm. Cartier Collection CC 61 A14. Sold to Mrs. W. B. (Nancy) Leeds.

The case was carved from a hollowed block of nephrite. On the side is a compartment for matches with a striking surface on the cover. The silk cord replaces the original silk-sheathed cotton wick (dipped in saltpeter to make it more flammable).

RIGHT 137. **Cigarette case** Cartier Paris, 1912. Agate, platinum, rose-cut diamonds, *calibré*-cut and cabochon sapphires. Monogram *HA*. 9.3 × 5.1 × 1.4 cm. Cartier Collection CC 74 A12. Provenance: reputedly owned by Lady Henriette Acton-Mitchell.

The case was carved from a hollowed block of agate.

WORLD WAR I AND THE 1920S

World War I played a major role in expanding demand for cigarettes among both men and women. For the troops, who experienced long periods of boredom and discomfort interspersed with episodes of terror and horror, cigarettes were a comforting reminder of home and normalcy—a soothing, portable pleasure. Commanders on both sides regarded cigarettes as essential to morale and distributed them as rations. During the war, women carried out a variety of roles and jobs previously performed by men; they felt entitled to the open enjoyment of privileges such as smoking. By war's end, smoking rates among both sexes were surging, and women were demanding the right to vote in both the United States and the United Kingdom. After the long privations of war, Europeans and Americans were ready to enjoy life and rebuild shattered economies. Restrictive social norms were thrown aside, and the Roaring Twenties began.

Women attended dance halls, drank cocktails, and publicly applied makeup and smoked cigarettes. Dress hems retreated, and waistlines disappeared; jewels to complement the new fashions included *sautoirs*, bandeaus, and bracelets. The final touch was a vanity case (*nécessaire*), cigarette case, or a clever amalgam of the two (see page 137). Cartier's cases, made for the social elite, were fashioned of precious materials such as enameled gold and diamonds mounted in platinum. A 1924 example, a cigarette-and-vanity case presented by the wealthy Duke of Westminster to his mistress Coco Chanel (fig. 138), is restrained in decoration. The barrel-shaped case, decorated with black and white enamel and a *C* monogram of diamonds and platinum, dangled from a finger ring and chain. Interior compartments were designed to hold both cigarettes and cosmetics. A tiny lighter with an inset clock is similar in style (see fig. 153, page 147).

Jacques Cartier presented his niece Marion (Pierre's daughter) with a similar, but more luxurious, model adorned with white enamel, lapis lazuli end panels, and an *MC* diamond monogram (fig. 139). The interior could hold a mirror, comb, powder, cigarettes, and perhaps a handkerchief. In 1920 Pierre Cartier gave his wife, Elma, a lovely rectangular vanity-and-cigarette case with a pink gold interior and an onyx exterior ornamented with a design in tiny diamonds, emeralds, and rubies (fig. 143). The two standing greyhounds probably symbolize Pierre and Elma; the puppy between them, their daughter, Marion (Pierre and Elma affectionately referred to one another as "my popular pup").[8]

Cartier's cigarette cases of the 1920s are among the firm's most extravagant products—iconic symbols of their era. Some were designed to dangle from the hand,

Thayaht, "De la fumée—Robe de Madeleine Vionnet," *La Gazette du Bon Ton*, no. 2, 1922, pl. 13. Bibliothèque des arts décoratifs, Paris.

ABOVE 138. **Cigarette and vanity case** Cartier New York, about 1924. Pink gold, platinum, enamel, rose-cut diamonds. Engraved inside: *Amour Ben d'or / '24*. 8.4 × 4.1 × 3 cm. Cartier Collection VC 39 C24. Sold to the Duke of Westminster.

The interior has multiple compartments. One, with a gold openwork retaining clip, holds cigarettes. There are also two lidded compartments: one with a striking surface for matches and the other for powder. Yet another compartment holds lipstick.

Hugh Grosvenor (1879–1953), 2nd Duke of Westminster, was nicknamed "Bend Or" after his grandfather's famous racehorse, which won the Epsom Derby in 1880. The monogram refers to Coco Chanel (1883–1971), to whom the vanity case was presumably given by the duke.

LEFT 139. **Vanity case** Cartier, about 1920. Gold, platinum, rose-cut diamonds, lapis lazuli, tortoiseshell, enamel. 12 × 4.6 × 3 cm. Pierre Cartier Foundation FPC 7.

The interior is fitted with a tortoiseshell-backed mirror, a cigarette compartment with a gold openwork retaining clip, a covered powder compartment with sifter, and a tortoiseshell comb.

OPPOSITE Fashion photograph with Cartier jewels by Edward Steichen, published in *Vogue*, Oct. 1, 1934. Steichen/*Vogue*. Condé Nast Archive.

140. **Cigarette case** Cartier Paris, 1934. Fluted and polished gold, buff-top and *calibré*-cut sapphires. 11.7 × 8.1 × 0.7 cm. Cartier Collection CC 19 A34. Sold to the Tikka Raja of Kapurthala.

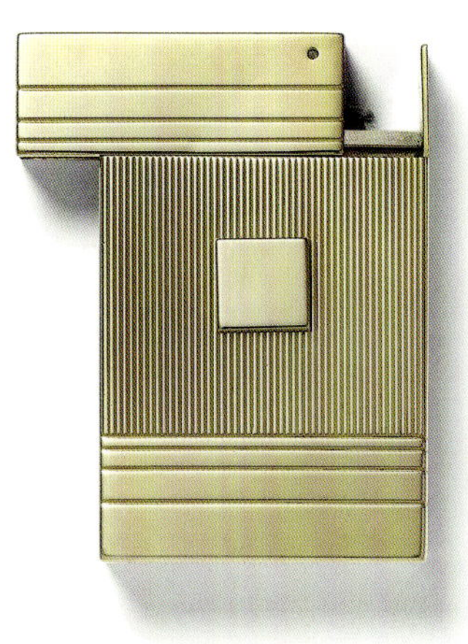

141. **Lighter** Cartier Paris, 1934. Gold. 4.5 × 3 cm. Cartier Collection LR 48 A34. Sold to Prince Bishmu of Nepal.

Pressing the central square of polished gold automatically triggers the lighter.

The urbane Maharaja Yeshwant Rao Holkar II of Indore wearing a Tank wristwatch on a leather cord, photographed by Man Ray, about 1930. Man Ray Trust.

while others are simple rectangles carried in the purse and displayed on the table. One of the most popular designs featured a Persian carpet–like pattern of leaves, flowers, and medallions in black or white enamel on a gold ground (fig. 147); a matching lighter was also available (fig. 146). Cases frequently incorporated vividly colored materials such as coral, lapis lazuli, turquoise, carnelian, nephrite, jadeite, and mother-of-pearl, as well as the rubies, sapphires, and emeralds seen so often in Cartier jewelry. Often the cases were made in exotic styles: Asian, Persian, and Egyptian looks were favorites. Some incorporated imported elements such as carved plaques (see fig. 59, page 64), inlaid lacquer panels, and ancient Egyptian faience. Cigarette holders could be equally colorful and ornate. One example, made of coral, lapis lazuli, emeralds, diamonds, and platinum, perfectly complements Egyptian-style cases (see figs. 74 and 75, page 84). A "Chinese" cigarette holder (fig. 145) has a nephrite bowl ornamented with a tiny jeweled dragon—a fitting mate to a glamorous case of rose quartz, lapis lazuli, and mother-of-pearl with gold dragons on black enamel (fig. 144) or to a hanging case with inlaid figural scenes, turquoise, coral, and enamel trim, and a sinuous, diamond-ornamented dragon on the summit (see fig. 99, page 105).

Cigarette cases for men in the 1920s and early 1930s were generally less flamboyant than their feminine counterparts. Made of silver or gold, they were flat and rectangular in shape, for display on a flat surface. Ornamentation was discreet but elegant: engraved or inlaid stripes (fig. 140), squared initials or crests (see fig. 201, page 185), and black enamel (see fig. 200, page 184). An exceptionally attractive cigarette and match case set ordered in 1932 is decorated with an engraved and enameled moiré pattern (fig. 142). To keep the fingers from becoming stained with nicotine, the fastidious

OPPOSITE 142. ***Moiré* cigarette case and match case** Cartier Paris, special order, 1932. Gold, enamel, sapphire cabochon. Inside the cigarette case, a hinged gold openwork retaining clip. Inscription added later. Cigarette case 14.9 × 8.6 × 1.2 cm, match case 6 × 4.3 × 1 cm. Cartier Collection CC 55 A32.

A
IVIS C. PEASE
CHERBOURG
PARIS
NEW YORK
LONDON
NEWPORT
CON ESTIMACION DEL
CONSEJO DE ADMINISTRACION
Y PERSONAL DE INDETEL
MEXICO 13-XI-61

OPPOSITE 143. ***Greyhound* vanity case** Cartier Paris, special order, 1920. Platinum; pink gold; onyx; rose-cut diamonds; *calibré*-cut emeralds, rubies, citrine, and amethysts. 9.5 × 7.7 × 2 cm. Pierre Cartier Foundation FPC 11. Ordered by Pierre Cartier.

The interior is fitted with a mirror and three compartments, including two with covers: one with lipstick holder, the other with powder sifter.

TOP 144. **Cigarette case** Cartier Paris, 1927. Gold, platinum, rose quartz, lapis lazuli, mother-of-pearl, rose-cut diamonds, navette-shaped emerald cabochons, enamel. 8.9 × 5.1 × 2.1 cm. Cartier Collection CC54 A27.

ABOVE 145. ***Dragon* cigarette holder** Cartier Paris, 1925. Platinum, rose-cut diamonds, *calibré*-cut sapphire cabochons, nephrite, ivory, enamel. Shaft and mouthpiece originally albatross bone. Length 21.9 cm. Cartier Collection CH 18 A25.

This cigarette holder was one of the items displayed by Cartier at the Exposition internationale des arts décoratifs et industriels modernes held in Paris in 1925.

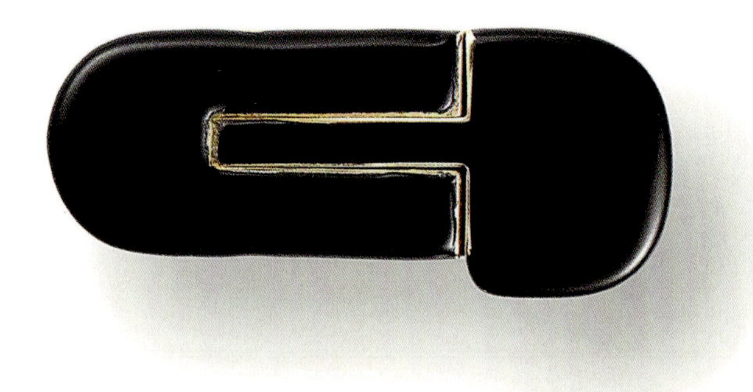

ABOVE 146. ***Lilliput* lighter** Cartier Paris, 1931. Pink gold, enamel. 3 × 3 × 1 cm. Cartier Collection LR 53 A31.

The term *Lilliput* is used in the Cartier Archives for objects of small size and is applied to lighters and pens.

OPPOSITE 147. ***Persian* cigarette case** Cartier Paris, 1924. Pink gold, enamel, onyx cabochons. 8.7 × 7.7 × 1 cm. Cartier Collection CC 64 A24.

This case has a "Kodak" system catch that opens automatically when the push-pieces on both sides are pressed.

ABOVE LEFT 148. **Cigarette holder** Cartier Paris, 1923. Amber; yellow and pink gold; ruby, emerald, sapphire, topaz, and amethyst cabochons; jet. Length 12.8 cm. Cartier Collection CH 01 A23.

ABOVE RIGHT 149. **Cigarette holder** Cartier London, 1930. Bakelite, platinum, baguette-cut and fancy-shaped diamonds. 12 × 1.7 cm. Cartier Collection CH 10 A30.

LEFT 150. **Cigarette clip-holder** Cartier Paris, 1925. Gold. Length 8.8 cm. Cartier Collection CH 09 A25. Sold to the Tikka Raja of Kapurthala.

Placed on the index or middle finger, this item held a cigarette away from the fingers to prevent unsightly nicotine stains.

smoker might use an amber holder studded with tiny colored stones (fig. 148) or an elegant gold clip holder (fig. 150).

Deluxe smoking equipment for the home included cleverly stacking agate ashtrays (fig. 151) and table lighters (larger than the lighters carried in the purse [fig. 153] or pocket). Tabletop boxes, for dispensing cigarettes to guests, ranged in style from spare and modern to intricate and lushly decorated. A 1927 smoker's set of silver, crystal, and ebonite decorated with coral cabochons has an unmistakably masculine feel (fig. 152). It features two rectangular crystal jars for holding cigarettes, an ashtray, and a sleek lighter. Its owner might have smoked with the aid of a black Bakelite cigarette holder, minimally ornamented with a platinum-and-diamond airplane motif (fig. 149). Its proportions are shorter and thicker than those of ladies' cigarette holders of the era. More massive is a silver box with gold trim and ebonite legs (see fig. 197, page 181). On the lid are the crossed flags of the New York Yacht Club and the Vanderbilt family, along with an engraved inscription in the handwriting of Pierre C. Mérillon. He presented the box to his hosts, Mr. and Mrs. William K. Vanderbilt II, in gratitude for a 1928–29 round-the-world cruise on the yacht *Ara*.

At the opposite end of the stylistic spectrum is an Asian-inspired tabletop box of silver and gold on ebonite legs (fig. 157). The legs recall a traditional Chinese stand for a vase or sculpture, while the box itself has a curved profile that terminates in cylinder forms. The sides are engraved with a pattern reminiscent of Japanese textiles and ornamented in the center with carved-jade medallions studded with coral and sapphire cabochons. The box's two lids resemble sections of an Asian painted scroll displayed between two rollers (see pages 150–51). Each lid is a framed square of *laque burgauté*, probably taken from a dismantled item of Chinese furniture. The *laque burgauté* is inlaid with mother-of-pearl delicately tinted purple, blue, and green. Both panels depict evening garden scenes. In one, a man gestures to a woman by the water's

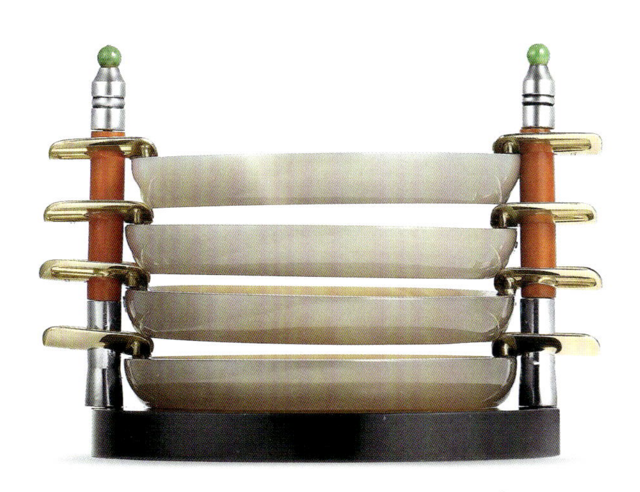

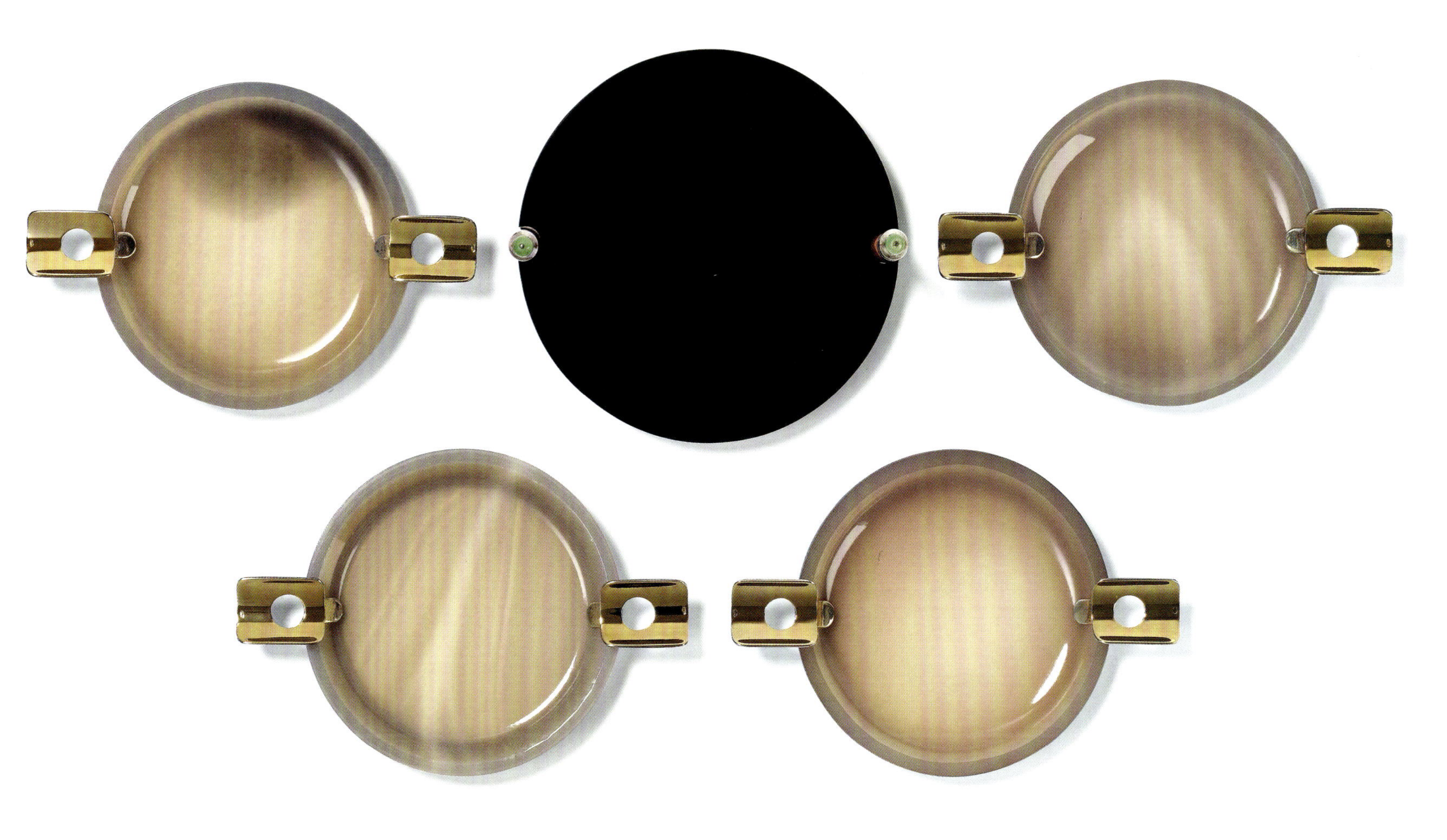

151. **Set of four ashtrays** Cartier Paris, about 1923. Agate, silver-gilt, jade beads, coral, onyx. 7 × 6 × 9.5 cm. Cartier Collection SA 03 C23.

A hole in the cigarette rests allows the ashtrays to be stacked on the uprights.

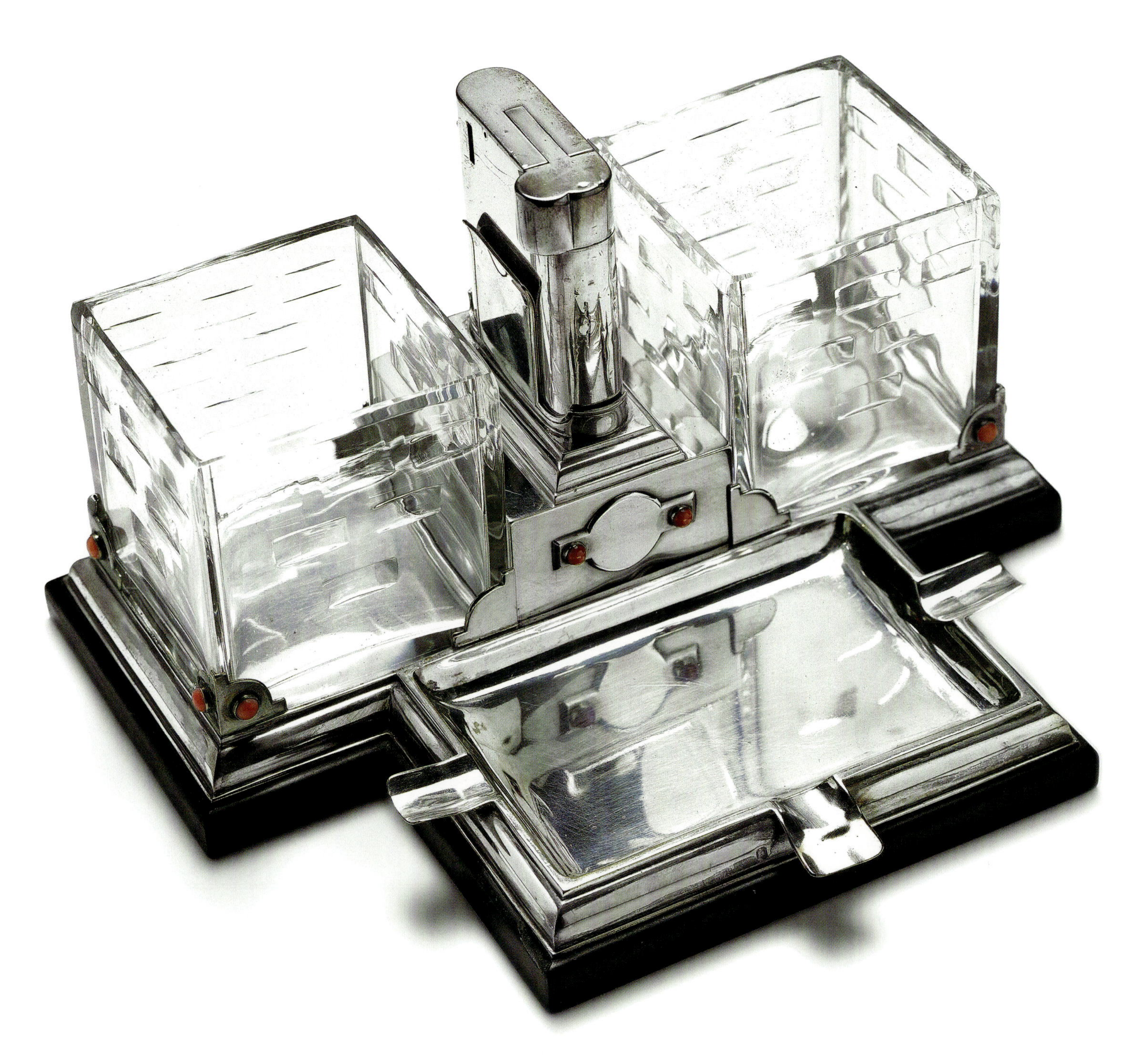

ABOVE 152. **Smoker's set** Cartier Paris, 1927. Silver, crystal, coral cabochons, ebonite. 7 × 18.5 × 15 cm. Cartier Collection SA 07 A27.

The set consists of two square jars, an ashtray with three cigarette rests, and a lighter.

OPPOSITE 153. **Lighter with watch** Cartier Paris, 1929. Gold, enamel. Round movement, Côtes de Genève decoration, rhodium-plated, 3 adjustments, 15 jewels, Swiss lever escapement, bimetallic balance, Breguet balance spring. At top left, a system for adjusting the flint. 4.5 × 3.2 × 1.4 cm. Cartier Collection LR 03 A29.

CARTIER
PARIS

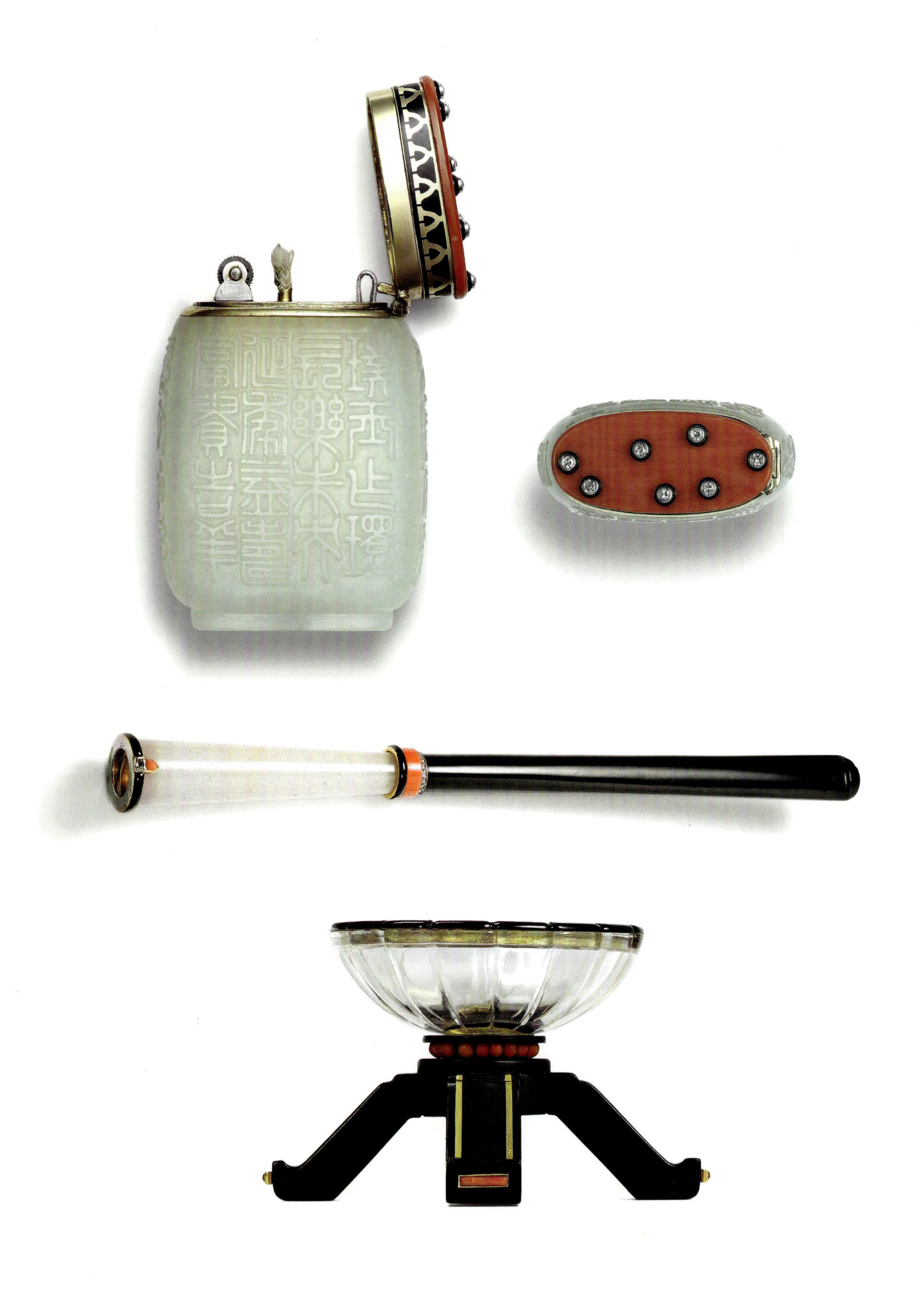

TOP 154. **Table lighter** Cartier Paris, 1939. Engraved white jade, gold, platinum, silver-gilt, coral, round old-cut and collet-set diamonds, enamel. Filling screw on bottom of flask. 6.5 × 4.5 × 2 cm. Cartier Collection LR 22 A39.

The jade flask, engraved with Chinese characters, came from the firm's stock of *apprêts*.

CENTER 155. **Cigarette holder** Cartier Paris, 1928. Gold, platinum, agate, jet, coral, rose-cut diamonds, enamel. Length 14.1 cm. Cartier Collection CH 17 A28.

ABOVE 156. **Ashtray** Cartier Paris, 1934. Rock crystal, gold, coral, ebonite, lacquer. 5.2 × 8.3 cm. Cartier Collection SA 05 A34.

edge. Inlaid sapphire cabochons represent the moon and stars, while a ruby serves as a lantern. The other panel shows a convivial candlelit meal at which four men are seated around a table attended by a servant. Inlaid cabochons represent a fan, tree fruits, and stars. A decade or so later, but very much in keeping stylistically, are an ashtray of rock crystal, ebonite, gold, and coral (fig. 156) and a table lighter made from a Chinese carved-jade flask (fig. 154). The sides of the flask-lighter's cover are gold with black enamel patterning and its top is a vivid orange coral studded with diamonds.

THE DEPRESSION ERA AND BEYOND

Cigarette cases and other smoking accessories were frequently given as gifts, either as tokens of personal affection (see fig. 138, page 136) or in recognition of achievement (see fig. 200, page 184). Cartier could accommodate a wide range of budgets. In 1928 Cartier New York produced a color brochure titled *For a Luxurious Smoke: Accessories, by Cartier* (see page 152 top). A silver cigarette-package holder could be purchased for as little as $9, while a ladies' two-color gold cigarette-and-vanity case is listed at $400. An elaborately decorated ladies' case could cost much more. After the 1929 stock market crash, Cartier emphasized the availability of relatively inexpensive gift items. A 1931 catalog offers crystal jewelry with sporting motifs, charm bracelets, cloth and leather handbags, and cigarette boxes and table lighters. A year later, as the Depression deepened, a Cartier catalog touted "gifts one dollar and upward." Among the "smokers articles for men" are a silver lighter with gold stripes for $55 and a cigarette case for $50. Suggested "smokers articles for ladies" include an $11 lacquer cigarette case with Japanese motifs. A stunning case with a geometric pattern of inlaid turquoise and lapis lazuli (fig. 160) made in

ABOVE AND OVERLEAF 157. **Table cigarette box** Cartier Paris, 1925. Silver; gold; *laque burgauté* plaques; moonstone; ruby, sapphire, and coral cabochons; jade; rose-cut diamonds; ebonite; enamel; wood (interior). 6 × 19.8 × 9.3 cm. Cartier Collection TB 11 A25.

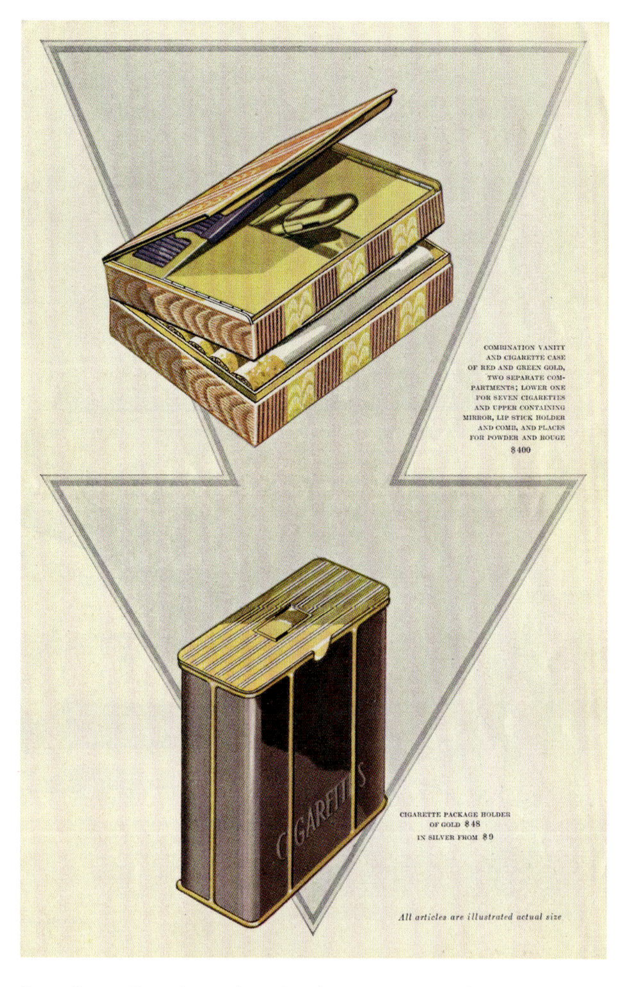

Page from "For a Luxurious Smoke: Accessories, by Cartier," Cartier New York, 1928. Cartier Archives.

1930 took seven years to sell,[9] probably a casualty of the reigning financial austerity.

Not all pocketbooks were affected by the Depression. A 1930 table cigarette box is carved of deep green nephrite with lapis lazuli feet (fig. 158). Mounts and hinges are gold with enameled Persian arabesques. Inset into the front of the box is a clock with a coral border and platinum hands set with diamonds. In 1932 Virginia Graham Fair Vanderbilt ordered a luxuriously elegant ladies' cigarette case, also in the "Persian" taste. Its gold surface is embellished with a spiraling flowering vine and rabbits in white enamel, overlaid by cavorting black antelopes. When the case is opened, a spring mechanism raises the end of a cigarette for easy withdrawal (see fig. 62, page 67). Another case, from 1936, is simply but richly decorated with reeded gold surfaces and translucent ends of faceted, *calibré*-cut sapphires (fig. 159).

Cinema played an important role in the twentieth-century popularization of cigarette smoking, both through movie scenes in which smoking occurs and through the cultural influence of its stars. The artistic and commercial potential of moving pictures, which were initially perceived as a passing novelty, was clear

158. **Cigarette box with clock** Cartier New York, 1930. Gold, platinum, silver, nephrite, coral, lapis lazuli, rose-cut diamonds, enamel, wood (interior). Round Lémania movement, rhodium-plated, 3 adjustments, 15 jewels, Swiss lever escapement, bimetallic balance wheel, Breguet balance spring. Winding crown under the box. 8.3 × 22.3 × 11.7 cm. Cartier Collection TB 13 A30.

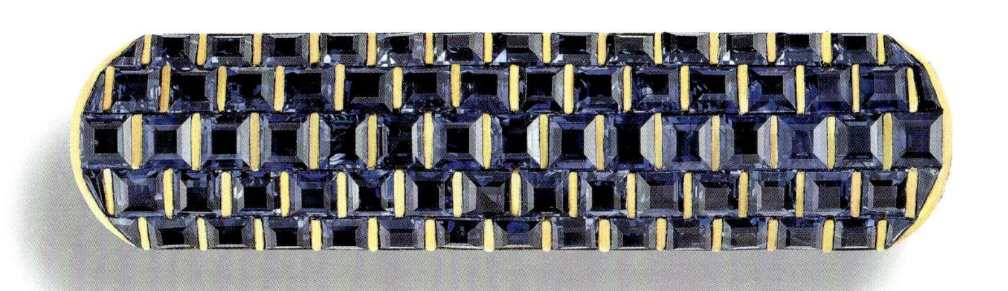

159. **Cigarette case** Cartier London, 1936. Fluted gold, faceted and *calibré*-cut sapphires, baguette-cut sapphire clasp. 8.9 × 6.8 × 1.7 cm. Cartier Collection CC 66 A36.

This case is set with 175 sapphires weighing a total of 67 carats.

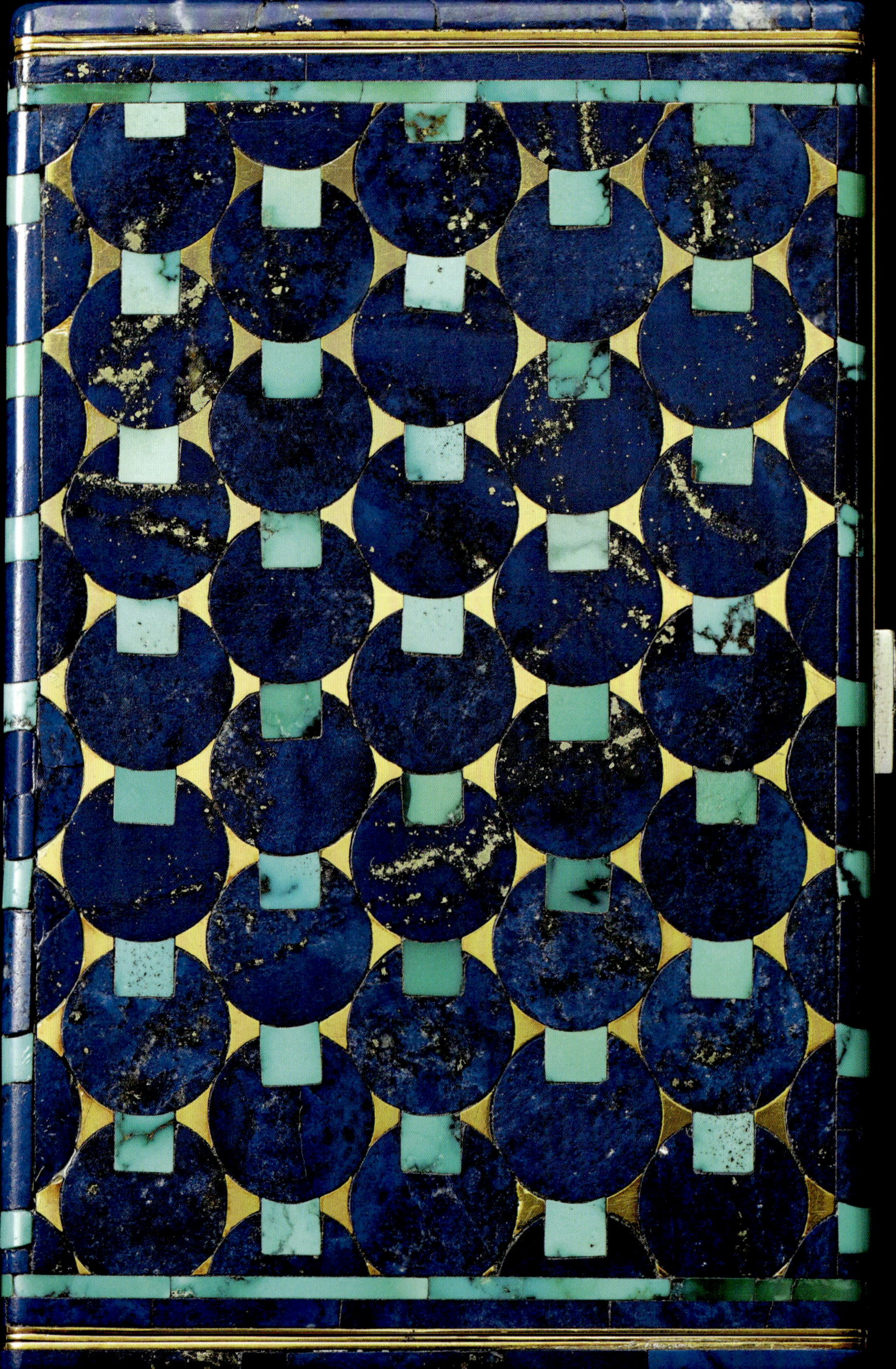

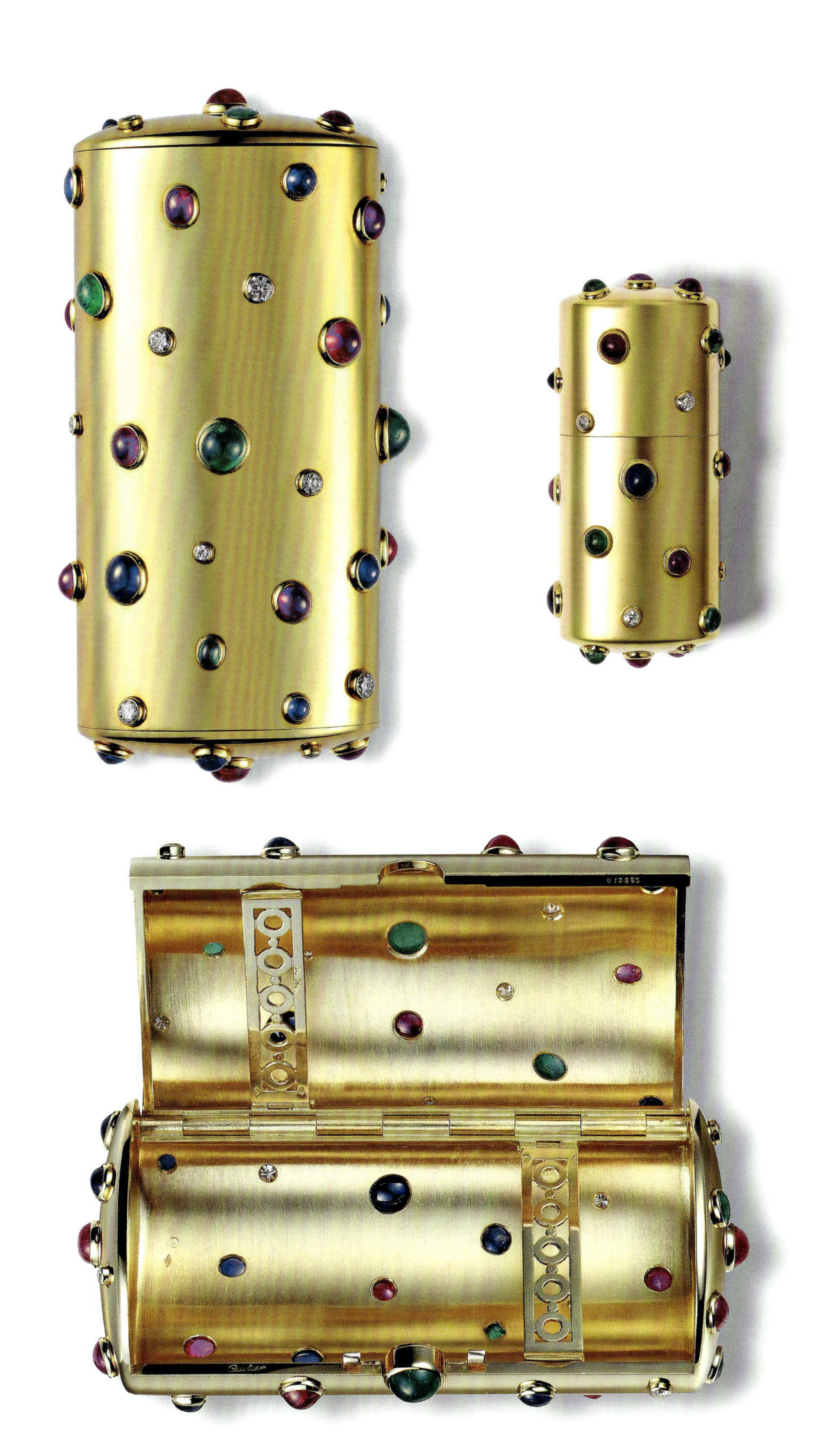

OPPOSITE 160. **Cigarette case** Cartier Paris, 1930. Gold, platinum, lapis lazuli, turquoise, baguette-cut diamond. 8.7 × 5.6 × 1.9 cm. Cartier Collection CC 47 A30.

ABOVE 161. **Cigarette case and lighter** Cartier Paris, 1947 (case) and 1950 (lighter). Gold; ruby, emerald, and sapphire cabochons; brilliant-cut diamonds. 7.8 × 4 cm (case), 5 × 2.5 cm (lighter). Cartier Collection CC 71 A47-50. Sold to a member of the Romanian royal family.

The interior of the case is fitted with two gold openwork retaining clips.

John Rawlings, shown here holding a Cartier cigarette case, was a Condé Nast photographer whose images often appeared in *Vogue*. Cartier Archives.

162. **Cigarette case** Cartier Paris, 1938. Gold, silver-gilt, wood. Engraved inside *Mary Magdalene Autumn 1938.* 11 × 8.4 × 1.7 cm. Cartier Collection CC 102 A38. Sold to Marlene Dietrich.

Marie Magdalene Dietrich (1901–1992), a German singer and cabaret artist, became a famous movie actress. She became a U.S. citizen in 1939 and during World War II she was a high-profile frontline entertainer.

by the 1910s. Projected in big-city and small-town theaters throughout the world, movies were a mass-communication mode and a cultural unifier. At first considered inferior to their stage counterparts, cinema actors and actresses were soon idolized by vastly larger audiences who were eager to learn about their personal lives and imitate their lifestyles, both on- and offscreen. In the silent-picture era (through the late 1920s) facial expressions and gestures, including those associated with smoking, were especially important in conveying both meaning and emotion. Stars such as Douglas Fairbanks, Theda Bara, Gloria Swanson, and Rudolph Valentino excited the romantic fantasies of a generation; their clothing, jewelry, homes, and travels were avidly chronicled in the press. Publicity photos often depicted stars with cigarettes, and they sometimes endorsed specific brands. In the films of later decades, smoking was, if anything, even more prominent—regularly used to telegraph attraction and desire. Marlene Dietrich, Humphrey Bogart, and Lauren Bacall were just a few of the actors whose film personas are inextricably linked with cigarette smoking. Cartier's prestige made it the preferred source of cigarette cases, holders, and lighters for many cinema stars, including Douglas Fairbanks, Mary Pickford, Marlene Dietrich, and Vivien Leigh. Marlene Dietrich's cigarette case, a masculine-looking model of gold and wood (fig. 162) is especially striking and a perfect complement to her carefully cultivated image (see page 128).

Cartier's women's cigarette cases from the 1930s and 1940s were sleek and glamorous, made of yellow gold decorated with colored gems (fig. 161). In the 1950s and 1960s cigarette smoking retained its popularity, but its glamour gradually declined, replaced by a grittier ethos. Sophisticates continued to purchase Cartier cigarette cases and lighters, but young people attracted to the style of Marlon Brando or James Dean were less likely to sport decorative gold or silver cases. Although zealots had decried tobacco on moral and medical grounds for centuries, scientific evidence of its ill effects on health became convincing by the 1970s. Smoking was slowly transformed in popular perception from an elegant pleasure to a dangerous addiction. While it is difficult to mourn the passing of an era when the majority of adults smoked—and suffered the negative health consequences of the habit—it is hard not to feel at least a twinge of regret at the disappearance of smoking's choreographed rituals and exquisite accessories.

MICHAEL HALL AND
MARGARET YOUNG-SÁNCHEZ

THE MASCULINE VIEW

FROM ITS FOUNDING IN 1847 ON, CARTIER SUPPLIED a clientele that was susceptible to the lure of objects made specifically for men. The firm's first use of platinum, in 1859, was for men's shirt buttons, followed by cuff links in 1874. In the twentieth century, platinum was used for a variety of men's items, including an elegantly simple pocket watch edged by *calibré*-cut sapphires and marked on the back with an enamel crown (fig. 163). The initially narrow range of men's objects increased only gradually until after World War I, when it expanded dramatically.

By the 1920s Cartier had recognized the new mood, the new money, and the new needs of a restless and changing postwar society. Louis Cartier's words were profoundly direct: "We must make it our business to build up an inventory that responds to the moral mood of the public by producing articles which have a useful function but which are decorated in the Cartier style."[1] Besides cuff links and shirt studs (see fig. 11, page 28), "useful" items included tie pins, shaving brushes, combs, hairbrushes, and penknives (fig. 165). Letter openers formed part of lavish desk sets (fig. 164) that included pens (fig. 167) and pencils (see fig. 187, page 173), blotters, clocks, calendars (fig. 166), photograph frames, stamp moisteners, paperweights, inkstands, and even barometers (see fig. 23, page 39) and small scientific instruments such as chronographs (stopwatches) (fig. 170) and opisometers (curvimeters, used for measuring distances on a map or globe).[2] Such objects—unisex, universal—could be used by both men and women, particularly the range of wildly imaginative and spectacular clocks, which were as suited to the feminine sitting room as to the masculine library.[3]

Cartier's Department S (for "silver"), which sold "elegant gifts and everyday consumer goods," aimed at exactly the right area of the market. Its products were designed for men or men and women equally, particularly watches and smoking accessories (page 161 top). They were superbly designed and executed,

OPPOSITE Clark Gable wearing a Cartier Tank watch, 1933. The Granger Collection, NY.

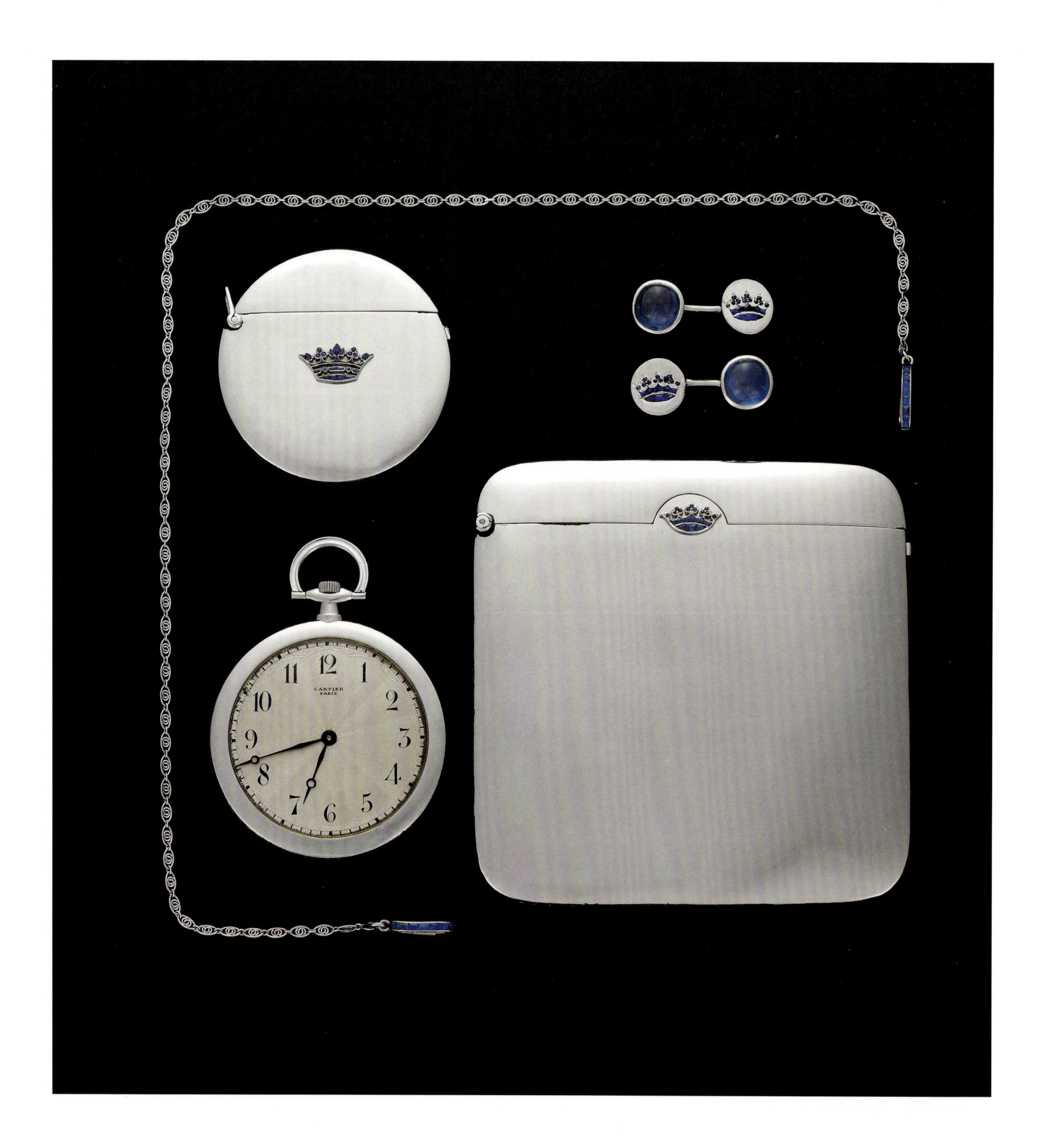

163. **Gentleman's set: pocket watch, chain, match case, cigarette case, cuff links** Watch: Cartier Paris, 1912. Platinum, sapphires, enamel, Cartier Paris movement. Width of cigarette case 8 cm, diameter of watch 4.4 cm. Cases, chain, and cuff links possibly by another maker. Private collection.

Page from a brochure featuring men's watches and accessories. Cartier Paris, 1931. Cartier Archives.

and had the cachet of the Cartier name. However, those who purchased these items for men were often women. Since the 1860s major reforms in Europe and America had allowed women to own property and manage their own finances. By the 1920s women had gained economic independence, and independently wealthy women were purchasing Cartier jewels in increasing numbers. These women, who had the means to buy lavish jewelry for themselves, could certainly select both jewelry and accessories for the men in their lives. Cartier offered a full line of luxury items suitable as gifts.

In 1933, shortly before she came of age and gained legal control of her Woolworth inheritance, Barbara Hutton went on a shopping spree at Cartier New York with her cousin James Donahue. She reportedly spent more than $98,000 on jewelry for herself and gifts for Donahue and her future husband Alexis Mdivani. These included a ribbed gold cigarette case with pavé-set sapphires, black-pearl-and-diamond

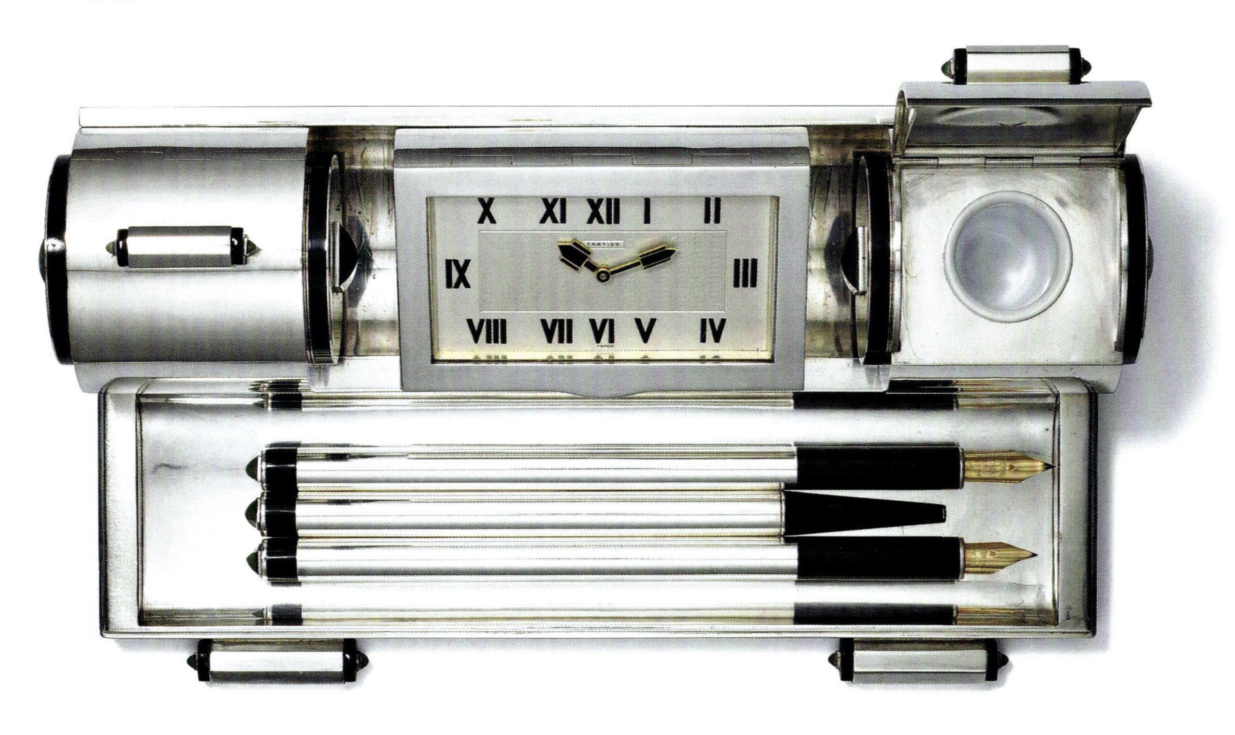

164, Desk set with clock Cartier Paris for Cartier New York, 1931. Silver, gold, nephrite cabochons, lacquer, enamel. Round European Watch & Clock Co. Inc. movement, Côtes de Genève decoration, rhodium-plated, 3 adjustments, 15 jewels, Swiss lever escapement, bimetallic balance, Breguet balance spring. 24 × 12.5 × 7.5 cm. Cartier Collection DI 29 A31.

The set holds two fountain pens and a matching mechanical pencil. The clock is mounted on the cover of a compartment that holds stamps, flanked by two inkwells.

LEFT 165. **Man's pocket utility kit** Cartier New York, about 1937. Gold, steel, copper. Coat of arms in polished reserved gold. Accessories: a steel knife blade, a copper key, and a telescopic mechanical pencil. Rectangular FHF 59 caliber Pery Watch Co. movement, silver-plated, 17 jewels, Swiss lever escapement, bimetallic balance, flat balance spring. Length 10 cm. Cartier Collection AG 50 C37.

CENTER 166. **Revolving clock** Cartier New York, 1930. Nephrite jade, sapphire, mother-of-pearl; with calendar, barometer, thermometer, and compass. 11.1 × 8.7 × 8.7 cm. Private collection.

RIGHT 167. **Telescopic fountain pen with perpetual calendar** Cartier New York, about 1926. Gold, enamel. Length closed 10.9 cm. Cartier Collection WI 23 C26.

cuff links with matching shirt studs, and a gold horse sculpture.[4]

England's Edward VIII (later the Duke of Windsor) and his American wife, Wallis Simpson, were two of Cartier's most important clients, purchasing both spectacular jewelry, often specially commissioned, and a full range of men's accessories (frequently bought by the duchess for the duke). At the landmark sale of the duchess's jewels, held in 1987, the duke's cigarette cases, pipe cleaner, pillbox, pocket watches, and dress studs with matching cuff links, all made by Cartier, came under the hammer. The androgynous, chic, and voguish couple's international style was exemplified by the duke's rectangular gold cigarette case set with enamel and precious stones showing the route of their European holiday in 1935, made to match a semicircular vanity case for the duchess, a brilliant combination conceived by Cartier's designers and craftsmen.[5]

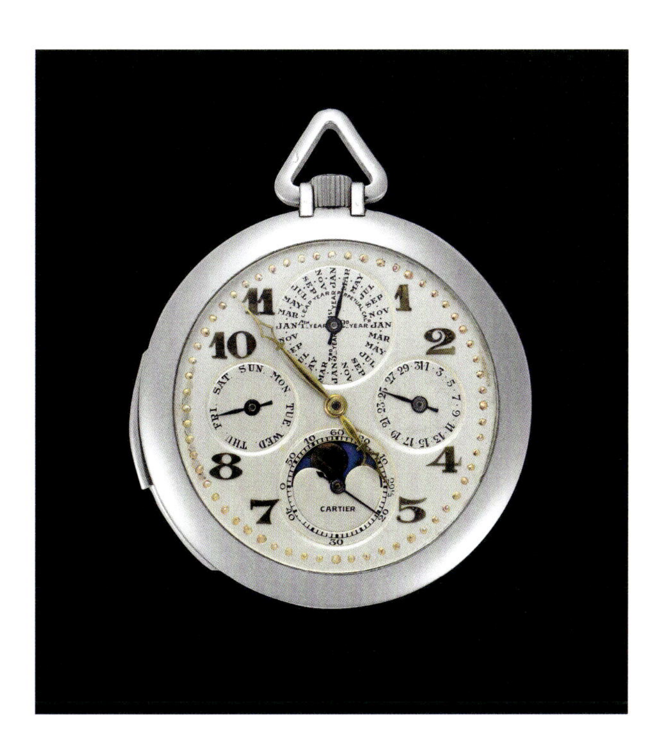

CARTIER WATCHES

Men have long prized fine watches for their precision and mechanical ingenuity. Watch "complications" such as chronographs (stopwatches); chronographs with split seconds (for timing two competitors in a race) (fig. 168); perpetual calendars, moon phases, and minute repeaters (chimes that sound the time) (fig. 169); and even a model that sounds the watches for a ship's crew (fig. 171) require engineering genius and extraordinary craftsmanship. These highly personal items are often inscribed with the owner's monogram or crest (figs. 172 and 173) and are frequently presented as gifts on significant occasions (figs. 170 and 179).

Cartier's men's pocket watches, or fob watches, which boasted increasingly refined components and stylish cases, were directly descended from eighteenth-century models. London and Geneva produced the finest mechanisms, although Paris had the advantage when it came to styles of decoration. "Mystery" pocket watches, with transparent crystal dials (fig. 175); "hunters," with protective cases; and "half hunters," with a small window in the case that revealed the dial (fig. 174), provided customers with a wide range of choices for a variety of uses and occasions, from everyday wear to sporting events and evening dress. Chains and fobs made in gold or platinum could be lavishly decorated with pearls or precious stones for evening wear, often to match studs and cuff links. Especially exquisite watches were set in transparent rock crystal (fig. 176). Understated elegance typifies Cartier's pocket watches, making them perfect for wear by sophisticated and discerning men.

Because of both the location of its shops and the role it played in haute couture, Cartier was at the center of fashion. A prime example of the firm's innovative

TOP 168. **Split-seconds chronograph pocket watch** Cartier Paris, 1910. Platinum. Encrusted on back of case in gold "W.K.V." Two small subsidiary dials for sweep seconds at 6 o'clock; 30 minutes register at 12 o'clock. Diameter 5 cm. Private collection. Provenance: William K. Vanderbilt II.

A split-seconds chronograph has two timing hands. When the timing button is pushed, both hands move together; when the "split-seconds" button is pushed, one hand stops to indicate elapsed time, while the other hand continues. Pushing the button again causes the "split-seconds" hand to catch up with the continuous sweep hand. The user can thereby time several events of varying duration.

ABOVE 169. **Minute-repeating pocket watch with perpetual calendar and phases of the moon** Cartier Paris, 1925. Platinum, yellow gold. Four subsidiary dials indicating weekday at 9 o'clock, the date at 3 o'clock, month combined with leap year indicator at 12 o'clock, and continuous seconds combined with phases of the moon at 6 o'clock. Diameter 4.7 cm. Private collection.

TOP 170. **Split-seconds chronograph pocket watch** Cartier New York, 1929. Gold. Round LeCoultre caliber 17/18JCCV movement, split-seconds chronograph, 30-minute totalizer, *fausses* Côtes de Genève decoration, rhodium-plated, 8 adjustments, 28 jewels, Swiss lever escapement, bimetallic balance, Breguet balance spring. Button at 11 o'clock starts and stops the split-seconds hand. Engraved on back of case: GRAND NATIONAL / 1931 / "GREEN CHEESE" / R.McK. / FROM / LIZ AND JOCK. Diameter 5 cm. Cartier Collection WPC 11 A29.

ABOVE 171. **Ship's-bell pocket watch** Cartier Paris, 1926. Gold, enamel. Round LeCoultre caliber 150 movement, ship's-bell chime on request, Côtes de Genève decoration, rhodium-plated, 8 adjustments, 29 jewels, Swiss lever escapement, bimetallic balance, Breguet balance spring. Diameter 5 cm. Cartier Collection WPC 19 A26.

Made with a minute repeater in 1926, this pocket watch was sold in 1928 to American yachting enthusiast William B. Leeds (son of tin industrialist William B. Leeds and his wife, Nancy, an important Cartier jewelry customer) with a striking mechanism that sounded shipboard time: the eight bells of the four-hour watches manned by each shift of the crew.

TOP 172. **Pocket watch** Cartier Paris, 1919. Platinum, rose-cut diamonds. Round LeCoultre caliber 140 movement, *fausses* Côtes de Genève decoration, rhodium-plated, 19 jewels, Swiss lever escapement, bimetallic balance, flat balance spring. Engraved on back of case: arms and motto, *Scutum opponebat scutis.* Diameter 4.6 cm. Cartier Collection WPO 21 A19.

ABOVE 173. **Pocket watch with chain and matchbox** Cartier, about 1910. Gold, enamel, pearls, rose-cut diamonds. Round LeCoultre caliber 142 movement, swan-neck regulator, *fausses* Côtes de Genève decoration, rhodium-plated, 8 adjustments, 18 jewels, Swiss lever escapement, bimetallic balance, Breguet balance spring. Matchbox with striking surface on the edge. Length of chain 32 cm, diameter of watch 4.6 cm. Cartier Collection WPO 30 C10.

response to changing technologies and lifestyles was the invention and development of the modern men's wristwatch. Cartier's first modern wristwatch for men was the Santos, designed by Louis Cartier in 1904 for his friend Alberto Santos-Dumont, the trailblazing Brazilian pilot, who needed a watch he could consult easily and quickly (see page 168 left). Its industrial functionality was reflected in its square shape and clearly visible screw ends (fig. 178). These were small and unobtrusive on the original models; later models feature larger screw heads, to emphasize the qualities of a functional instrument rather than a fashionable accessory, befitting the "moral mood" of a pioneer aviator.

However, the Santos did not go into regular production until 1911, by which time the barrel-shaped Tonneau was also being made. The Tortue, introduced in 1912, recalls the curved, flattened form of a turtle's shell (fig. 179). The distinctive cabochon sapphire set in the winding crown (a reminder that Cartier was first and foremost a jeweler) became a hallmark of Cartier's watch designs. The Tank watch evolved naturally from these models. The projecting lugs that held the straps echoed the tracks of either the rhomboid British Mark I tank or the Renault FT-17 tank, first seen in late 1916 and early 1917 (fig. 180).[6] With the design of the Tank, Louis Cartier overcame the inherent conflict between the new rectangular watch shape and the traditional circular watch face. As World War I drew to a close and a new world order emerged, here was the future—Cartier's modernism in burnished gold.

Over the next two decades new models emerged that combined distinctive shapes, novelty, and technical innovations: the Tank Cintrée (figs. 181 and 182) was followed in 1927 by a golfer's watch that included a scorecard and a tiny pencil and in 1931 by a waterproof watch. The Losange of 1936 (fig. 183), while clearly derived from the Tank of twenty years before, was a Cartier interpretation of surrealism. The Losange sold well for many years; an example was bought by the actor Stewart Granger in 1963.

What made these technical developments possible was the partnership between Cartier and the Parisian watchmaker Edmond Jaeger, a collaboration that dated back to 1903, if not before. From 1907 until his death in 1922, Jaeger worked exclusively with Cartier, and his firm had a contract with Cartier until 1933. Jaeger overcame the technical difficulties involved in producing ultrathin but superbly accurate mechanisms. In 1929 Cartier applied for a patent for a reversible watch with a frame that could be lifted up, allowing the watch face to pivot and turn toward the wrist. Eventually called the Basculante (fig. 184), it was not produced commercially until 1932, but by then Jaeger and Swiss watchmaker LeCoultre had devised

OPPOSITE

TOP LEFT 174. ***Éclipse* pocket watch with two dials** Cartier Paris, 1925. Gold. Round LeCoultre caliber 140 movement, *fausses* Côtes de Genève decoration, rhodium-plated, 8 adjustments, 19 jewels, Swiss lever escapement, bimetallic balance, flat balance spring. Diameter 4.4 cm. Cartier Collection WPO 13 A25.

The two shutters slide open to reveal the dial when the winding crown is pressed.

TOP RIGHT 175. **Mystery pocket watch** Cartier Paris, 1931. Platinum, crystal, enamel. Rectangular LeCoultre caliber 409 basic movement with additional plate, Côtes de Genève decoration, rhodium-plated, 3 adjustments, 15 jewels, Swiss lever escapement, bimetallic balance, flat balance spring. 4.1 × 4.1 cm. Cartier Collection WPC 23 A31.

CENTER 176. **Pocket watch with transparent back** Cartier New York, 1929. Platinum, gold, rock crystal, rose-cut diamonds. Round LeCoultre caliber 139 movement, *fausses* Côtes de Genève decoration, silver-plated, 8 adjustments, 19 jewels, Swiss lever escapement, bimetallic balance, flat balance spring. 5.8 × 4.7 × 0.6 cm. Cartier Collection WPO 36 A29.

BOTTOM 177. **Coin watch** Cartier Paris, 1937. Gold. Round LeCoultre caliber 9HPVB movement, *fausses* Côtes de Genève decoration, rhodium-plated, 8 adjustments, 18 jewels, Swiss lever escapement, bimetallic balance, flat balance spring. Diameter 3.4 cm. Cartier Collection WPO 57 A37.

The case was made from a gold U.S. $20 coin minted in 1900 and opens by pressing the edge below "1900."

CARTIER

1900

LEFT Pioneering Brazilian aviator Alberto Santos-Dumont, 1907.

ABOVE 178. ***Santos* wristwatch** Cartier Paris, 1916. Platinum, gold, sapphire cabochon, leather strap. Round LeCoultre caliber 126 movement, *fausses* Côtes de Genève decoration, rhodium-plated, 8 adjustments, 18 jewels, Swiss lever escapement, bimetallic balance, Breguet balance spring. Case 3.4 × 2.5 cm. Cartier Collection WCL 88 A16.

a more successful method of achieving reversibility.[7] After 1933 Cartier continued to buy mechanisms from LeCoultre. The company later retailed watches by other Swiss manufacturers, including Vacheron Constantin, Patek Philippe, and Rolex.

Cartier imaginatively incorporated its distinctive, white enamel–faced watches with Roman numerals and parallel black lines—the Railroad—into a wide range of men's accessories and novelties: belt buckles (fig. 190), lighters, billfolds (fig. 186), cuff links (fig. 188), and the tops of pens and pencils (fig. 189). Novelty watches were set within the thickness of gold coins (fig. 177) and some embedded in whiskey bottles. Yet another novelty was a platinum-and-steel pocket watch with a roulette-wheel face (fig. 185). These popular items were aimed at developing a broader market for Cartier products without compromising the firm's high aesthetic standards and superb craftsmanship.

Several innovations intended for one Cartier line were later applied to another. The deployant buckle, patented in 1909 jointly by Cartier and Edmond Jaeger, allowed the wristband to be expanded without opening it. This clasp proved to be useful as a security device on fine jewelry, including jeweled bracelets. The "Kodak" system travel clock has a cover, patented by Cartier in 1926, that springs open like a camera shutter, and the lid folds back to support the clock in the display position.[8] This ingenious device was also used on cigarette cases: the case inscribed for André Citroën, the automobile manufacturer, for instance, has a "Kodak" catch (see fig. 200, page 184). Another innovation, instigated by Jeanne Toussaint, who, from the early 1920s on, was one of the guiding forces in the firm for product development and design,[9] was the idea of linking rolls of gold to form hollow bands, first as a jewelry design and then as part of articulated straps for wristwatches.[10] Fabriclike woven gold and platinum used for evening bags also translated well into watchbands and gave new impetus to sales during the difficult years of the late 1930s.

TOP 179. ***Tortue* single-button chronograph wristwatch** Cartier New York, 1929. Gold, leather strap. Round LeCoultre caliber 133 movement with single-button chronograph, 30-minute totalizer, *fausses* Côtes de Genève decoration, rhodium-plated, 8 adjustments, 25 jewels, Swiss lever escapement, bimetallic balance, Breguet balance spring. Case 3.5 × 2.7 cm. Cartier Collection WCL 42 A29. Sold to Edsel Ford.

After her husband's death, Eleanor Ford respected his wishes by giving this watch to his close friend and colleague Arthur Backus.

ABOVE 180. ***Tank Normale* wristwatch** Cartier London, 1922. Gold, sapphire cabochon, leather strap. Round LeCoultre caliber 123 movement, Côtes de Genève decoration, rhodium-plated, 8 adjustments, 19 jewels, Swiss lever escapement, bimetallic balance, Breguet balance spring. Case 3.1 × 2.3 cm. Cartier Collection WCL 133 A22.

OVERLEAF LEFT, CLOCKWISE FROM TOP LEFT

181. ***Tank Cintrée* wristwatch** Cartier Paris, 1936. Yellow and pink gold, sapphire cabochon, leather strap. Round LeCoultre caliber 122 movement, Côtes de Genève decoration, rhodium-plated, 2 adjustments, 18 jewels, Swiss lever escapement, bimetallic balance, flat balance spring. Case 4.6 × 2.2 × 0.5 cm. Cartier Collection WCL 39 A36. Provenance: Juan Perón (President of Argentina 1946–55, 1973–74).

182. ***Tank Cintrée* wristwatch** Cartier New York, 1941. Platinum, sapphire cabochon, European Watch & Clock Co. Inc. movement. Length of case 4.3 cm. Private collection.

183. ***Losange* wristwatch** Cartier Paris, 1936. Gold, leather strap. Round LeCoultre movement, *fausses* Côtes de Genève decoration, rhodium-plated, 2 adjustments, 18 jewels, Swiss lever escapement, bimetallic balance, flat balance spring. Case 3.6 × 2.3 cm. Cartier Collection WCL 109 A36.

184. **Reversible *Basculante* wristwatch** Cartier Paris, 1936. Yellow and pink gold, leather strap. Rectangular LeCoultre caliber 111 movement with cut corners, rhodium-plated, 2 adjustments, 18 jewels, Swiss lever escapement, bimetallic balance, flat balance spring. Case 3.8 × 2 cm. Cartier Collection WCL 96 A36.

OVERLEAF, RIGHT, CLOCKWISE FROM TOP LEFT Warren Beatty, Cary Grant, Andy Warhol, and Rudolph Valentino, all wearing Tank watches.

CARTIER
FRANCE

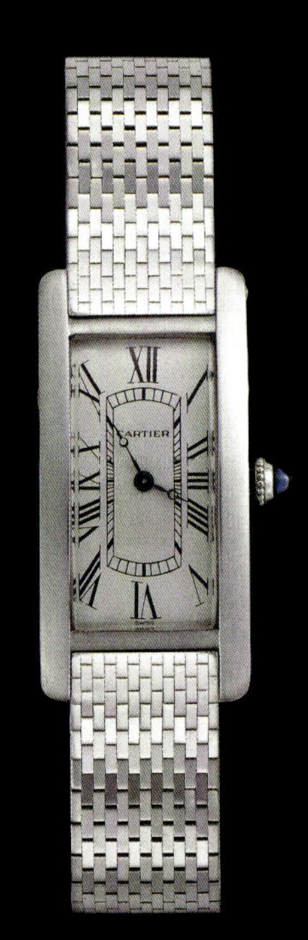
CARTIER

CARTIER

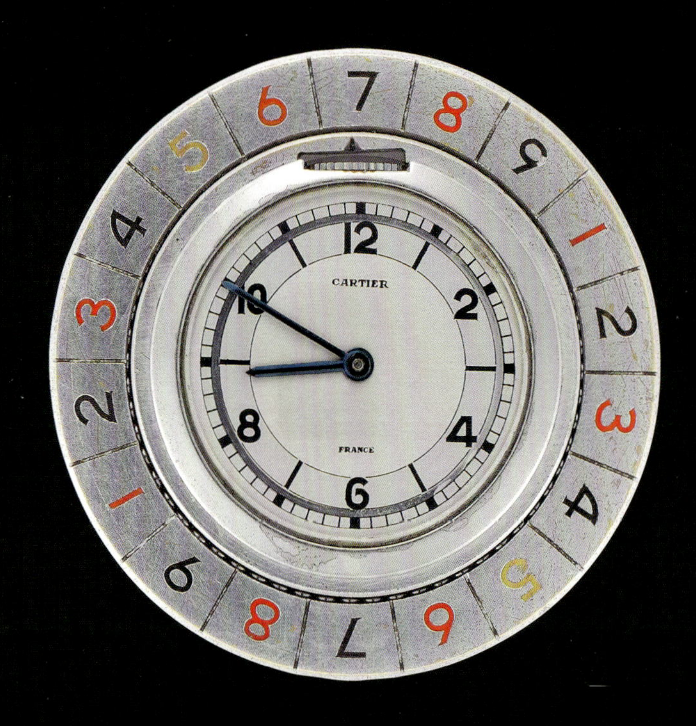
CARTIER
FRANCE

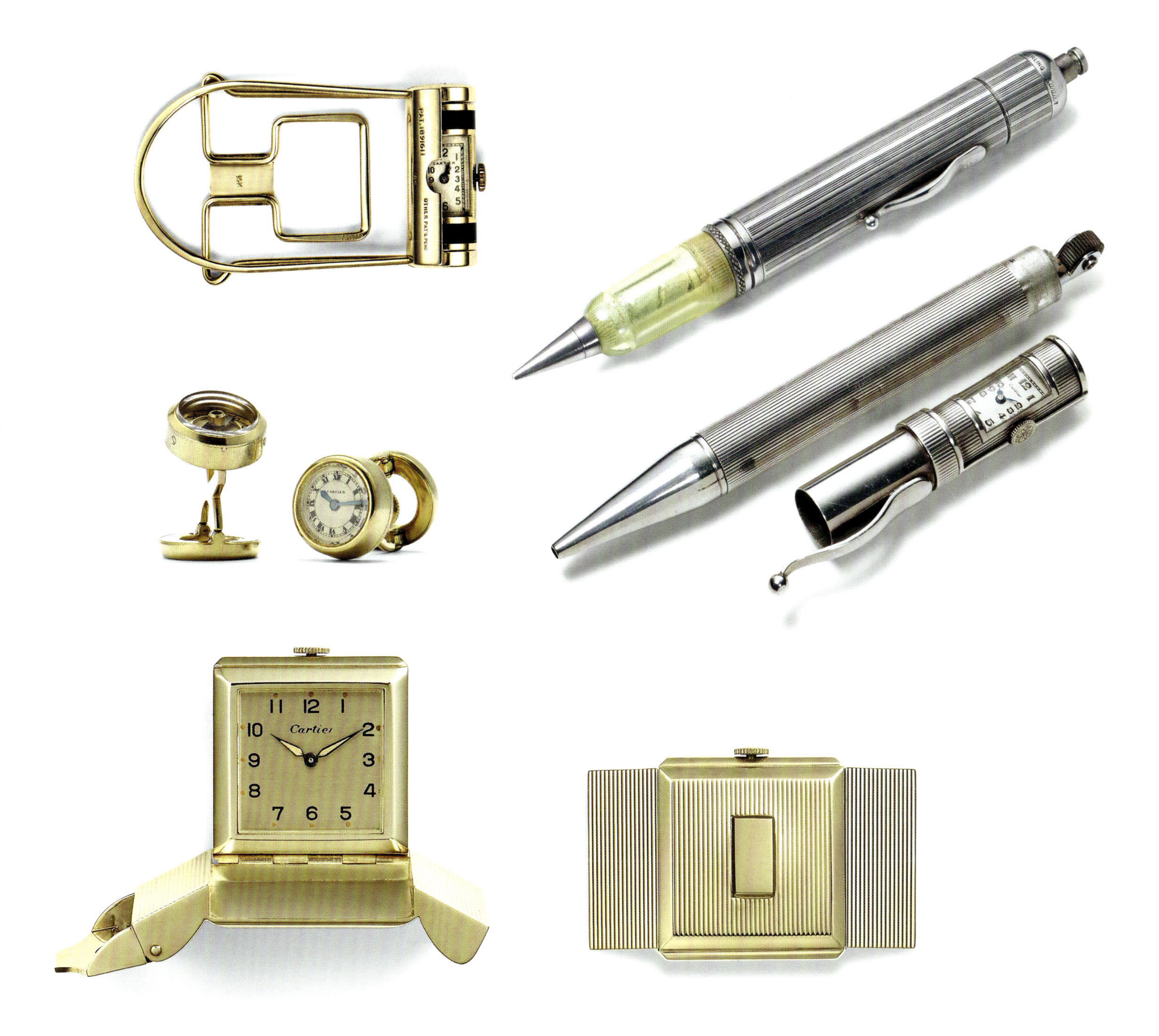

OPPOSITE 185. **"Roulette" pocket watch** Cartier London, 1937. Circular-shaped revolving steel case mounted on ball bearings. Round movement, bimetallic balance, flat balance spring. Diameter 5.1 cm. Private collection.

The owner of this "gambler's companion" watch could spin the wheel to aid in selecting a bet.

TOP LEFT 186. **Billfold with watch** Cartier New York, about 1933. Gold, enamel. Rectangular Pery Watch movement with cut corners, rhodium-plated, 17 jewels, bimetallic balance, flat balance spring. 5.7 × 3.4 × 1.2 cm. Cartier Collection WO 18 C33.

The watch pivots to protect the dial when the billfold is carried in a pocket.

TOP RIGHT 187. **Mechanical pencil with light** Cartier, about 1930. Silver, plastic screen. Plastic screen to filter light from the battery-driven bulb. Push-piece on top turns light on; cone-screw mechanism to advance the lead. Length 13.7 cm. Cartier Collection WI 30 C30.

A similar model was sold to British writer Noël Coward in 1934.

CENTER LEFT 188. **Cuff links with watch and compass** Cartier Paris, 1945–47. Gold. Swivel system. Round JLC caliber 426 movement, rhodium-plated, 16 jewels, Swiss lever escapement, monometallic balance, flat balance spring. Diameter 1 cm. Cartier Collection BC 13 A45-47.

CENTER RIGHT 189. **Mechanical pencil with lighter and watch** Cartier, about 1933. Silver. Shaft with lighter at end, cap with pivoting watch, cone-screw mechanism to advance the lead. Rectangular FHF caliber 59 movement with cut corners, silver-plated, 17 jewels, Swiss lever escapement, bimetallic balance, flat balance spring. Length 13.6 cm. Cartier Collection WI 13 C33.

BOTTOM 190. **Belt buckle with watch** Cartier New York, 1950. Gold. Round Concord Watch Co. Swiss movement, rhodium-plated, 17 jewels, Swiss lever escapement, monometallic balance wheel, Breguet balance spring. 5.7 × 2.8 cm. Cartier Collection WO 15 A50.

This style is also known as a golfer's watch. As early as the 1920s several watchmakers began offering models to be worn on the belt to protect the watch movement from the shock of the wrist swinging a golf club.

ACCESSORIES AND COMMEMORATIVE OBJECTS

The imagination of Cartier's designers ran riot in the decades after World War I as the firm produced myriad objects men never knew they needed. Of necessity, these objects were restrained in ornamentation. Men's accessories are by their nature small, personal, and intimate, and can only really be appreciated by the wearer or by those in close proximity to him. A 1928 pair of enameled cuff links (fig. 191) could be said to constitute an inside joke—the road symbols with which they are decorated can be translated as "train crossing," "intersection," "dangerous curves," and "bumps ahead." Besides wristwatches, pocket watches, and smoking accoutrements, pocket chess sets, flashlights (fig. 192) and night lights, folding tape measures, key rings, and toothpicks were designed by Charles Jacqueau, who with Georges Rémy was the most original and influential of Cartier's designers. But for men's accessories, as for jewelry, Cartier made a conscious decision not to credit individual designers, which allowed the firm to maintain a unified style.

The firm also produced notebooks and diaries, billfolds, suspenders, cocktail sets (fig. 194), swizzle sticks to reduce the fizz of Champagne (fig. 193), and travel kits containing brushes and combs of all sizes and descriptions—all quotidian objects fashioned in precious materials. Some were more mundane than others—ivory containers for dental floss vied with silver yo-yos, a special order produced for major client William K. Vanderbilt II in 1925. Vanderbilt also received more substantial objects from Cartier, such as a table cigarette box inscribed with the signature of his guest on a round-the-world cruise in 1928–29 on his yacht *Ara* (fig. 197), and a split-seconds chronograph in a platinum case (see fig. 168, page 163).

Commemorative objects, public and private, were another area in which Cartier excelled. For example, the firm paid tribute to the first solo transatlantic flight, made in May 1927 by Charles Lindbergh in the *Spirit of St. Louis*, the engine of which was manufactured by Wright Aeronautical. A scale model of the

191. **Cuff links** Cartier Paris, 1928. Gold, royal blue enamel "road sign" motifs. Diameter 1.4 cm. Cartier Collection BC 06 A28.

192. **Flashlight** Cartier, about 1930. Gold, ivory. 5.4 × 1.3 cm. Cartier Collection IO 39 C30.

193. **Champagne swizzle sticks** Cartier, about 1930. Silver, gold, rock crystal, carved ivory. 21.5 × 8.8 cm. Cartier Collection IO 41 C30.

194. **Travel bar kit** Cartier New York, about 1930. Silver. 20 cm (height of shaker), 20.5 cm (height of flasks), 12.5 cm (height of lemon press), 4.5 cm (height of tumblers). Cartier Collection SI 09 C30.

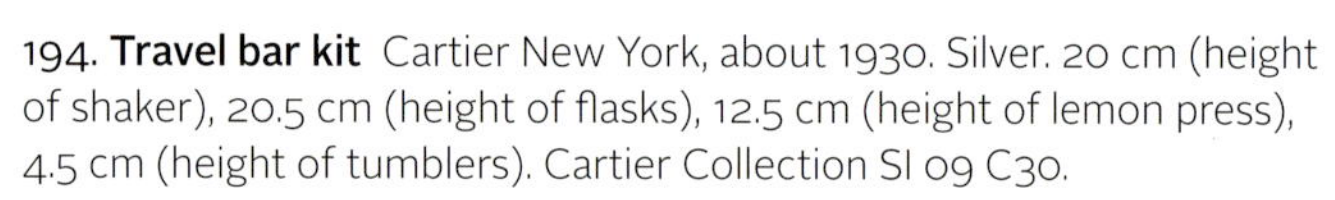

The set is composed of a shaker, two flasks, a lemon press, and six cups with gilt interiors. When traveling, the kit is carried in a black leather case.

J.C.C
J.C.C
J.C.C

"whirlwind motor" in brass, steel, and red enamel, with a mahogany propeller, was ordered from Cartier soon afterward (fig. 196).[11]

The firm honored other modern acts of heroic achievement as well. An especially meaningful and moving commemorative is the clock presented to President Franklin D. Roosevelt by Pierre Cartier in 1943, near the end of World War II (below and fig. 195). The clock's face incorporates five dials set to simultaneously display the hour in Washington, D.C.; London and Paris; Berlin and Rome; San Francisco; and Tokyo. The clock would "mark the hour of victory," Cartier wrote to the president. His longing for war's end was undoubtedly heartfelt; his brothers, Jacques and Louis, died in 1941 and 1942, respectively, and the future of Cartier's Paris and London branches was threatened.

Cartier commemorated yet another form of pioneering travel in 1969, when the French newspaper *Le Figaro* commissioned the firm to make three gold models of the *Apollo 11* lunar module for the mission commander, Neil Armstrong, and his fellow astronauts Edwin "Buzz" Aldrin and Michael Collins (fig. 199).[12]

Personal commemorative objects sometimes incorporated signatures and handwritten inscriptions

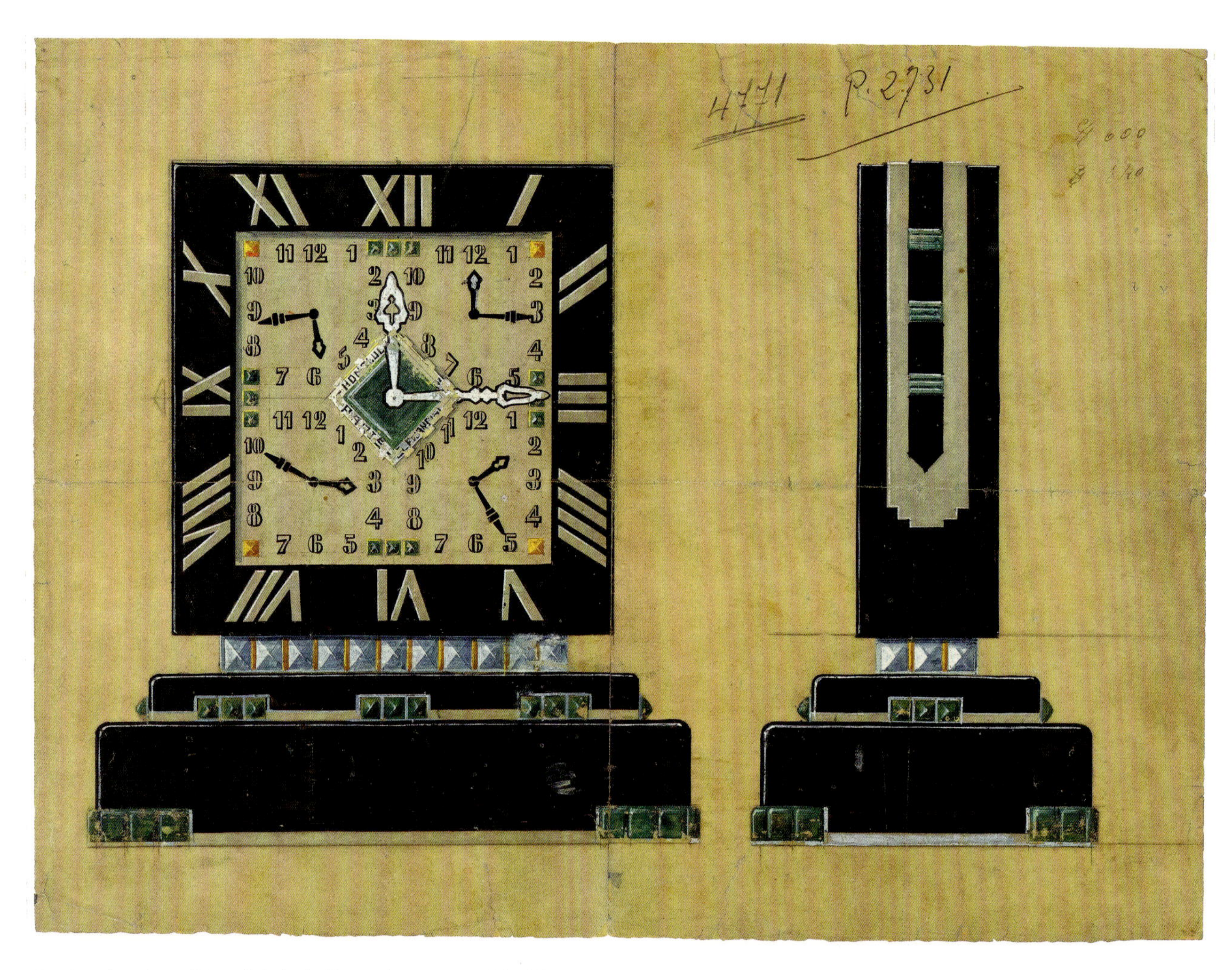

Design drawing of five-dial clock (fig. 195). Later modified for presentation to President Roosevelt. Cartier Archives.

OPPOSITE 195. **Five-dial clock** Cartier New York, 1930. Ebonite, silver, nephrite, enamel, European Watch & Clock Co. Inc. movement. Engraved: *"L'HEURE DE LA VICTOIRE / DANS LE MONDE."/ HOMMAGE À SON ARTISAN / LE PRESIDENT DES ÉTATS UNIS / FRANKLIN D. ROOSEVELT ("THE HOUR OF VICTORY / IN THE WORLD" / IN HONOR OF ITS ARCHITECT / PRESIDENT OF THE UNITED STATES / FRANKLIN D. ROOSEVELT).* 22 × 20 × 11 cm. Private collection. Provenance: Franklin D. Roosevelt.

Cartier
TOKYO
"L'HEURE DE LA VICTOIRE
DANS LE MONDE"
HOMMAGE Á SON ARTISAN
LE PRESIDENT DES ETATS UNIS
FRANKLIN D. ROOSEVELT

ABOVE 196. **Replica of Charles Lindbergh's Wright Whirlwind engine** Cartier New York, about 1927. Brass, steel, gold, enamel, mahogany, glass display case, mirrored base. A gold plaque on the engine is engraved: *Lawrence Model, Wright Whirlwind Motor, Made in the Workshop of Cartier*. 31.8 × 46.4 × 23.5 cm. Cartier Collection OV 12 C27.

This object is a replica of the Wright Whirlwind engine that powered the *Spirit of St. Louis* in which Charles Lindbergh made the first solo flight across the Atlantic in 1927. His nonstop flight from Roosevelt Field, New York, to Le Bourget outside Paris lasted 33½ hours.

OPPOSITE 197. **Table cigarette box** Cartier Paris, 1929. Silver, gold, onyx, ebonite, cedar (interior bottom), enamel. The top is engraved: *Yacht Ara / to / the Commodore / and / Mrs W. K. Vanderbilt / "en souvenir" / of the trip around the world / November 1928 – May 1929 / Pierre* [and in the corners:] *New York / Saigon / Bombay / Monaco.* 32.5 × 22.2 × 10.5 cm. Cartier Collection TB 04 A29. Sold to Mr. Pierre Clinch Mérillon.

Pierre Clinch Mérillon (1899–1991) was the son of a French banker and the American heiress Cornelia Stewart Clinch. He had the cigarette box engraved and then gave it to Mr. and Mrs. William K. Vanderbilt II to thank them for a worldwide cruise on their yacht. The flags are those of the New York Yacht Club (with white star) and the Vanderbilts.

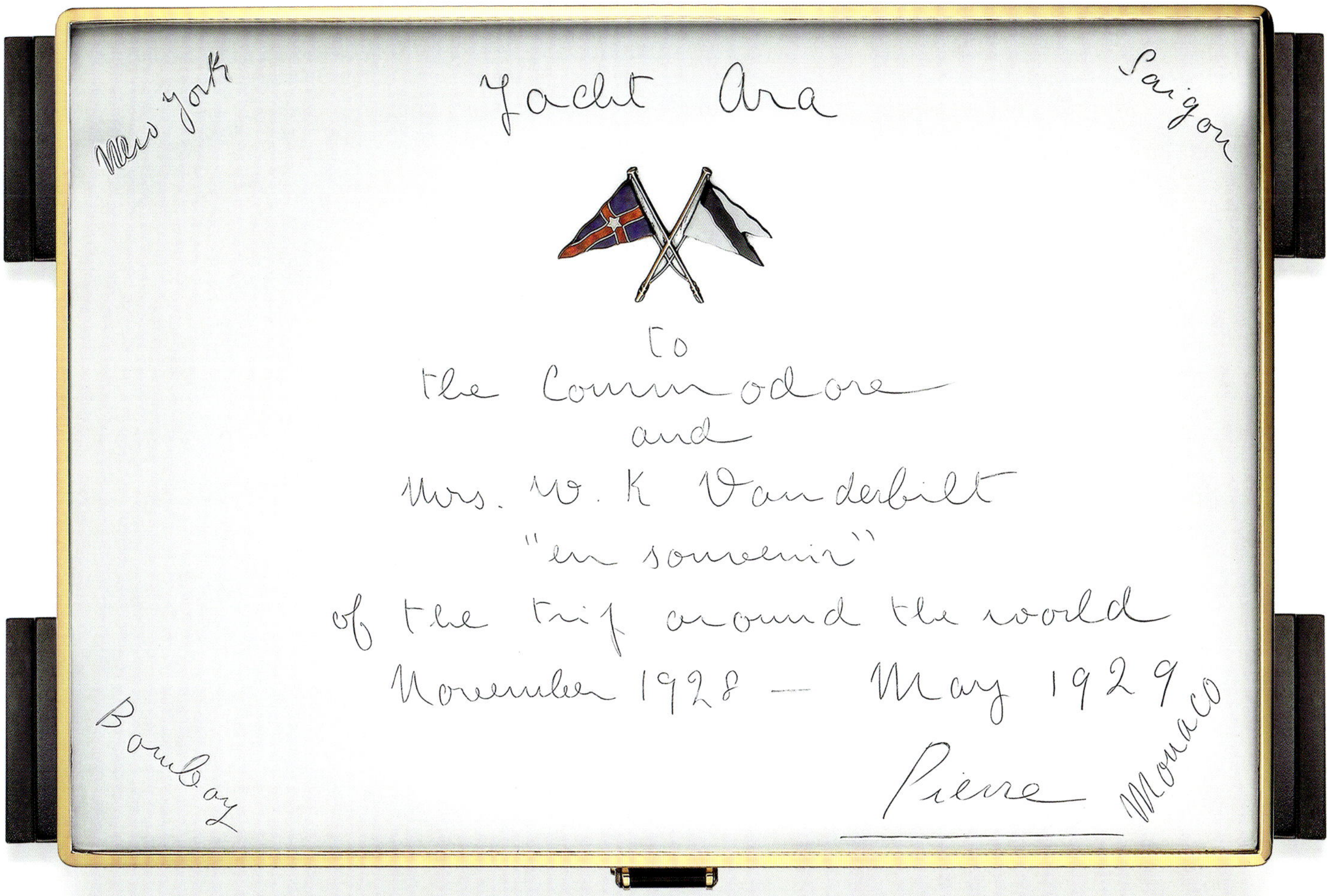

Yacht Ara

New York

Saigon

to
the Commodore
and
Mrs. W. K Vanderbilt
"en souvenir"
of the trip around the world
November 1928 — May 1929

Bombay

Pierre

Monaco

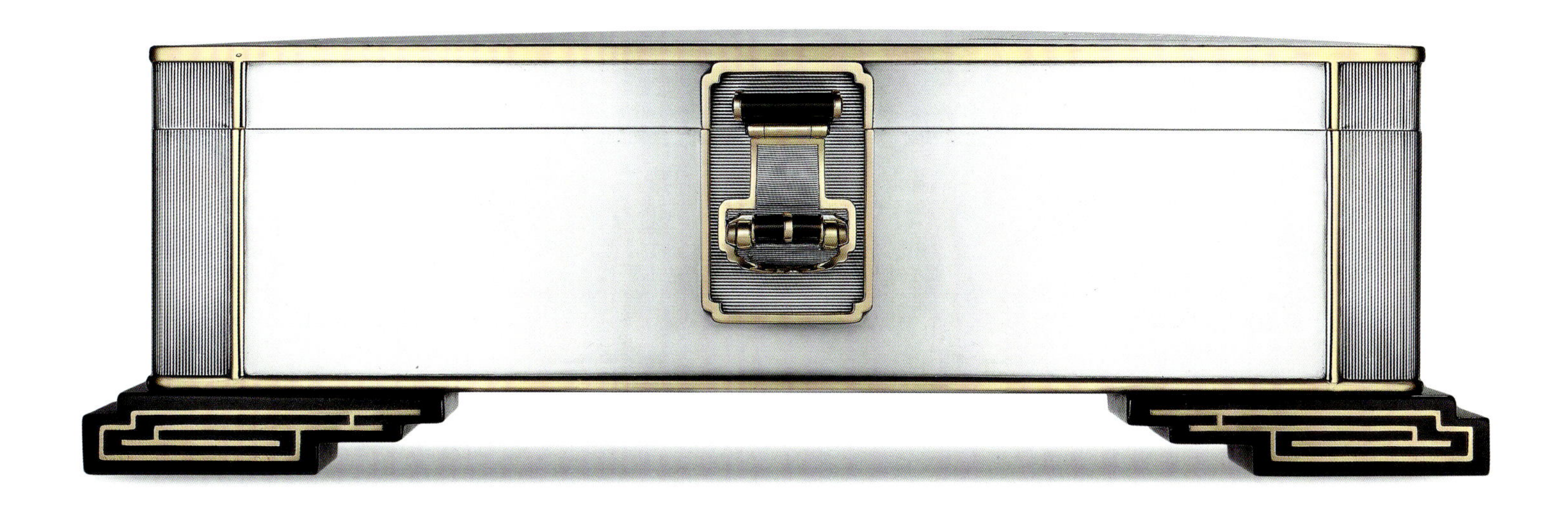

transferred by engraving: in 1932 Winston Churchill presented his son, Randolph, on the occasion of the young man's twenty-first birthday, with a cigarette case in the form of a gold envelope with an enamel stamp. Many cigarette cases were decorated with commemorative inscriptions. One, sold to Willis McCormick of Queen Aeroplane Company in 1912, contains the signatures of numerous aviation pioneers, including Alberto Santos-Dumont (fig. 198). A case presented by Pierre Cartier to aviator Dieudonné Costes (see page 184 right) is inscribed with the route of his history-making 1928 transcontinental journey (fig. 201). Another inscribed case commemorates André Citroën's automobile trek across the Sahara (fig. 200).

In the 1920s Cartier expanded the range of raw materials it used, adding both color and texture to its products. Beautiful and exotic materials came to the fore, particularly gemstones—red and pink coral, lapis lazuli, turquoise, alabaster, black onyx, and various shades of jadeite and nephrite—along with mother-of-pearl, tortoiseshell, and even kingfisher feathers.[13] Cartier also utilized synthetic products such as purpurine, a pseudo-hardstone made of glass that was used by Fabergé; moreover, the firm knew the secrets of how to heat chalcedony to alter its color, and it made use of the newly invented Bakelite.[14]

Cartier's enameling techniques, perfected in the early years of the century in response to the extraordinary quality of Russian enamelers, were particularly well employed in the decoration of cigarette cases, lighters, clocks, watch cases, and other flat surfaces in need of discreet, masculine embellishment. Technically difficult to perfect, enameling and the Russian technique of niello were ideal for luxury objects.

The Wall Street crash of 1929 and subsequent Depression greatly affected some of Cartier's customers, but the firm produced many affordable items (jewelry and accessories alike), with the result that sales of those items rose by at least 50 percent between 1928 and 1930.[15] This was especially important because Cartier's core business—pearls—suffered a serious decline in the 1930s as cultured pearls from Japan, called "white beads" by their detractors,

198. Cigarette case Cartier Paris, 1912. Silver, green, and pink gold; sapphire cabochon. 8.9 × 8.5 cm. Cartier Collection CC 98 A12. Sold to Willis McCormick, president of Queen Aeroplane Company.

The inside of the case is engraved with the signatures of approximately thirty figures from the early days of aviation, including Maurice Chevillard, Igo Etrich, Jacques Mortane, Alberto Santos-Dumont, Jules Védrines, Gabriel Voisin, Roland Garros, Raymond Saulnier, and Jacques Schneider.

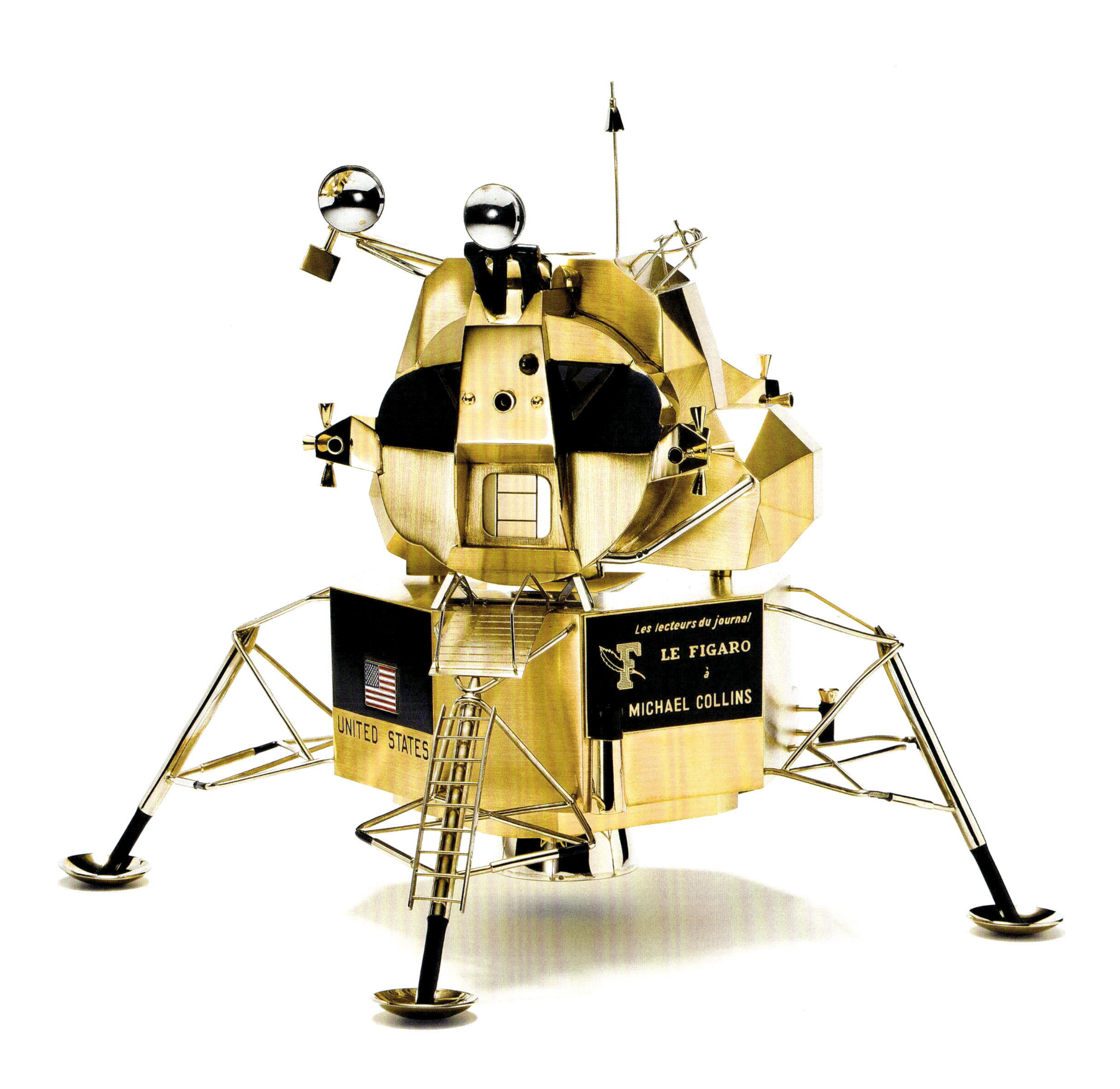

199. **Lunar Excursion Module (exact replica)** Cartier Paris, 1969. Yellow and white gold, lacquer, enamel. Engraved: *United States* and *Les lecteurs du journal Le Figaro à Michael Collins* [From readers of *Le Figaro* newspaper to Michael Collins] 15 × 10 × 25 cm. Cartier Collection OV 11 A69.

Each of the three models contained a microfilm bearing the names of the *Le Figaro* readers who contributed to the subscription drive that financed the commemorative gifts.

ABOVE 200. **Cigarette case** Cartier Paris, 1922. Gold, enamel. "Kodak" system opening, released by pressing the two push-pieces on the sides. Inside cover engraved: *Paris, / le 5 Décembre 1922 / Bonne chance / André Citroën / Paris / le 16 Février 1923 / Bravo!!* [Paris, December 5, 1922 / Good luck / André Citroën / Paris, February 16, 1923 / Bravo!!] 9.9 × 7.2 × 1.2 cm. Cartier Collection CC 86 A22. Sold to André Citroën.

A graduate of the prestigious École Polytechnique, engineer André Citroën (1878–1935) launched the automobile firm that still bears his name. Like Henry Ford, he made cars more widely accessible, mass-producing a single model, his Type A. Also innovative in publicity and marketing, Citroën organized and promoted an automotive crossing of the Sahara Desert from Algiers to Timbuktu from December 1922 to February 1923.

Aviator Dieudonné Costes.

became readily available. They almost destroyed the market for natural pearls, which had formed 60 percent of Cartier's business in Paris alone, a business that had been carefully fostered by Jacques Cartier with many visits to pearl fisheries in the Persian Gulf and secondary markets in India.[16] The promotion of accessories during this difficult period is easily understood. Cartier's designers and craftsmen were already in place and the Cartier name was thoroughly established as the leading brand of luxury objects in the world's fashion, social, and financial capitals—Paris, London, and New York.

OPPOSITE 201. **Cigarette case** Cartier New York, about 1928. Gold, enamel. Inside, a hinged gold openwork retaining clip and an inscription and facsimile signature: *Au Capitaine Dieudonné Costes / En souvenir de son envolée, qui en deux / coups d'ailes a relié l'Europe, l'Afrique / et l'Amérique. / Son compatriote et admirateur / New York, le 16 Février, 1928 / P. C. Cartier* [*To Captain Dieudonné Costes / in memory of his flight, who with two flaps of his wings linked Europe, Africa / and America. / From his compatriot and admirer / New York, February 16, 1928 / P. C. Cartier*]. It is accompanied by a map with blue enamel arrows indicating the pilot's route. 12.8 × 7.7 cm. Cartier Collection CC 16 C28.

Dieudonné Costes (1892–1973) was a French aviator who made the first nonstop flight across the South Atlantic in 1927. He also made the first east-to-west nonstop flight across the North Atlantic in 1930.

NEW YORK
FEVR. 11 1928
WASHINGTON
MONTGOMERY
N. ORLEANS
MEXICO
GUATEMALA
BARANQUILLA
CARACAS
COLON
PANAMA
GUAYAQUIL
LIMA
LA PAZ
ASSOMPTION
SANTIAGO
MONTEVIDEO
BUENOS-AIRES
RIO DE JANEIRO
NATAL
ST. LOUIS
PARIS
OCT. 10, 1927
ROME
ATHENS
BANDER A BBAS
KARACHI
CALCUTTA
HANOI
TOKIO
Au Capitaine Dieudonne Costes
En souvenir de son envolée, qui en deux
coups d'ailes a relié l'Europe, l'Afrique
New York, le 16 Fevrier, 1928.
P. C. Cartier

MEN'S JEWELRY

For Cartier's male clientele in Europe and America, the wearing of jewelry was generally circumscribed by accepted norms of good taste, although princes and kings often wore elaborate official jewelry and badges. For most men, opportunities for the use of precious stones were restricted, with the obvious exception of cuff links (fig. 203). Sometimes Cartier used small diamonds, including rose-cut stones, which were less ostentatious than brilliant cuts, for accents and initials on men's accessories. Cartier swiftly adopted the newly invented and reinvented rectangular cuts—the emerald, the baguette, and the *calibré*—which had a strong, masculine feel, as did the well-established cabochon, principally for colored stones.[17] The distinctive Cartier blue-green color combination was featured in the *calibré*-cut sapphires and emeralds used in the cuff links bought by King Alexander I of Yugoslavia in 1929 (fig. 202). On studs and cuff links, for discreet initials, and on thumbpieces for opening cases of every description, the use of stones on men's accessories became a hallmark of Cartier: the extra luxury.

At first glance, Cartier's greatest productions, the fine jewels—*haute joaillerie*—might seem to have been made exclusively for women. But that is not the case. The magnificent Cartier jewelry with the finest, most important stones—both diamonds and colored gems—was actually made for men. The native rulers of British India, more than a hundred princes, were historically possessed of vast treasuries of cut and uncut precious stones and natural pearls; they also had the taste, desire, and money to wear them in fashionable

TOP 202. **Cuff links** Cartier Paris, 1929. Platinum, faceted rectangular emeralds, faceted and *calibré*-cut sapphires. Double clip-hook system. Button 1.1 × 1.3 cm. Cartier Collection BC 10 A29. Sold to Alexander I, King of Yugoslavia, who presented them to King Carl II of Romania. Alexander was assassinated by a Macedonian separatist in Marseille on October 9, 1934.

ABOVE 203. **Cuff links** Cartier, about 1920. Platinum, sapphires. Diameter 1.3 cm. Pierre Cartier Foundation FPC 8.

The sapphires are carved with the profiles of Elma and Marion Cartier, wife and daughter of Pierre Cartier.

European settings. Cartier responded by resetting historic stones, often carved colored gems, for the princes themselves (the firm also acquired stones in India to set in jewels for their Western clients, particularly carved emeralds of the highest quality and largest size). The forms of Indian men's jewelry were copied as well—the *sarpech* became aigrettes or tiaras, the *bazuband* worn on the upper arm translated into

bangles and bracelets—while the motifs of sixteenth-century Mughal India were transformed into a wide variety of modern idioms. In 1922 the Bombay millionaire Sir Dhunjibhoy Bomandji sent Cartier 859 of his own diamonds (only twenty-eight of which were not used) to make a large, flexible diamond *bazuband* that could also be flattened, disassembled, and worn as a brooch (see fig. 80, page 91). The most spectacular pieces were those created anew in platinum, such as the Bomandji *bazuband* and the multistrand diamond necklace made for the Maharaja of Patiala from his own stones in 1928 (see fig. 78, page 89). Less expensive but no less glamorous was the fifteen-piece dressing table set Cartier created for the maharaja at the same time, set with faceted mirrors and detailed in black enamel and red coral.[18]

One other accoutrement made by Cartier should be mentioned: the ceremonial swords of members of the Académie française. The green-and-gold uniform of the forty members is adorned with a court sword. In 1931, when the Duc de Gramont was elected to the Académie, Cartier was commissioned to make his sword, and twenty-seven other Académie members have received Cartier swords since then. Jacqueau, the greatest of Cartier's designers of men's accessories, designed the sword of André Maurois in 1938, and Rémy designed fifteen swords before he retired in 1975. The poet and artist Jean Cocteau designed his own sword for Cartier to make when he was elected in 1955 (right and below). Writer and historian Daniel-Rops, upon taking his Académie seat in 1956, congratulated Rémy on "the magic and charm of an ornament which, in consequence, spreads the renown of Cartier across the globe," a magic and charm that still persists.[19]

ABOVE Jean Cocteau at home, wearing the garb of the Académie française and holding the sword he designed, 1956. Cartier Archives.

BELOW Academician's sword and scabbard made for Jean Cocteau by Cartier Paris, 1955.

JANET ZAPATA

THE AGE OF GLAMOUR

GLAMOUR. THE VERY WORD SUMMONS UP ELEGANT events, stylish gowns, dazzling jewels. Both an attribute and a state of mind, glamour is the quality of being "fascinating, alluring or attracting, especially by a combination of charm and good looks." This definition neatly encapsulates a certain kind of lifestyle that was enjoyed during the middle third of the twentieth century, when glamour reigned supreme, but was the antithesis of the economic tenor of the Great Depression throughout the United States and most of Europe. France was somewhat protected from the worst of the Depression because of its self-sufficient economy, based on small and medium-size businesses and, most important, on the fact that French investors tended to put their money not in stocks but in gold. By the end of the 1920s, France was accumulating significant gold reserves, which in effect buoyed the jewelry market and enabled makers to satisfy their customers' demands both in Europe and the United States.

To understand the ethos of the times, it is important to look back to earlier decades. Shortly after the turn of the century, couturier Paul Poiret changed fashion by streamlining dresses and then introducing the high Empire waistline, which eliminated the need for tightly laced corsets. When American ballroom dancer Irene Castle arrived in Paris with her husband and dance partner, Vernon, in 1912, she transformed the concept of the ideal woman. Her slim, lithe figure charmed Parisian society as she glided through the latest ballroom dances, embodying a newly active and visible feminine persona.[1] During World War I, women entered the workforce and in so doing were liberated from constrictive clothing. The straight flapper dresses of the 1920s perpetuated this sense of freedom, and women claimed ever greater personal autonomy.

OPPOSITE Fashion photograph of a model wearing Cartier diamond earrings and a diamond brooch to secure the tulle scarf around her neck, 1957. Cartier Archives.

THE NEWLY LIBERATED WOMAN: GLAMOUR IN THE 1920S AND 1930S

Fashion photograph by Edward Steichen, published in *Vogue*, Sept. 15, 1933. Steichen/*Vogue*. Condé Nast Archive.

Jewelers responded to the new slim, sleek fashions by introducing several new cuts of gemstones, including the baguette, trapezium, table, and square cuts. They also engraved the surface of gemstones with figurative motifs. In fine jewelry, the setting came to equal the gemstones in importance. Cartier was at the forefront of this new aesthetic, offering its clientele the superb jewelry that had long been its standard in styles that reflected the changing times.

Spearheading Cartier's jewelry design was Jeanne Toussaint, who was named director of Cartier's fine jewelry department in 1933. Under her tutelage, the firm's jewelry evolved from abstract confections to figurative and bold designs. A modern woman, she lived an avant-garde life and carried on a romantic relationship with Louis Cartier. Daring and unafraid, she came up with the ideas for some of Cartier's most outstanding jewels. Her taste was legendary, and her devotion to Cartier helped promote the eminence of the house. She became one of the driving forces in jewelry styles for several decades.

In the 1930s women no longer wanted the schoolboy figure of the previous decade. Rather, they wanted curves, which were facilitated by new uplift bras. One of the driving forces behind this trend was Hollywood. The stars of the silver screen epitomized glamour and radiated sex appeal. The clothes, makeup, and mannerisms of such screen idols as Greta Garbo, Marlene Dietrich, Joan Crawford, and Jean Harlow were emulated by their adoring fans and gave women a new concept of femininity. According to the English author, critic, and art historian James Laver, "Film is the most perfect visual medium for the exploitation of fashion and beauty that ever existed."[2]

Fashion affected jewelry forms and how they were to be worn (see page 188). Coco Chanel designed

Christmas card featuring the Cartier New York boutique's entrance, about 1930. Cartier Archives.

simple suits that could be dressed up with abundant costume jewels, and Elsa Schiaparelli created broad-shouldered, form-fitting suits and dresses with matching jackets. No one styled this sleek look better than the Duchess of Windsor, who was wont to add a silk sash to a plain dress, pin a jewel to her shoulder, wrap a bracelet around her wrist, or drape a necklace around her neck—thus making use of the many gifts she received from the duke. It was a time of individuality, when jewels, more than ever, became statements of a woman's personality.

Jewelry designers of the 1930s were not afraid to experiment, and their eager clientele was receptive to the bold, new designs that evolved from the flat, rectilinear styles of the 1920s. Diamonds continued to be popular and were often juxtaposed with oversize colored gemstones chosen for their hues—emerald, turquoise, aquamarine, peridot, lapis lazuli, and citrine.

Cartier was at the forefront of the new design direction. A gorgeous necklace owned by actress Merle Oberon features diamond-and-platinum rondelles and a fringe of large Indian emerald beads (fig. 205 and page 192 right). It is perfectly complemented by a branchlike diamond-and-emerald brooch from the same era (fig. 204). A tiara from 1937 is made up of a band of *calibré-* and baguette-cut citrines that encircles the head; its centerpiece, set with a 62.35-carat stone, also functions as a clip brooch (fig. 206). Convertible jewelry that could be worn in numerous ways was particularly in demand at the time, perhaps a reflection of an economy in which buyers wanted more versatility out of a single jewel. Rectangular citrines are also featured in a chic gold bracelet-watch (fig. 207). Two years later, Cartier introduced a novel item, the handcuff bracelet, which was made of rectangular *calibré*-cut citrines counterbalanced by

204. Brooch Cartier Paris, 1951. Platinum, white gold, brilliant- and single-cut diamonds, pear-shaped cabochon emerald drops. 10.2 × 4.8 cm. Private collection.

Each emerald is studded with a collet-set diamond.

Actress Merle Oberon and gossip columnist Walter Winchell, Stork Club, New York, 1940.

conical-shaped amethysts (fig. 209). An art moderne bracelet and ring (fig. 208) are dominated by large citrines set into ample gold mounts accented with diamond-set scrolls on either side; the diamonds counterbalance the dramatic golden color of the citrines.

At about the same time, Cartier created an inventive watch in keeping with the house's continued interest in making out-of-the-ordinary timepieces. Instead of a traditional watchstrap or gold band, polished-gold spring-hinged links, like kernels of corn, wind around the wrist. The rectangular watch face is offset parallel to the band (fig. 210).

Magazines such as *Vogue*, *Harper's Bazaar*, and *Vanity Fair* played a role in publicizing the latest fashions by commissioning photographs of couturier designs—which were often accessorized with jewelry. Cartier pieces appeared in such fashion spreads, and *Vogue* featured four Cartier pieces set with citrines on the cover of its August 1, 1938, issue (see page 196 left). Cartier also placed advertisements for its latest designs in these magazines and others.

Aquamarines were seen in jewelry made during the first decade of the twentieth century but thereafter largely took a hiatus until the 1930s. By the middle of that decade, Cartier jewelry incorporated these and other large-scale colored gemstones because they complemented the era's fashions, which had a softer, more feminine shape. Despite their renewed popularity, very few aquamarine pieces by Cartier have come to light: one example is an openwork platinum-and-diamond

OPPOSITE **205. Necklace** Cartier London, 1938, lengthened by Cartier Paris in 1963. Old European- and single-cut diamonds, slightly baroque-shaped emerald cabochon drops. Private collection. Sold to film director and producer Sir Alexander Korda (1893–1956).

Alexander Korda gave this necklace to his second wife, Merle Oberon (1911–1979), an actress best known for her performance in *Wuthering Heights*. In 1963 Cartier Paris lengthened the chain by adding 29 diamond rondelles.

ABOVE, CLOCKWISE FROM TOP

206. **Tiara** Cartier London, 1937. Gold; platinum; round old- and baguette-cut diamonds; one large octagonal emerald-cut 62.35-carat dark citrine; *calibré*-, baguette-cut, and hexagonal citrines. Diameter 17 cm, clip-brooch 5.8 × 4.7 cm. Cartier Collection HO 14 A37.

The central motif can be detached from the tiara and worn as a brooch, pointing downward.

207. **Bracelet-watch** Cartier Paris, 1938. Gold, dark and lighter citrines. Rectangular LeCoultre caliber 403 Duoplan movement, rhodium-plated, 15 jewels, Swiss lever escapement, bimetallic balance, flat balance spring. Diameter 5.7 cm, width of case 1.1 cm, width of bracelet 2.5 cm. Cartier Collection WWL 71 A38.

208. **Bracelet and ring** Cartier New York, about 1938. Gold, approx. 250-carat and 70-carat citrines, diamonds. Bracelet 7 × 6.4 × 4.8 cm, ring 3.5 × 3.5 × 2.9 cm. Private collection.

OPPOSITE 209. ***Handcuff* bracelet** Cartier Paris, 1939. Gold, amethyst cabochons, *calibré*-cut citrines. Diameter 7.5 cm. Cartier Collection BT 105 A39.

Cartier

tiara that incorporates large, blossomlike ovals made of aquamarines (fig. 211). Another diamond-and-aquamarine tiara from 1937 (fig. 213; purportedly worn at the coronation of George VI) has a very different, more geometric look. That same year, Cartier made a cuff bracelet (fig. 212) set with perfectly matched aquamarines, an indication that the stones were cut from the same rough crystal of flawless quality. The stones probably came from one of the world-renowned mines in Minas Gerais, Brazil, which produced some of the finest gem material available anywhere. Finding such perfectly matched gemstones was difficult. As a 1936 letter from Cartier London to Cartier New York notes, "We have . . . a number of partly completed necklaces, which we were unable to finish owing to the lack of the necessary aquamarines."[3]

Peridot, a beautiful green variety of olivine, is not a gemstone often seen in Cartier jewelry. The most prized are those exhibiting a dark green color without undertones of yellow or brown. Cartier incorporated mining magnate Chester Beatty's peridots into a necklace with diamond-set scrolls accenting the geometric-cut gemstones; emerald-cut and cabochon peridots accent an accompanying bracelet (fig. 214).

Turquoise has been considered a gem since ancient times. Egyptians mined it more than six thousand years ago. In the Americas, the Aztecs cherished its

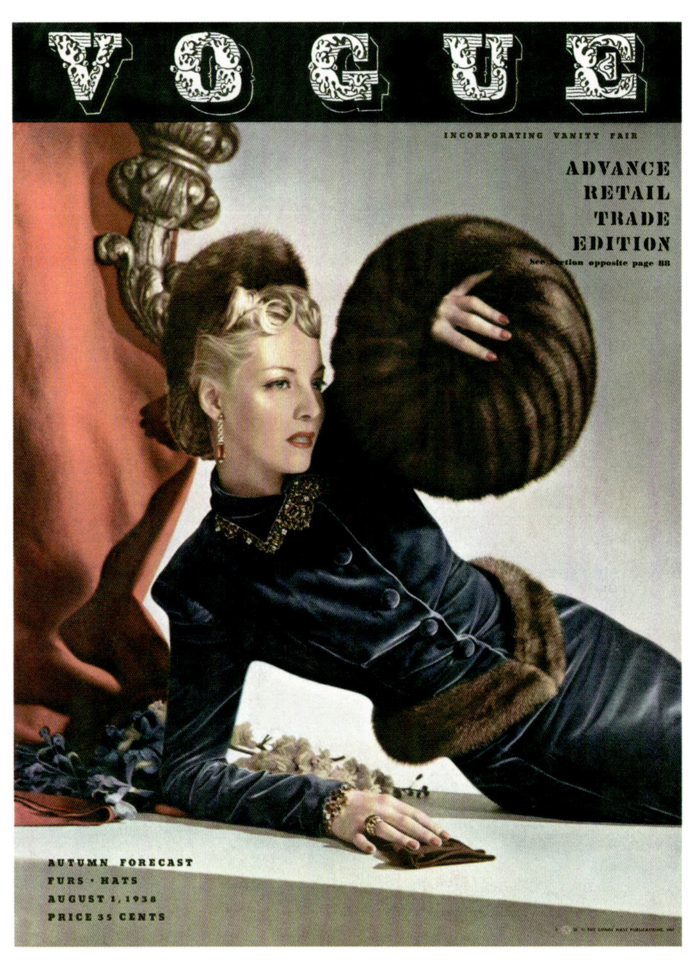

Cover of *Vogue*, Aug. 1, 1938, featuring Cartier citrine jewelry, photographed by Horst P. Horst. Horst/*Vogue*. Condé Nast Archive.

ABOVE 210. **Bracelet-watch** Cartier Paris, 1936. Gold. Rectangular LeCoultre caliber 403 Duoplan movement, rhodium-plated, 2 adjustments, 15 jewels, Swiss lever escapement, monometallic balance, flat balance spring. Length of case 2.3 cm. Cartier Collection WWL 103 A36. Sold to the Pasha of Marrakech.

OPPOSITE 211. **Tiara** Cartier London, 1938. Platinum, diamonds, aquamarines. Millegrain setting, height 5.5 cm, diameter 15.5 cm. Qatar Museums Authority.

TOP 212. **Bracelet** Cartier New York, 1937. White gold, platinum, aquamarines. Height 3 cm. Private collection.

ABOVE 213. **Tiara** Cartier London, 1937. Platinum, round old-cut diamonds, oval and fancy-cut aquamarines. Height at center 5 cm. Cartier Collection HO 12 A37.

In 1937 Cartier London received orders for no fewer than twenty-seven tiaras, most of them to be worn at the coronation of King George VI in May of that year. The central motif can be removed from the tiara and worn as a brooch, pointing downward.

OPPOSITE 214. **Necklace and bracelet** Cartier London, special order, 1936. Cartier Collection JS 06 A36. Provenance: Mrs. A. Chester Beatty.

Necklace: Platinum, round old- and baguette-cut diamonds, one emerald-cut 63.48-carat peridot, emerald-cut peridots of various shapes. Diameter 15 cm, front height 6.1 cm.

Bracelet: Platinum, round old- and baguette-cut diamonds, one emerald-cut 68.93-carat peridot, cabochon and square faceted peridots. 17 × 3 cm.

sky-blue color. The finest turquoise exhibits a uniform, medium-blue color, as exemplified by the leaf-carved gemstones on a tiara (fig. 216) made for Phyllis Brand, a sister of Lady Astor and the wife of Robert Henry Brand, a director of Lazard Brothers and Lloyds Bank who also served in the British government. Each gem on this tiara is engraved to delineate the veining. Turquoise cabochons and diamonds also adorn the baton clasp on a 1937 lapis lazuli–beaded bracelet. Each lapis bead in the central row is artfully set with a diamond, providing sparkle to the design (fig. 215).

But of course it is diamonds, the best and finest diamonds, with which the name Cartier is synonymous. At the turn of the twentieth century, Cartier created important bracelets, necklaces, brooches, corsage ornaments, *lavallière* necklaces, and tiaras in the garland style. Thirty-some years later, the firm continued to make jewelry in the all-white look but with updated designs. Forms became sharply delineated, and gemstones were fashioned in the new geometric cuts. On the 1934 Halo head ornament, for instance, baguette-cut diamonds form lotus-flower stems, and the flowers gradually diminish in size from the center to the upturned scrolling buds at the base (fig. 217). The head ornament was formerly in the collection of Her Highness the Begum Aga Khan, Andrée Carron, wife of Sir Sultan Muhammad Shah, Aga Khan III.

The central section of an all-white bangle from 1937 features three large diamonds surrounded by smaller stones and separated by baguette-cut diamonds (fig. 218). A bracelet also created in 1937 has a wide gold band that is in strong visual contrast to a diamond-set "buckle" that originally could be detached and worn as a brooch (fig. 219).

Earrings are one type of jewelry that often does not stand the test of time. Either they are reconfigured in another form or one of the pair is, sadly, lost. A pair of diamond-and-emerald earrings from 1934 (fig. 221) provides a rare glimpse at design in mid-decade. Each has a diamond at the apex, from which is suspended an articulated chevron motif set with baguette-, square-, and marquise-cut diamonds. An emerald drop of outstanding color and clarity completes the composition. These earrings were formerly in the collection of Mrs. Charles Wrightsman, who is, according to the 2012 Sotheby's catalog of her jewelry collection, "an icon of taste and style and, most importantly, a philanthropist of unequalled generosity," as well as "one of the most remarkable art collectors of our age."[4]

In 1936 Cartier repeated the chevron theme on a ruby-and-diamond necklace (fig. 220). But whereas the chevron dominated the design of the earrings, here it serves as a divider between the double row of rubies at the front of the necklace and the single row at the back. The chevrons are artfully placed so they rest just above the collarbone, enabling the jewels to lie comfortably on the neck. This short necklace

215. **Bracelet** Cartier Paris, 1937. Platinum, white gold, silver, round old- and single-cut diamonds, lapis lazuli beads, turquoise cabochons. Length 20.3 cm. Cartier Collection BT 01 A37.

216. Tiara Cartier London, special order, 1936. Platinum, old- and single-cut diamonds, carved turquoises. Height at center 4.8 cm. Cartier Collection HO 06 A36. Sold to the Honorable Robert Henry Brand.

Banker and senior civil servant Robert Henry Brand (1878–1963) was a director of Lazard Brothers and Lloyds Bank.

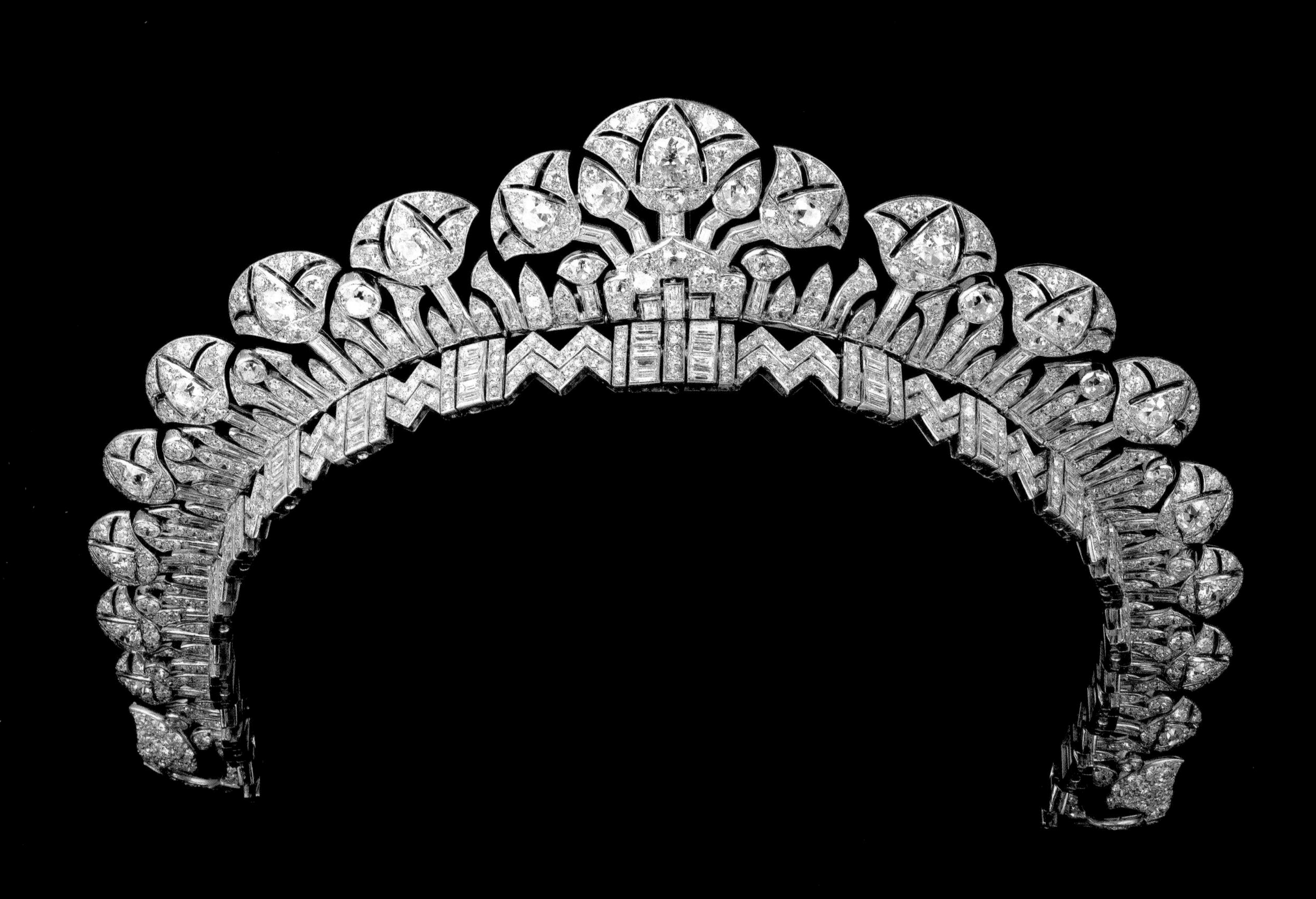

OPPOSITE 217. ***Halo* tiara** Cartier London, 1934. Platinum, round old- and baguette-cut diamonds. Height at center 4 cm. Cartier Collection HO 10 A34. Sold to HH the Begum Aga Khan.

Born Andrée Carron, Princess Andrée Aga Khan was the third wife of Sir Sultan Muhammad Shah, Aga Khan III (whom she divorced in 1944) and mother of Prince Sadruddin Aga Khan.

The upper part forms a halo of stylized lotus flowers, while the lower part with its zigzag motifs can be detached to form a bandeau.

TOP 218. **Bangle** Cartier Paris, 1937. Platinum; cushion-shaped, square-, baguette-, brilliant-, round old-, and single-cut diamonds. 5.7 × 7 × 2.6 cm. Cartier Collection BT 48 A37.

ABOVE 219. ***Buckle* bangle** Cartier London, 1937. Yellow and white gold; platinum; brilliant-, baguette-, and single-cut diamonds. 6.1 × 5.5 × 3.1 cm. Cartier Collection BT 91 A37.

ABOVE 220. **Necklace** Cartier London, 1936. Platinum, baguette-cut and square-shaped diamonds, cushion-shaped and oval faceted rubies. Length 40 cm. Cartier Collection NE 32 A36.

This necklace was originally longer (the back part had an additional ten rubies and ten diamond spacers).

TOP 221. **Ear clips** Cartier London, 1934. Platinum; baguette-cut, square-cut, and marquise-shaped diamonds; emerald drops. Length 6.4 cm, width 2.5 cm. Each emerald is 25 carats. Private collection. Provenance: Mrs. Charles Wrightsman.

complements the low necklines and bare shoulders of 1930s fashion.

The mid-1930s was also a time of luxurious international travel. Splendid aircraft flew the rich and famous to exotic locations. The deluxe ocean liner the *Queen Mary* was launched in 1936. Its sumptuous accommodations included five dining areas, cocktail bars, swimming pools, a squash court for those who wanted to stay physically fit, a hospital for emergencies, and a grand ballroom, where the latest fashions and most lavish jewels were in conspicuous view. The fun continued on land, at such playgrounds of the wealthy as the French Riviera, Saint-Tropez, the Lido, and Saint Moritz, where jewels were de rigueur.

Jeanne Toussaint was one of the designers who brought gold jewelry back as a fashion statement. The word *ordinary* was not in her vocabulary. On a gold, lapis lazuli, and diamond suite from 1937 (fig. 222), each jewel is adorned with a cluster of beads and each bead is inset with either a collet-set inverted square-cut diamond or a square-shaped sugarloaf lapis lazuli. The bracelet is made up of a grouping of twenty-three beads connected to a gas-pipe band, a style that would become ubiquitous in the next few years.

Before handbags became popular, the well-dressed lady carried a vanity case. This was an essential accessory for the modern woman, who could no longer do without her cosmetics, whether she was in town, in the country, or traveling. The vanity case contained a powder compact, lipstick, comb, and mirror. It replaced either a small purse worn suspended from a chatelaine that hung from the belt or the more traditional cloth bag carried in the hand. The surfaces on vanity cases could be plain, engraved with a design, chased with figurative scenes, enameled, or set with gemstones. These small, bejeweled objects evolved into works of

222. **Jewelry suite: bracelet, ear clips, ring, and brooch** Cartier Paris, 1937. Gold, platinum, sugarloaf square-cut lapis lazuli, inverted square-cut and old mine-cut diamonds. Length of bracelet 17.5 cm, diameter of brooch 3.8 cm. Private collection.

223. **Clock** Cartier Paris, 1941. Gold, platinum, mother-of-pearl, single-cut diamonds, topazes. Round 8-day movement decorated with vertical stripes, 2 adjustments, 15 jewels, Swiss lever escapement, bimetallic balance, Breguet balance spring. Hand-setting and winding mechanism hidden underneath the base. 21.5 × 11.5 × 12.5 cm. Cartier Collection CDB 03 A41.

The upper part is adorned with an ancient Egyptian bas-relief of fossilized wood showing a canopic jar.

art that were not only functional but also enjoyable from a purely aesthetic perspective.

In creating vanity cases, as in designing the finest jewels, Cartier's jewelers paid attention to the minutest detail. One large case (see fig. 51, page 59) owned by Beatrice Mills, daughter of the financier and philanthropist Ogden Mills and wife of the eighth Earl of Granard, is rectangular with a ribbed surface and black enamel edging. A crown, two palmettes, and her initials, all set with diamonds, further adorn the case's upper surface. A smaller vanity case in similar style is semicircular in form and edged with diamonds; it was purchased by Frederick William Vanderbilt (fig. 224). A third case, elegantly simple, was owned by Mary Millicent Rogers, famous on both sides of the Atlantic for both her beauty and her taste in jewelry (fig. 225).

The era of international travel and luxury spending came to an abrupt halt when Adolf Hitler invaded Poland on September 1, 1939. A few days later, Great

OPPOSITE, TOP 224. **Vanity case** Cartier New York, special order, 1936. Gold; platinum; baguette-, single-, and brilliant-cut diamonds. Monogram *ADV*. 8.6 × 4.7 × 1.6 cm. Cartier Collection VC 82 A36. Ordered by Frederick William Vanderbilt.

OPPOSITE, BOTTOM 225. **Powder box** Cartier Paris, 1937. Gold, platinum, rose- and single-cut diamonds. 7 × 7 × 0.9 cm. Cartier Collection PB 35 A37. Sold to Mr. Ronald Balcom.

Ronald Balcom was a New York stockbroker. In 1936, he married Mary Millicent Rogers, the Standard Oil heiress.

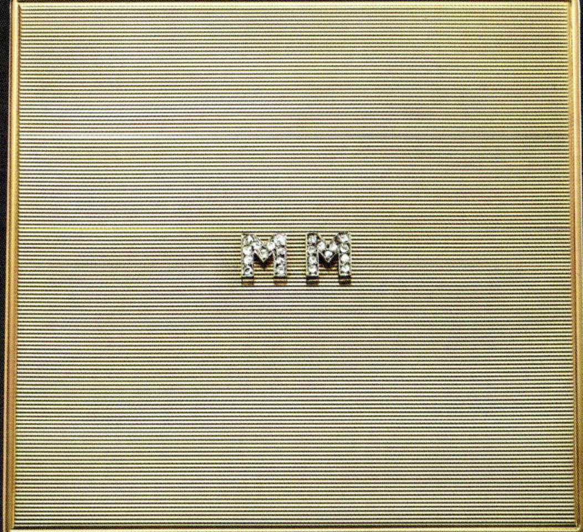
MM

Britain and France retaliated by declaring war on Germany. World War II had begun. In 1940, the Bank of France banned all trading in gold. In spite of the hostilities, Cartier continued to make limited quantities of jewelry and objets d'art at its Paris, London, and New York locations. The Paris workshop still created unusual timepieces, including an Egyptian-inspired, easel-style rectangular clock, veneered in mother-of-pearl and adorned with an ancient Egyptian bas-relief of fossilized wood bearing the image of a canopic jar (fig. 223). The brown tones of the bas-relief are reiterated in the topaz border surrounding it and in the *calibré*-cut topaz hour markers. Diamond-set platinum hands in the shape of a lotus flower and bud complete the Egyptian theme.

A set of four multicolored sapphire floral-bouquet brooches with matching ear clips (fig. 226) was made in Cartier's London workshop in 1944. It was purchased by Anthony

ABOVE 226. ***Floral bouquet* brooches and ear clips** Cartier London, 1944. Platinum, multicolored sapphires, diamonds. Length of each brooch 4.5 cm. Private collection. Provenance: Anthony Joseph Drexel Biddle Jr.

RIGHT 227. **Bracelet-watch with double-shutter cover** Cartier New York, 1942. Gold, platinum, ruby cabochons, brilliant-cut diamonds. Rectangular LeCoultre caliber 406 movement, rhodium-plated, 5 adjustments, 15 jewels, Swiss lever escapement, monometallic balance, flat balance spring. Case 3.3 × 1.1 cm. Cartier Collection WWL 88 A42.

The case opens by squeezing the oval flanges.

FAR RIGHT 228. **Blossom ear clips** Cartier London, about 1945. Gold, platinum, ruby beads, carved emeralds, collet-set diamonds. Private collection.

Joseph Drexel Biddle Jr. of Philadelphia, a socialite, career military man, and U.S. ambassador to Poland at the start of World War II. The New York workshop continued to design jewelry, accessories, and watches, including a bracelet-watch with a double-shutter cover set with cabochon rubies (fig. 227). Faceted rubies resembling petals are used in a stunning pair of earrings from the same era (fig. 228). The ruby petals surround vivid green, engraved emerald centers accented with diamonds. Despite such singular extravagances, the luxury trade did not regain its former vitality until the war ended in 1945.

GLAMOUR'S NEW LOOK: THE LATE 1940S AND 1950S

In 1947 couturier Christian Dior introduced a collection that became known as the New Look after *Harper's Bazaar* editor in chief Carmel Snow exclaimed, "It's such a new look!" It was characterized by small, rounded shoulders, a heart-shaped neckline, a narrow waist, and a flared, voluminous skirt. In Dior's words:

> We were emerging from a time of war, of uniforms, and of women soldiers built like boxers. I designed flower-like women, with delicate shoulders, blossoming bosoms, narrow liana-like waists and skirts as wide as corollas ... I wanted my dresses to be built and molded round the curves of a woman's body, and to stylize its contours. I accentuated the waist and the volume of the hips; I set off the bust to its best advantage.[5]

The New Look provided ample space at the neck and shoulders for wearing jewels. Gold bracelets—not the modest, pretty examples from the early 1930s but big, bold statement pieces, sometimes worn in multiples—became popular (right). In

Cover of *Vogue*, June 15, 1942, photographed by Horst P. Horst. On the model's hand are a diamond-and-gold bracelet-watch and a sapphire, ruby, and diamond ring, both by Cartier. Condé Nast Archive.

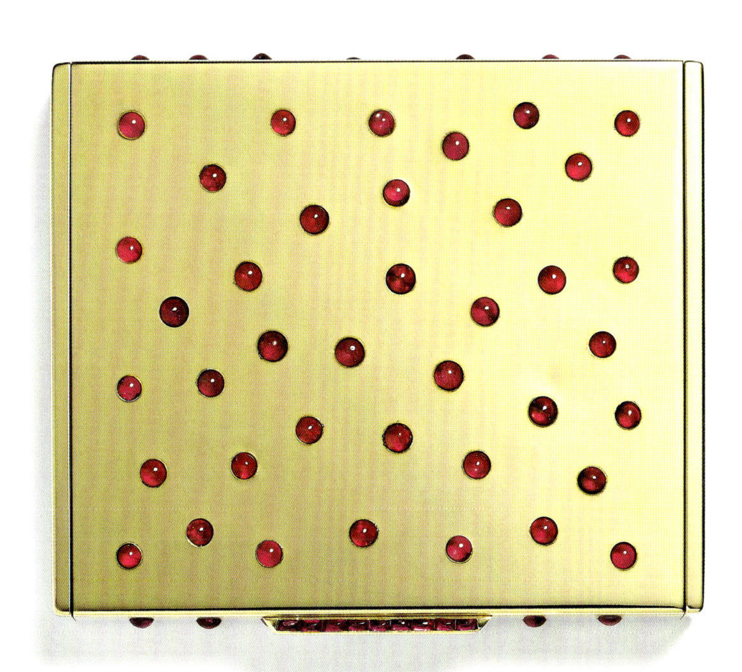

OPPOSITE Page from *Vogue,* April 1, 1947. The model's jewels are by Cartier. Condé Nast Archive.

TOP 229. **Ring** Cartier Paris, 1948. Gold, ruby beads. 2.9 × 3.2 cm. Cartier Collection RG 39 A48. Provenance: Daisy Fellowes.

ABOVE 230. **Powder compact** Cartier New York, 1946. Gold, cabochon and *calibré*-cut rubies. Interior fitted with a mirror and a covered compartment engraved with the monogram *GL*, the initials *V+L*, and the date *1952*. 7.7 × 6.6 × 1.4 cm. Cartier Collection PB 30 A46. Sold to Vivien Leigh in 1952.

Born in India, Vivian Hartley (1913–1967) was later known as Vivien Leigh. She won an Oscar in 1940 for Best Actress for her unforgettable role as Scarlett O'Hara in *Gone with the Wind*. That same year she married Laurence Olivier, forming one of the most fashionable couples in London society.

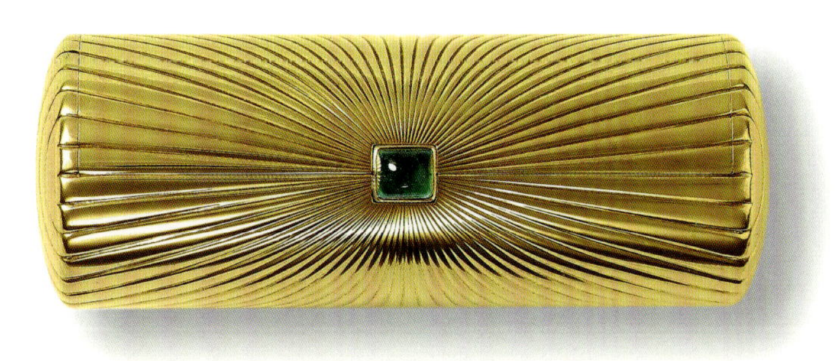

TOP AND CENTER 231. **Cigarette case** Cartier Paris, 1948. Gold, emerald cabochon. Interior fitted with two compartments with gold openwork retaining clips. 8.4 × 3.1 × 4.6 cm. Cartier Collection CC 43 A48.

ABOVE 232. **Lighter** Cartier Paris, 1945. Gold, emerald cabochon. 4.5 × 4 × 1.5 cm. Cartier Collection LR 14 A45.

OPPOSITE 233. **Bracelet** Cartier Paris, 1945. Yellow and red gold. 19 × 2.6 cm. Cartier Collection BT 63 A45.

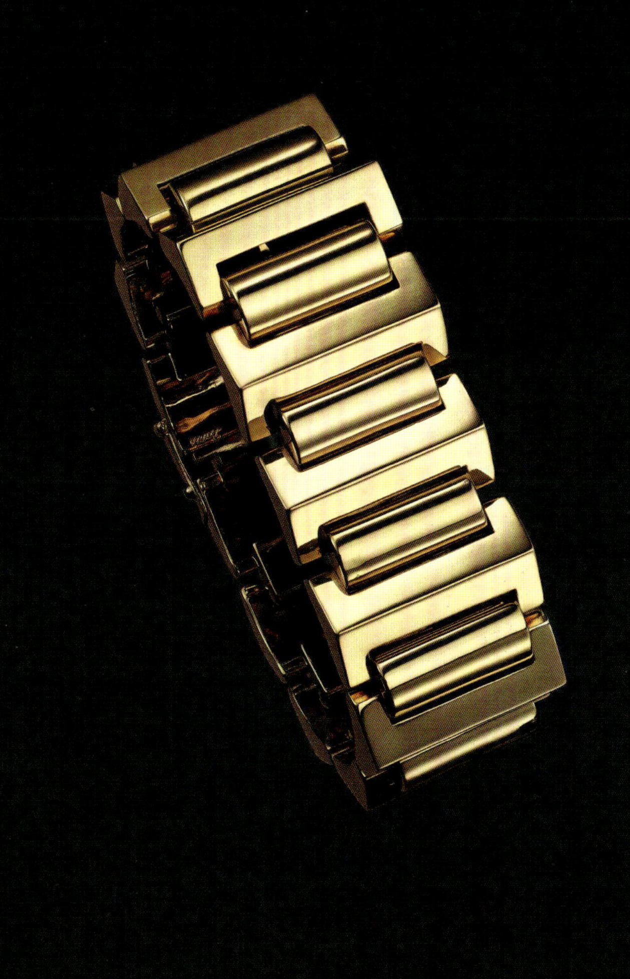

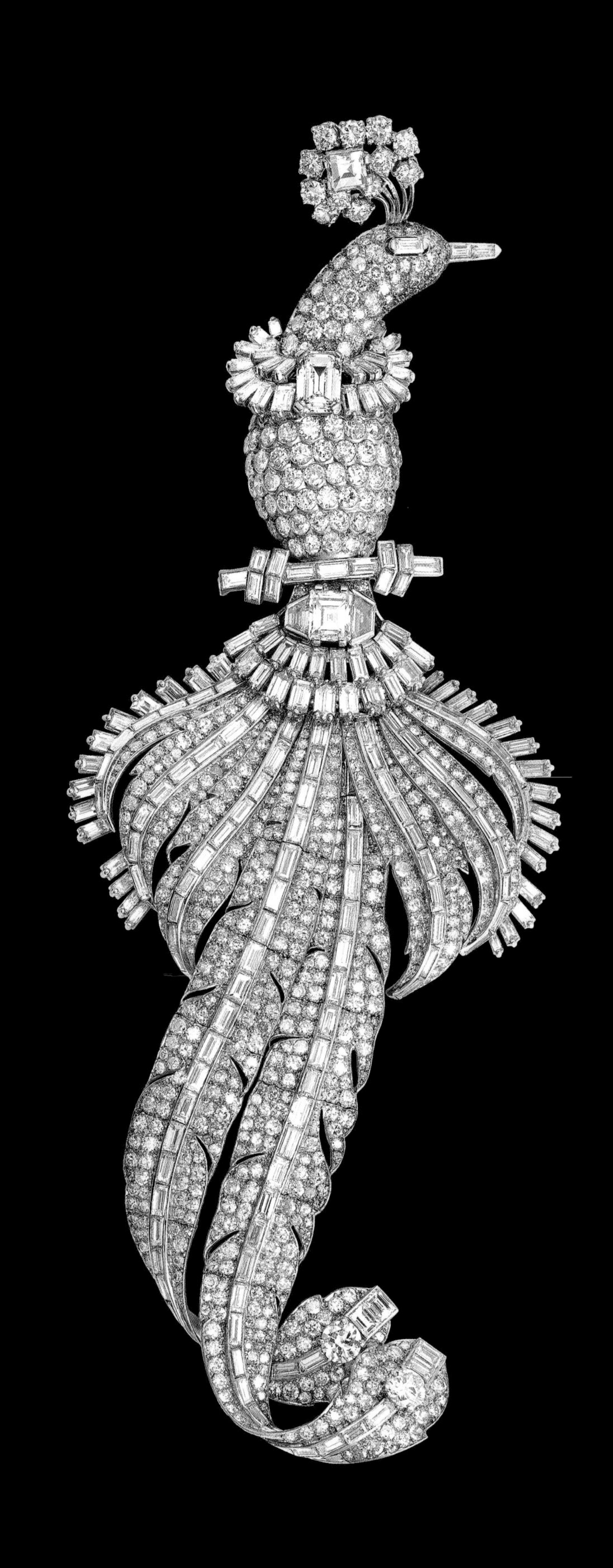

1945 Cartier created a striking yellow-and-red-gold bracelet made of long triangular sections alternating with tubelike links (fig. 233). A lovely ring made in 1948 features densely clustered ruby beads (fig. 229). The house designed a stylish ruby-studded powder compact (fig. 230) in 1946 that was purchased by the actress Vivien Leigh (best known for her role as Scarlett O'Hara in *Gone with the Wind*) in 1952. Other gold accoutrements included a cigarette case and a lighter (figs. 231 and 232) featuring a radial design emanating from a cabochon emerald push-piece.

Within a few years of the war's end, diamonds came roaring back. Cartier created an all-white bird brooch (fig. 234) that was a stupendous eight inches long and set with 994 diamonds, weighing a total of 90.29 carats. Perfectly suited for the New Look, the brooch was meant to be worn pinned to the shoulder, with the bird's head twisted to one side. The design is ingenious. The bird is positioned on a perch made of baguette diamonds that demarcates its body from its glorious, lyre-shaped tail feathers below. The use of a variety of diamond cuts (square, emerald, baguette, brilliant, and fancy) lends dynamism to the design. This brooch was featured in a François Kollar fashion photograph, shown pinned to a Robert Piguet dress (right).

Parures, or matched suites of jewelry, became popular in the 1950s, a throwback to the nineteenth century. Cartier created several examples, including a 1951 diamond-and-ruby necklace, bracelet, and earrings parure in the Indian style (fig. 235). The shape of the pendants on the earrings and the five elements of the necklace is reminiscent of an Indian amulet. A similar suite was featured in a fashion photo in the December 1950 issue of *Album du Figaro*. The later suite was owned by Lady Lydia Deterding (née Koudoyaroff), who was born in Russia and lived a grand life there with her first husband, General Bagratouni, a Russian diplomat, before immigrating to Paris. After their divorce, she married Sir Henri Deterding, a founder of Royal Dutch Petroleum. She

Fashion photograph of Cartier diamond Bird brooch on a Robert Piguet dress by François Kollar. RMN—Grand Palais/Art Resource, NY.

OPPOSITE 234. ***Bird* brooch** Cartier Paris, special order, 1948. Platinum; white gold; emerald-, square-, baguette-, brilliant-, and fancy-cut diamonds. Height 20.2 cm. Cartier Collection CL 316 A48.

The client provided many of the diamonds for this brooch. The exceptional dimensions (almost 8 inches long, weighing 156.45 g) make this brooch a unique post–World War II piece of high jewelry.

PRECEDING PAGES 235. **Necklace, bracelet, and pair of earrings** Cartier Paris, special order, 1951. Platinum; gold; brilliant-, baguette-, modified baguette-, and fancy-cut diamonds; cushion-shaped and round faceted Burmese rubies. Lengths: necklace 37 cm, bracelet central motif 6.2 cm, earrings 6 cm. Cartier Collection JS 11 A51. Made as a special order for Lady Deterding.

ABOVE 236. ***Egg* vanity case** Cartier Paris, 1958. Gold; platinum; baguette-, brilliant-, and single-cut diamonds. Interior with a powder compartment with Plexiglas cover, a cigarette compartment with gold openwork retaining clip, and a mirrored cover. 11.1 × 8.2 × 5.9 cm. Cartier Collection VC 86 A58. Sold to Lady Deterding.

had an innate sense of style and continued to acquire jewelry after she and Deterding divorced in 1936. Another Cartier item of hers is an egg-shaped vanity case. Decorated with engine turning (fig. 236), it hangs from a gold suspension chain. The interior includes a compartment for powder, another for cigarettes, a mirrored compartment, and an attached comb—all essential items for a night on the town.

In the late 1940s and 1950s, Cartier placed full-page advertisements for its precious gemstone jewelry in *Vogue*. One 1946 ad featured three spectacular necklaces: the first made of all diamonds; the second, of diamonds and rubies; and the third, of rubies and emeralds.[6] Another ad highlighted a diamond-and-emerald necklace with eleven suspended emeralds, and yet another put the spotlight on an important all-diamond necklace. Several advertisements for Cadillac also promoted Cartier, including one that showcased the Alexander II emerald necklace, which features a square-cut emerald weighing approximately 45 carats set into a platinum-and-diamond mounting and seven additional square-cut emeralds, and another that pictured two smartly dressed couples in front of Cartier's Fifth Avenue store (right).[7]

In the 1950s the anxieties of the previous decade receded and prosperity was on the rise. As a larger segment of the population began to enjoy the benefits of increasing income, fine jewelry was no longer the province of the rich alone but was becoming accessible to members of the middle class, who were eager to emulate the trendsetters of the day. Events such as the storybook marriage of the American actress Grace Kelly to Prince Rainier III of Monaco on April 19, 1956, captivated the world. Jacqueline Kennedy, a quiet, elegant socialite, was catapulted into international prominence when her husband, Senator John Fitzgerald Kennedy, was elected president of the United States in 1960. The social environment had changed; formal entertaining was replaced by cocktail parties, for which everyone wanted to dress in the latest fashions. Glamour was once again "in," amply supported by a broad range of jewelry styles, from sumptuous diamond creations to colorful, artfully designed confections.

Cadillac advertisement illustrating the Cartier boutique on Fifth Avenue, New York, 1956. Cartier New York Archives.

In 1955 Cartier combined turquoise and diamonds on a five-part gold wire necklace (fig. 239). The triangular central section resembles a gentleman's cravat. The chain is formed of plaited gold in a manner similar to that of a turquoise-and-diamond bangle (fig. 238). Turquoise also adorns a *toi et moi* (you and me) ring, highlighted with sapphires and diamonds (fig. 237). Gold, once the preferred metal for daytime wear, was now acceptable for evening.

TOP 237. ***Toi et moi* ring (Crossover ring)** Cartier Paris, 1967. Gold, platinum, brilliant-cut diamonds, 3.56-carat sugarloaf sapphire cabochon, round faceted sapphires, turquoise cabochons. 3 × 2.5 cm. Cartier Collection RG 17 A67.

ABOVE 238. **Bangle** Cartier Paris, 1953. Yellow and white gold, brilliant-cut diamonds, turquoise cabochons. 6.5 × 7.1 cm. Cartier Collection BT 104 A53. Sold to a member of the Rothschild family.

OPPOSITE 239. **Bib necklace** Cartier Paris, 1955. Gold wire and plaited gold, brilliant-cut diamonds, turquoise cabochons. Length of central motif 7.6 cm. Cartier Collection NE 31 A55.

The central pendant is hinged, allowing it to conform to the wearer's body.

Design drawing of *Palm tree* clip brooch (fig. 240). Cartier Paris, 1957. Cartier Archives.

Cartier created several different versions of the palm tree brooch. One, made in 1939 entirely of diamonds, features an articulated trunk set with brilliant-cut diamonds. Various-shaped diamonds form the fronds, and six briolette diamonds serve as the coconuts. An example from 1950 has baguette-cut diamonds forming the trunk, which rises from a base of five marquise-cut diamonds; four pear-shaped diamonds hang from fronds of brilliant-cut and baguette-cut diamonds. Perhaps the most dynamic is a diamond-set palm tree with a cluster of seven ruby coconuts, weighing 23.10 carats in total, bursting from diamond-set fronds (fig. 240 and above). The articulated trunk is set with brilliant-cut and baguette-cut diamonds.

The variety of animal-style jewelry from the 1950s and 1960s parallels the fascination for the same subject during the Victorian period. Cartier created an exotic dolphin bangle as a special order in 1969, replicating the mammal's streamlined, fusiform body—wide in the middle and tapered at either end—which enables it to swim quickly. The bangle is fashioned out of gold and set with 1,028 brilliant-cut diamonds that highlight the engraved, scaly body (fig. 241).

Among the most spectacular Cartier jewels is the diamond necklace set with a 98.57-carat deep blue sapphire, known as the Bismarck sapphire, once owned by Countess Mona von Bismarck. In the introduction to the Sotheby's catalog of the sale of her jewelry, fashion editor Diana Vreeland writes, "In a rather miraculous way, everything that was hers was out of the ordinary. By day, I never saw her without her enormous pearls gleaming on her immaculate skin. By night, her superb jewels, sometimes a magnificent diamond necklace, sometimes a chain of emeralds or her parure of rubies, would be backdrop to her unforgettable elegance."[8] In 1967 Mona presented her huge sapphire necklace (see fig. 242, page 231) to the National Museum of Natural History of the Smithsonian Institution in Washington, D.C.[9]

From the 1930s to the 1960s, Cartier created beautiful, often spectacular, one-of-a-kind treasures that, like the women who owned them, have become icons of a time when glamour was not just a state of mind but also a way of living. The jewelry and objets d'art, like their predecessors from the Renaissance, will be desirable five hundred years from now and will forever conjure a time when glamour meant living life to the fullest and never settling for anything less.

OPPOSITE, TOP 240. ***Palm tree* clip brooch** Cartier Paris, special order, 1957. Platinum, white gold, brilliant- and baguette-cut diamonds, seven cushion-shaped rubies weighing 23.10 carats in total. 11.5 × 7 × 2.8 cm. Cartier Collection CL 34 A57.

OPPOSITE, BOTTOM 241. ***Dolphin* bangle** Cartier Paris, special order, 1969. Engraved gold, 1,028 brilliant-cut diamonds weighing 33.73 carats in total, pear-shaped emeralds. 9 × 8.1 × 5.7 cm. Cartier Collection BT 115 A69.

A swivel system on each side allows the bracelet to open.

STEFANO PAPI

ICONS OF STYLE

FOR MORE THAN A HUNDRED YEARS THE NAME Cartier has signified glamour, power, and effortless elegance—qualities embodied in the exquisite pieces of jewelry created for some of the most iconic figures and symbols of gracious living of the twentieth century. Royalty, aristocrats, film stars, socialites, and heiresses all wished to possess the creations of this famous house. It was not just the meticulous craftsmanship and magnificent materials that attracted Cartier's clients, but also its position at the vanguard of twentieth-century jewelry design.

This reputation was secured around 1900, when Cartier rejected the forms of contemporary art nouveau jewels and became the champion of the garland style, a fashion characterized by delicate leaves, flowers, ribbons, and bows, as well as symmetrical forms that harked back to the rococo pattern books and architecture of the eighteenth century. This light but ornate Edwardian-era style is epitomized by the high choker and large *devant de corsage* worn by some of the most well-known women of the period, from queens and countesses to actresses and singers. One of the most significant examples was the *résille* choker created in 1904 for Queen Alexandra, the consort of the British king Edward VII. It consisted of a supple network of platinum and diamonds with a large central stone and a fringe of emerald and ruby drops (see pages 31 and 226). Three years earlier, in 1901, the firm made a choker for Lady de Grey, later Marchioness of Ripon, an influential patron of opera and ballet who was instrumental in bringing Diaghilev's Ballets Russes to London. In 1907 Princess Marie Bonaparte, heiress to the fortune of the Blanc family of Monte Carlo, married Prince George, second son of King George I of Greece, prompting the creation of some of Cartier's most magnificent garland-style jewels. The centerpieces were Princess Marie's beautiful tiara, designed as an olive wreath set with diamonds and a pear-shaped motif suspended in the middle

OPPOSITE Daisy Fellowes wearing her Hindu necklace (see fig. 252, page 243) and a Schiaparelli jacket, 1936, photographed by Cecil Beaton. Courtesy of the Cecil Beaton Studio Archive at Sotheby's.

François Flameng (1856–1923), *Queen Alexandra*, 1908. Oil on canvas. The Royal Collection, RCIN 405360. The queen wears her 1904 Cartier diamond *résille* necklace. Royal Collection Trust.

(opposite and see fig. 17, page 34), and a comb, also designed with olive leaves and pearls, that was later transformed into a tiara (see fig. 4, page 21). This spectacular array of jewels was on display in the window of Cartier's boutique in rue de la Paix (see page 35 left). Many women of the era drew inspiration from its classical style. Cartier jewels also featured in the collections of leading performers of the day, including Carolina "La Belle" Otero, Spanish star of the Folies Bergère (see page 36), and the Italian opera singer Lina Cavalieri, who often wore her jewels when she performed.

Across the Atlantic, Cartier's garland style was proving similarly popular among high society. The ladies of the wealthiest American families, including the Vanderbilts, the Astors, and the Leedses, competed for the most glamorous jewels. These tacit competitions were played out at functions and social gatherings of many kinds, in particular at the Metropolitan Opera, where the U-shaped auditorium was nicknamed "the diamond horseshoe"—a reference to the spectators' sparkling parures.[1] Society reporters were particularly interested in the style of ladies such as Grace Vanderbilt, the pinnacle of New York high society, whose effervescent personality and innate skill as a hostess dictated trends of the early 1900s (see page 30 left). She was always immaculately presented, and her Cartier collection, including her stunning 1909 diamond necklace and an early art deco hat pin (later transformed into a brooch) had few rivals (see fig. 54, page 61).

Another notable character was the vastly wealthy Mary Scott Townsend, a pillar of Washington society. At the opening of the opera season she was often seen in her sparkling tiara, created in 1905, along with a 1906 high choker and *devant de corsage*. Made by Cartier Paris, the *devant de corsage* epitomized the belle epoque fashion for this kind of bodice ornament, with its delicate design of lily sprays, buds, and leaves in a platinum setting (see fig. 16, page 33).

THE 1920S

During the period leading up to the outbreak of World War I, Cartier simplified the intricate forms of the garland style, rendering them more linear and bold and ornamenting them with platinum, diamonds, black onyx, and rock crystal. Necklaces were elongated, anticipating the *sautoirs* that became fashionable in the 1920s. By contrast, the *devant de corsage* gradually diminished in size and eventually went out of fashion altogether. After the war, lines became even bolder, and, thanks to the use of vibrantly colored stones, dramatic chromatic contrasts were created. By the time of the 1925 Exposition internationale des arts décoratifs et industriels modernes, the art deco style was already well established and Cartier was a leading exponent of it. The company's *sautoirs* are still considered some of the outstanding creations of the period, especially the one belonging to the philanthropist and socialite Marjorie Merriweather Post, who inherited the Postum Cereal Company (later General Foods) from her father at the age of twenty-seven in 1914 and went on to become the richest woman in America. Her *sautoir* (now owned by the Smithsonian Institution) was created by the London branch of Cartier in 1928–29 and was formed of lines of tumbled emerald drops separated by a barrel-shaped motif of pavé-set diamonds. From the buckle-shaped pendant that she sometimes wore with it was suspended a cascade of emeralds dominated by a large hexagonal emerald (see pages 71 right and 228). Over the years this generous philanthropist with a passionate interest in history built up a collection of historical pieces. She eventually left it to museums and her own foundation so that the general public might widen its knowledge of this art form. During her lifetime she loved to mix these historic jewels with Cartier creations made especially for her.

Princess Marie Bonaparte wearing her 1907 Cartier diamond-and-platinum tiara (see fig. 17, page 34). Cartier Archives.

Perhaps the most dedicated champion of Cartier's *sautoir* was the flamboyant Polish opera singer Ganna

Marjorie Merriweather Post dressed as Juliet and wearing her Cartier Indian-style emerald necklace and brooch at the Everglades Ball, March 7, 1929. Courtesy of Hillwood Estate, Museum & Gardens.

Ganna Walska wearing a 1923 Cartier emerald necklace and 1928 earrings, June 17, 1936. Courtesy of Ganna Walska Lotusland.

American divorcée Linda Lee Thomas was already famed for her beauty and sense of style when she met Cole Porter in Paris. After their 1919 marriage, they traveled and entertained extensively.

Walska (above left). Most renowned for her six marriages and for Lotusland, the gardens she created in Montecito, California, Walska also had a passion for jewelry. After her second husband died in 1920, she married Alexander Cochran, an extremely wealthy carpet manufacturer and yachtsman from Yonkers, New York, who at the age of forty-six was considered the richest bachelor in New York. His wedding present to Walska was an invitation to go to Cartier and choose anything she desired. Nonetheless, the union ended in divorce in July 1922, and within two weeks Walska married the millionaire American industrialist Harold McCormick, who himself had recently been divorced from Edith Rockefeller, daughter of John D. Rockefeller, founder of Standard Oil. McCormick spent considerable sums of money promoting the opera career of his new wife, despite the fact that her voice was not of the finest caliber. In her jewelry collection, the most stunning pieces were those created by Cartier.

Walska's passion for oriental jewelry led her, in 1929, to add one of Cartier's chimera bangles to her collection of jewels. These bangles were among Cartier's most famous creations of the 1920s; the inspiration behind them came from the makara, the mythical Indian sea serpent. Cartier further orientalized the form by molding it into a fluid sculpture of vibrant coral, decorated with diamonds and colored stones. Walska chose one with two large, fluted emerald beads of 48.43 carats in total, which were held between the jaws of the mythical creature; the back was decorated with black, blue, and green enamel (see fig. 81, page 92).

Another icon of that period was the stylish and beautiful wife of Cole Porter, Linda Lee Porter (above right). While Ganna Walska was busily championing oriental-style jewels, Mrs. Porter was developing a fascination with the Egyptian Revival style. About the same time that Walska bought her chimera bangle, Mrs. Porter ordered, at Cartier Paris, a diamond, turquoise, and lapis lazuli bracelet, the centerpiece of which was an ancient Egyptian faience bead in the form of the eye of the falcon god Horus (see fig. 68 right, page 79). Her personal fashion sense was very sophisticated; she favored bold designs that served as the backdrop for Cartier's innovative creations, as detailed in George Eells's 1967 biography of Cole Porter.[2] Eells describes Mrs. Porter as "admired for the chic of her sapphire blue satin dress which had been designed especially to show off a Cartier ornament, a huge lapis-blue scarab set with two old faience turquoise Egyptian wings, held together in a setting with long diamonds" (see fig. 68 left, page 79). Just a few years later she embraced Cartier's tutti frutti jewelry, eventually acquiring two strap bracelets and a clip brooch (see figs. 119 and 120, page 117).

THE 1930S

The 1930s saw the emergence of three iconic figures: Mrs. Harrison (Mona) Williams, later Countess von Bismarck; Barbara Hutton, at that period Countess von Haugwitz-Hardenberg-Reventlow; and Mrs. Wallis Simpson, later Duchess of Windsor, for whom the king of England renounced the throne. These eminent women were gently mocked in an amusing ditty penned by Cole Porter, "Ridin' High," from the musical *Red, Hot and Blue* (1936):

> *What do I care*
>
> *If Missus Harrison Williams is the best-dressed woman in town?*
>
> *What do I care*
>
> *If Countess Barbara Hutton has a Rolls-Royce built for each gown?*
>
> *Why should I have the vapors*
>
> *When I read in the papers*
>
> *That Missus Simpson dined behind the throne?*
>
> *I've got a cute king of my own.*[3]

Voted in the Paris dressmakers' annual lists of 1933 and 1934 as one of the twenty best-dressed women in the world, Mona Williams owned jewelry that always added further glamour to her flawless style (opposite, top right). Cecil Beaton, a close friend who immortalized her in countless photographs, once described her as "one of the few outstanding beauties of the thirties ... who represented the epitome of all that taste and luxury can bring to flower."[4] She set the trend for stylish, colorful art deco pieces, which she loved to mix with antique items. Cartier also created jewelry for her in such a way that she could easily mix nineteenth-century pieces with contemporary designs. For example, some of her jewels were mounted with old-cut diamonds so they would look well when worn together with antique pieces. In the 1920s, while traveling with her husband, Mrs. Williams acquired a magnificent 98.57-carat sapphire that was set as a *sautoir* by Cartier New York (opposite, bottom). In 1959 she had it updated with a new diamond chain by Cartier Paris (fig. 242). She also owned an exquisite platinum, rock crystal, and diamond bracelet set with carved sapphire leaves and emerald berries that flank a vivid green jadeite carving (see fig. 115, page 114).

Barbara Hutton, the "poor little rich girl" of Noël Coward's 1925 song, was one of Cartier's best clients. When she was still only in her teens, her father took her to Cartier to select a jewel of her choice.

BELOW **242. Necklace** Cartier New York, 1927 (transformed in 1959). Platinum, diamonds, sapphires. Department of Mineral Sciences, National Museum of Natural History, Smithsonian Institution, G6757.

The central sapphire weighs 98.57 carats.

RIGHT A triple portrait of Mona Williams, later Mona von Bismarck, by Edward Steichen, 1934. The bracelet she is wearing can be seen on page 114 (fig. 115).

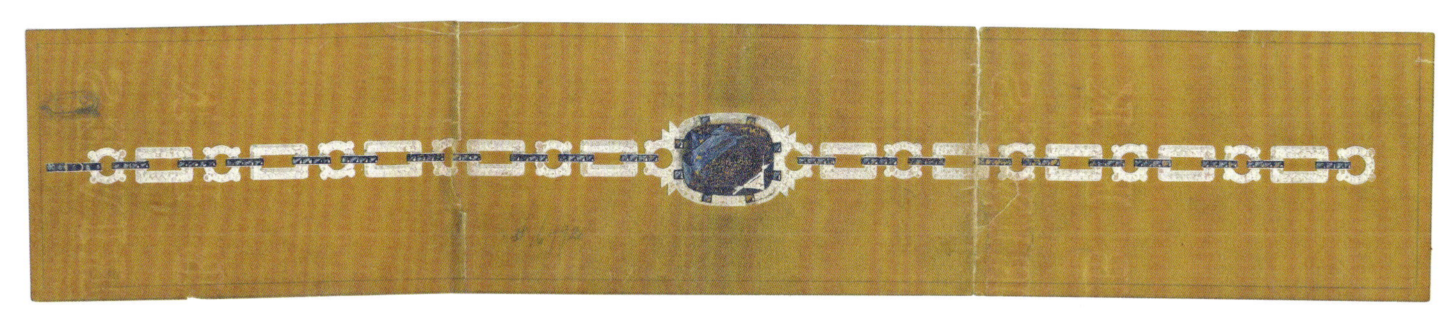

ABOVE Cartier design drawing of Mona von Bismarck's 1927 sapphire-and-diamond necklace. In 1959 she had the necklace transformed into the style shown in figure 242, and in 1967 gave it to the Smithsonian Institution. Cartier New York Archives.

Demonstrating an early instinct for recognizing beautiful stones, she chose a ruby ring that was the most expensive ruby in Cartier's stock and at $50,000 cost her father more than ten times what he had expected to spend.[5] She not only loved jewels but knew a great deal about them and spent much time admiring their natural beauty and the Cartier creative genius that went into fashioning them. It was widely thought that she sought in jewelry the perfection and durability that she failed to find in her personal life.

For her 1933 wedding to the Georgian prince Alexis Mdivani, she commissioned from Cartier a Balinese-style head ornament with delicate diamond trefoil motifs that were echoed in her lace veil. At the civil ceremony two days before, she wore a pale gray Chanel outfit and her Cartier engagement ring of black pearl.[6] Her father gave her what was described in the press as "one of the rarest strands of pearls ever sold by Cartier," a necklace of fifty-three pearls once worn by Queen Marie Antoinette of France.[7] He also gave her arguably the rarest and most magnificent jadeite bead necklace in the world, with a ruby and diamond clasp, created by Cartier in 1934. These were not Hutton's only historic acquisitions. She also purchased from Cartier, for $1,000,000, Grand Duchess Maria Pavlovna's emeralds, which had previously been owned by Edith Rockefeller. The publicity of this purchase and other extravagances reported in the major newspapers engendered bad feelings, especially among the employees of Woolworth, the company that generated her vast fortune. In 1947, by now the wife of Russian prince Igor Troubetzkoy (whom she married after divorcing the actor Cary Grant), she instructed Cartier to reset the emeralds in a lovely convertible necklace/tiara (above) in the oriental style, mounted in yellow gold instead of platinum, following a new trend set by the Duchess of Windsor. In 1967, now married to Laotian prince Pierre Raymond Doan Vinh na Champassak, she indulged her taste for exquisite belongings by purchasing a lapis, gold, and diamond mystery clock (fig. 243).

The Duchess of Windsor was the most important personality to dominate contemporary taste in jewelry in the 1930s. The relationship between Mrs. Wallis Simpson, as she was then known, and King

Barbara Hutton playing a lute at her home in Morocco, photographed by Cecil Beaton, 1961. The emeralds in her Cartier tiara were once owned by Grand Duchess Maria Pavlovna. Courtesy of the Cecil Beaton Studio Archive at Sotheby's.

OPPOSITE 243. **Mystery clock with single axle** Cartier Paris, 1967. Gold, platinum, lapis lazuli, rock crystal, single- and rose-cut diamonds. Rectangular 8-day movement, gold-plated, 13 jewels, Swiss lever escapement, bimetallic balance, Breguet balance spring. Hand-setting and winding mechanism underneath the base. Height 15.5 cm. Cartier Collection CM 17 A67. Provenance: Princess Doan Vinh na Champassak (Barbara Hutton).

Prince Pierre Raymond Doan Vinh na Champassak was Barbara Hutton's last husband.

Edward VIII remains one of the most romantic, controversial, and speculated-about love stories in history. Her jewelry collection was unique; not only were her pieces chosen—and, to some extent, created—by a king for the woman he loved, but many items were also inscribed with intimate messages referring to times they had spent together. The jewels represented some of the finest designs of that period. The most fascinating aspect of her collection is that the duchess, who showed a strong preference for Cartier creations, and her husband were active participants in designing their pieces; they presented Jeanne Toussaint at Cartier with ideas that she would then develop.

Cartier was no stranger to accommodating the occasionally idiosyncratic desires of its customers. But under the leadership of Toussaint, the firm created a full-fledged menagerie for the Duchess of Windsor, with whom Toussaint had a close artistic relationship. Highly regarded for her impeccable taste, well-balanced sense of proportion, and delicate brand of craftsmanship, Toussaint supervised the creation of jewels in the shapes of all sorts of creatures, from fantastical birds of paradise to dragonflies and ladybugs. A truly iconic piece was the magnificent flamingo brooch (fig. 244) made for the Duke and Duchess of Windsor in 1940 on the eve of the fall of France. Designed by Peter Lemarchand, the clip was pavé set with brilliant-cut diamonds; the plumage was set with *calibré*-cut emeralds, rubies, and sapphires. Many of the stones came from the duchess's own collection: she often had her jewels dismantled for reuse. An example is an extraordinary bib necklace in a dropped, articulated design of yellow gold set with cabochon and step-cut rubies and emeralds.[8] Created in 1945, it was made by breaking up two gem-set brooches, two pairs of earrings, and an emerald ring. Large pieces of this kind perfectly complemented the bold, simple designs of her evening gowns. One particularly dramatic necklace created for her in 1947, set with amethysts and turquoises (fig. 246 and page 236 left and right), exemplified the fashion not only for large necklaces but also for unusual combinations of colors.

This René Bouché drawing of the Duchess of Windsor with her Cartier Tiger lorgnette appeared in the May 1955 issue of *Vogue*. Condé Nast Archive.

The Windsors and Jeanne Toussaint shared a fascination with felines. Toussaint was particularly known for her love of panthers: her Paris apartment was strewn with their skins, which prompted her companion, Louis Cartier, to give her the nickname the Panther. Many of her creations were inspired by the animal's elegance and posture. The earliest example, from the late 1920s, depicts the panther in two-dimensional form, but later pieces were three-dimensional. The first of these, a brooch created in 1948, features an

OPPOSITE, TOP 244. ***Flamingo* brooch** Cartier Paris, special order, 1940. Platinum; gold; brilliant-cut diamonds; *calibré*-cut emeralds, sapphires, and rubies; sapphire cabochons, citrine. 9.7 × 9.6 cm. Cartier Collection CL 312 A40. Sold to the Duke of Windsor. The duke and duchess supplied many of the stones used in this brooch.

OPPOSITE, BOTTOM 245. ***Tiger* lorgnette** Cartier Paris, special order, 1954. Gold, black enamel, marquise-shaped emeralds. 8.5 × 2 cm closed. Cartier Collection OI 08 A54. Ordered by the Duchess of Windsor.

A hinge on the bridge of the glasses allows them to fold in half, and another hinge next to the tiger's head allows them to fold a second time along the side of the tiger's body. A brocade pouch bears the inscription: *Please return to HRH The Duchess of Windsor / Reward.*

ABOVE Design drawing of the Duchess of Windsor's bib necklace (fig. 246). Cartier Archives.

RIGHT The Duchess of Windsor wearing her bib necklace at a gala held in the Orangerie at Versailles, 1953. The Granger Collection, New York.

animal made of yellow gold with black enamel spots and emerald eyes crouching over a cabochon emerald of over ninety carats. The Duke of Windsor purchased it for the duchess to replace jewelry stolen in 1946.[9] The duchess loved the brooch so much that, one year later, the couple purchased a similar one (fig. 248). The panther on this brooch is made of platinum and diamonds, its spots studded with sapphires, and its eyes fashioned of pear-shaped yellow diamonds; the animal crouches on a Kashmir cabochon sapphire weighing 152.35 carats. This became one of the duchess's favorite pieces and an icon of the French house. From these beginnings, the duchess assembled a whole family of feline pieces: a 1952 outstretched-panther bracelet made of platinum and onyx (fig. 247), a lorgnette designed as a tiger in gold-and-black-champlevé enamel (fig. 245), a tiger bracelet in yellow gold with yellow diamonds and stripes of *calibré* onyx, a matching tiger brooch, and yet another panther brooch. The duchess did a great deal to popularize "great cat" jewels, and contemporaries commissioned their own versions, such as Barbara Hutton's 1957 brooch (fig. 249), its design based on the badge of the Order of the Golden Fleece.

OPPOSITE 246. **Bib necklace** Cartier Paris, special order, 1947. Twisted gold; platinum; brilliant- and baguette-cut diamonds; heart-shaped, emerald-cut, and oval faceted amethysts; turquoise cabochons. 20 × 19.5 cm. Cartier Collection NE 09 A47. This necklace was sold to the Duke of Windsor, who supplied all the stones except the turquoises.

Born in Baltimore, Wallis Warfield (1896–1986) first married Earl Winfield Spencer, followed by American businessman Ernest Simpson. She divorced him to marry Edward VIII, who was forced to abdicate the British throne. In March 1937 the new king, George VI, named his brother Duke of Windsor. The couple lived in Paris for the rest of their lives.

ABOVE 247. **Bracelet** Cartier Paris, 1952. Platinum, white gold, brilliant- and single-cut diamonds, navette-shaped emeralds (eyes), *calibré*-cut onyx. Length approx. 16.5 cm. Private collection. Provenance: Sold to the Duchess of Windsor.

OPPOSITE 248. ***Panther* clip brooch** Cartier Paris, 1949. Platinum, white gold, single-cut diamonds, pear-shaped yellow diamonds, 152.35-carat Kashmir sapphire cabochon, sapphire cabochons (spots). 6 × 3.7 × 3 cm. Cartier Collection CL 53 A49. Sold to the Duchess of Windsor.

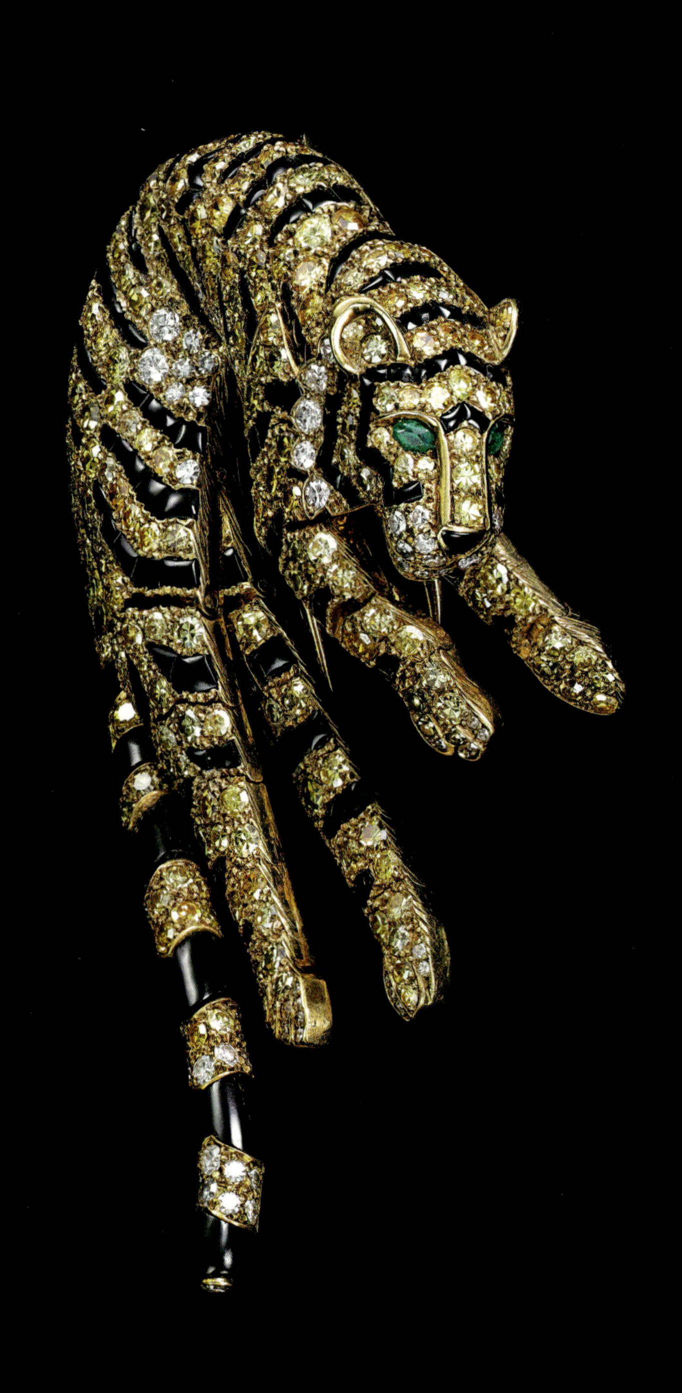

OPPOSITE 249. ***Tiger* clip brooch** Cartier Paris, 1957. Gold, single- and brilliant-cut diamonds ranging from fancy intense yellow to near colorless, marquise-shaped emeralds, fancy-shaped onyx. Head, legs, and tail are articulated. 7 × 4.5 × 1.5 cm. Cartier Collection CL 140 A57. Sold to Barbara Hutton.

Barbara Hutton (1912–1979) was the granddaughter of the founder of the Woolworth retail chain, and one of the richest women in the world.

TOP 250. **Pair of *Tiger* ear clips** Cartier Paris, special order, 1961. Gold, single- and brilliant-cut diamonds ranging from fancy intense yellow to near colorless, marquise-shaped emeralds, fancy-shaped onyx. Heads, legs, and tails are articulated. 2.9 × 4.6 cm. Cartier Collection EG 07 A61. Sold to Barbara Hutton.

ABOVE 251. **Handbag** Cartier Paris, special order, 1961. Gold; tiger: black enamel and marquise-shaped emeralds; single- and brilliant-cut diamonds; black satin. Black satin lining, six pockets, a mirror, and a black satin card holder. 26.9 × 20 cm. Cartier Collection EB 15 A61.

Ordered by Barbara Hutton, this handbag features the initial of Princess Nina Mdivani, Hutton's former sister-in-law, to whom it was given as a gift.

Daisy Fellowes (center) wearing her Hindu necklace at a dinner at the Hôtel Lambert, 1950.

Instead of the traditional ram's fleece, the brooch is in the form of a tiger made of yellow diamonds with black onyx stripes and emerald eyes. The dramatic curve of the animal was echoed in matching ear clips (fig. 250) made in 1961, followed by a bracelet the year after. Hutton also purchased a handbag with a stalking-tiger clasp as a gift for Princess Nina Mdivani (fig. 251).

Along with Harrison, Hutton, and the Duchess of Windsor, the much-admired Daisy Fellowes, heiress to the Singer sewing machine fortune and daughter of a French duke, also came to be an admirer of Cartier creations. Although initially uninterested in her appearance, she was purportedly distressed by a portrait she had commissioned soon after her marriage to Prince Jean Amédée Marie Anatole de Broglie in 1910. From that time on she set about creating a new persona for herself, far removed from the plain and uninteresting person she saw staring back at her from the canvas. According to her grandson Comte de La Moussaye, she took a particular dislike to the line of her nose, which she immediately had reshaped, horrifyingly without the aid of an anesthetic.[10] She then bought a whole new wardrobe of clothes and appointed a new hairdresser. Educating herself in the arts and in literature was another element in her re-creation of herself as a lady of high society, as was the acquisition, over her lifetime, of a superb jewelry collection. Widowed in 1918, she married the Honorable Reginald Fellowes in 1919. Through her own efforts, Mrs. Fellowes achieved a remarkable transformation and was by then regarded as one of the most elegant and fascinating women in Europe (see page 224). The incredibly long list of jewels that she acquired from Cartier served to confirm this reputation. One notable example was the famous Tête de Bélier (ram's head), a 17.47-carat pink diamond, which was stolen in 1939 and has never reappeared. Her passion for the multicolored gem-set jewelry known as tutti frutti led to the creation of one of Cartier's most iconic pieces in this style, unmatched to this day: the sensational Collier Hindou (Hindu collar) (fig. 252 and left). This necklace was created in 1936 by dismantling a 1928 necklace and a 1929 bracelet, also by Cartier. The original design, with its dramatic fringe of carved flower heads, foliage, and buds decorated with diamonds, is preserved in the Cartier archives in Paris.[11] It is complemented by a 1936 Indian-style white jade and gold vanity case decorated with multicolored stones (fig. 254). Years later, Fellowes purchased an elegantly simple necklace of feathered-gold half hoops studded with diamonds (fig. 253).

OPPOSITE 252. ***Hindu* necklace** Cartier Paris, special order, 1936, altered in 1963. Platinum; white gold; marquise-, baguette-, and round old-cut diamonds; carved sapphires, sapphire beads, and a sapphire cabochon; carved emeralds, emerald beads, and emerald cabochons; carved rubies, ruby beads, and ruby cabochons. Length 43 cm open. Cartier Collection NE 28 A36. Made for Daisy Fellowes.

Each emerald, ruby, and sapphire bead is studded with a collet-set diamond. Originally made in the Indian style, with black cord ties and a removable central clip, this necklace was transformed after Fellowes's death at the request of her daughter the Comtesse de Castéja.

OPPOSITE 253. **Necklace** Cartier Paris, 1953. Gold, diamonds, platinum. Length 38.1 cm. Private collection. Sold to Daisy Fellowes.

Born Marguerite Séverine Philippine Descazes (1890–1962), Daisy married French prince Jean Anatole de Broglie and, after his death, English financier Reginald Fellowes. She was the Paris correspondent for the influential magazine *Harper's Bazaar* from 1933 to 1935.

ABOVE 254. **Vanity case** Cartier Paris, special order, 1936. Gold, silver-gilt, gray jade, rubies, emeralds, colored stones, pearls, rose-cut diamonds. 20.8 × 12 × 3 cm. Cartier Collection VC 05 A36. Provenance: Daisy Fellowes.

The interior is fitted with a mirror, a lipstick holder, and five compartments, including two with covers. The ancient jade appliqué was supplied by the client, and Cartier supplied the handle. The vanity case was delivered with two sheaths of black reindeer leather for safe storage.

STYLE AFTER WORLD WAR II

In the postwar period the film actress María Félix was among Cartier's famous clients. Described as the most beautiful face in the history of Mexican cinema, in the 1940s she was the very incarnation of a femme fatale, with her sultry, dark features and strong, fiery personality. She married four times, and her flamboyant lifestyle constantly made the headlines, both in her native Mexico and around the world. In the 1950s she moved to Europe and lived in Paris, where she became a part of the elite beau monde and patronized the most important fashion houses of the period. Her fourth and last husband, the Swiss businessman Alex Berger, left her a stable of thoroughbred racehorses at Chantilly, near Paris; she then became a prominent figure on the European racing scene, attending all the major events, and even had saddles and bridles made by Hermès. She was always immaculately attired and wore extravagant jewels that were almost barbaric in their size and dramatic impact. She had a passion particularly for those molded into the shape of mythical creatures. In 1957 she ordered a pair of stunning coral, emerald, and diamond chimera bangles. They perfectly complemented her Cartier evening bag (fig. 257), another acquisition of that year, whose clasp—built into an engine-turned gold frame—was formed by twin carved-coral chimera heads decorated with diamonds, cabochon emeralds, and sapphires. Also made of coral, complemented with pearls, emeralds, and onyx, is a 1972 necklace remodeled from an earlier bracelet (fig. 258).

However, these are tame in comparison to Félix's two most spectacular purchases. The first, created in 1968, was a snake necklace; its completely articulated, three-dimensional body—with the scales on its underside decorated with red, green, and black enamel—was set with 2,473 baguette- and brilliant-cut diamonds and weighed a total of 178.21 carats (fig. 256). On August 19, 1973, in Deauville, she wore this exceptional necklace to great effect against a pale rose chiffon Chanel evening gown decorated with ostrich feathers. Cartier's second spectacular creation for her was made in 1975: a necklace designed as two fully articulated crocodiles that could be detached from each other and worn as two separate brooches (fig. 255). One was set with cabochon-emerald eyes

María Félix (1914–2002), photographed by Lord Anthony Snowdon, 1980. The Mexican actress became a celebrity in Mexico and France by starring in films by Emilio Fernández, Jean Renoir, and Luis Buñuel. She is wearing her Crocodile necklace commissioned from Cartier in 1975. Camera Press London.

OPPOSITE 255. ***Crocodile* necklace** Cartier Paris, special order, 1975. Gold; 1,023 brilliant-cut fancy intense yellow diamonds, weighing 60.02 carats in total; two navette-shaped emerald cabochons; 1,060 emeralds, weighing 66.86 carats in total; two ruby cabochons. Lengths of crocodiles 30 cm and 27.3 cm. Cartier Collection NE 43 A75. Made for María Félix.

The two crocodiles are completely articulated and flexible. When worn around the neck, the feet can be replaced by clawless paws that will not irritate the skin.

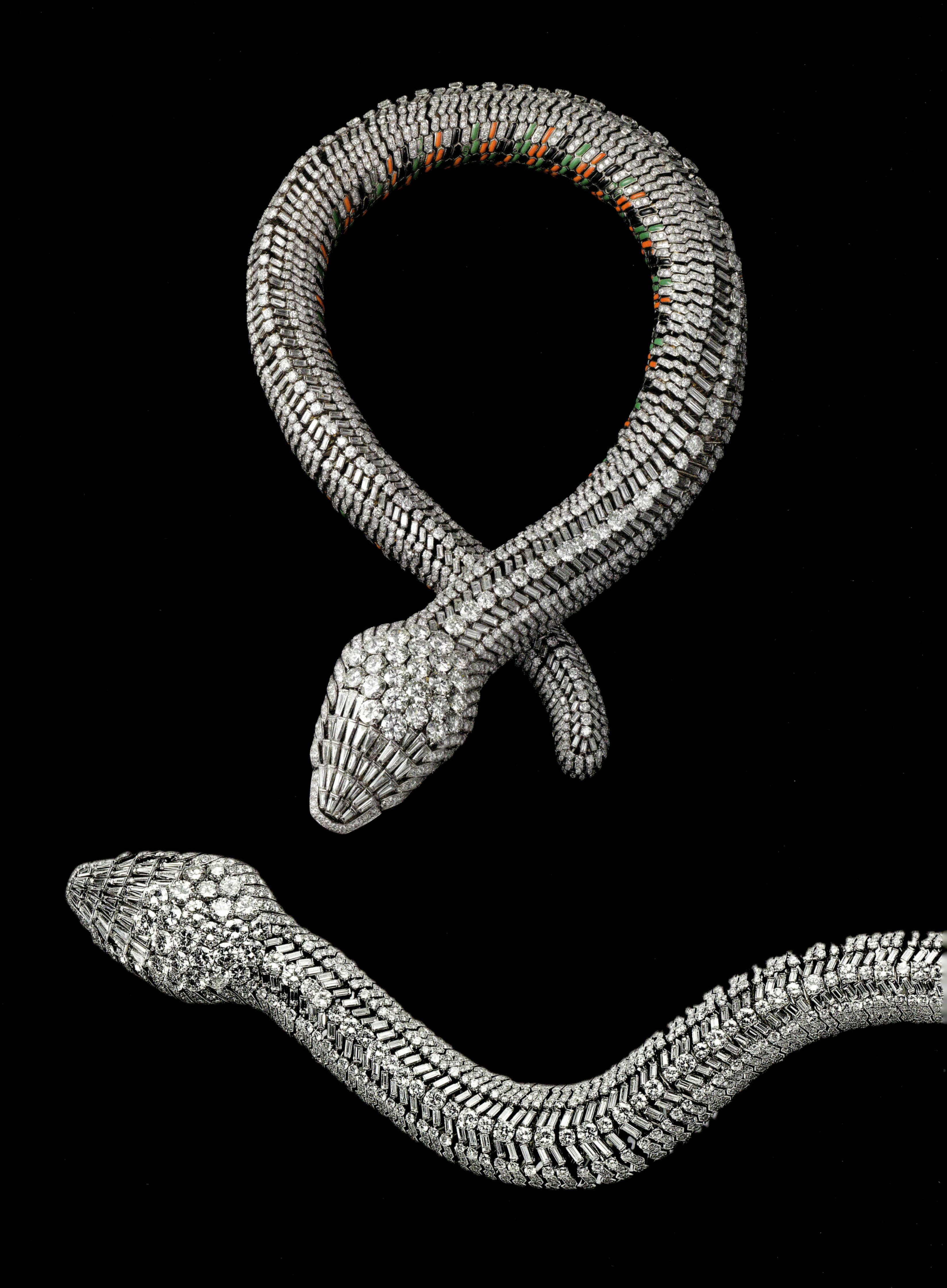

256. ***Snake* necklace** Cartier Paris, special order, 1968. Platinum; white and yellow gold; 2,473 brilliant- and baguette-cut diamonds, weighing 178.21 carats in total; two pear-shaped emeralds; enamel. Length 57 cm. Cartier Collection NE 10 A68. Made for María Félix.

ABOVE 257. **Evening bag** Cartier New York, 1957. Gold; platinum; carved coral; old-, baguette-, and brilliant-cut diamonds; emerald and sapphire cabochons; black velvet. Dark-gold satin lining, four pockets. 18 × 17 cm. Cartier Collection EB 25 A57. Provenance: María Félix.

OPPOSITE 258. **Necklace** Cartier, Paris, 1940; transformed 1972. Coral, pearls, onyx, emeralds, diamonds, platinum, enamel. Length approx. 40 cm. Private collection. Sold to María Félix.

RIGHT 259. ***Poodle* brooch** Cartier Paris, 1958. Platinum, white gold; brilliant-, round-, and baguette-cut diamonds; rubies (eyes); onyx (nose). 4 × 4.5 cm. Palais Princier de Monaco, P 011253. Provenance: HSH Princess Grace of Monaco.

FAR RIGHT 260. ***Bird* brooch** Cartier London, 1946. Carved gold, gold wire, emerald (eye), pearls, one coral cabochon. 3 × 2.5 cm. Palais Princier de Monaco, P 011253. Provenance: HSH Princess Grace of Monaco.

261. ***Prism* Clock** Cartier Paris, about 1955. Gold, platinum, brilliant-cut diamonds. On the top an appliqued crown of brilliant-cut diamonds. 8 × 4.8 × 4.8 cm. Palais Princier de Monaco, P 005989. Provenance: HSH Princess Grace of Monaco.

Princess Grace and Prince Rainier of Monaco with their children Caroline and Albert, about 1960. Palais Princier de Monaco.

and more than a thousand brilliant-cut yellow diamonds weighing a total of sixty carats. The other had cabochon-ruby eyes and was encrusted with more than a thousand circular-cut emeralds (see page 247). Félix remained a true diva and style icon until the end: in 1984, at the age of seventy, she was still showing up on best-dressed lists.

In Hollywood, meanwhile, Cartier's creations were much favored by the stars of the movie world. In 1956 Grace Kelly was given a Cartier engagement ring by her fiancé, Prince Rainier III of Monaco: a step-cut diamond of 10.48 carats set between two baguette diamonds (fig. 262). Upon their marriage, on April 19 of that year, she became Her Serene Highness Princess Grace of Monaco. In her new formal role she needed jewels, and Cartier became the chief supplier. One of her most elegant pieces was a diamond rivière set with three detachable diamond clips, each one embellished with a cabochon ruby (fig. 263). The princess loved to wear it as a headpiece along with an elegant diamond necklace—the front of which featured three rows of alternating baguette and large brilliant-cut diamonds, the back a rivière of brilliant-cut diamonds (fig. 265)—and a lovely diamond bracelet (fig. 266). These stunning pieces were the foundation of Princess Grace's jewelry collection and perfectly complemented her classic beauty. She wore several of them to great effect while attending a gala at the Élysée Palace with Prince Rainier as honored guests of the French president Charles de Gaulle on October 13, 1959. Resplendent in a Lanvin gown of ivory silk organdy, worn with a sash, star, and badge of the Monegasque Order of Saint-Charles (fig. 264), she looked the very essence of elegance. For her personal jewels and accessories, Princess Grace favored yellow gold items made by Cartier. These include an elegant prism clock inscribed: "je ne marque que les heures heureuses" (I mark only happy hours) (fig. 261) and a charming pin that depicts a mother bird atop

262. **Engagement ring** Cartier Paris, 1956. Platinum, one 10.48-carat emerald-cut diamond, two baguette-cut diamonds. 2.3 × 1.6 × 1.1 cm. Palais Princier de Monaco, P 01 1276. Provenance: HSH Princess Grace of Monaco.

Official portrait of Her Serene Highness Princess Grace of Monaco, 1959. Her engagement ring, necklace, bracelet, and head ornament are by Cartier. Palais Princier de Monaco.

TOP 263. **Set of three clip-brooches** Cartier Paris, 1955. Platinum, brilliant- and baguette-cut diamonds, three cabochon rubies weighing approximately 49 carats in total. 4.6 × 5 cm and 3.6 × 4.2 cm. Palais Princier de Monaco, P 011322. Provenance: HSH Princess Grace of Monaco.

ABOVE 264. **Star of the Order of Saint-Charles** Cartier Paris, special order, 1956. White gold, brilliant-cut diamonds, *calibré*-cut rubies, natural pearls, enamel. Star dated at back 19 April 1956; case stamped *19 April 1956*. Palais Princier de Monaco, P 011759. Provenance: HSH Rainier III.

The client supplied the star of the Order of Saint-Charles. Cartier embellished it with *calibré*-cut rubies and eight natural pearls.

OPPOSITE, TOP 265. **Necklace** Cartier Paris, 1953. Platinum, brilliant- and baguette-cut diamonds weighing approximately 64 carats in total. Length 38 cm. Palais Princier de Monaco, P 0111495. Provenance: HSH Princess Grace of Monaco.

OPPOSITE, BOTTOM 266. **Bracelet** Cartier Paris, 1955. Platinum, brilliant- and baguette-cut diamonds. 7 × 1.5 cm. Palais Princier de Monaco, P 011406. Provenance: HSH Princess Grace of Monaco.

her nest (with four eggs inside) (fig. 260). Another very personal item is a diamond, platinum, and white gold poodle brooch (fig. 259).

The princess's near contemporary—just slightly more than two years younger—was another equally striking Hollywood star: Elizabeth Taylor. This legendary actress adored jewels, and her husbands loved to satisfy her whims. One of the most treasured jewels in her collection was a ruby-and-diamond parure created by Cartier in the early 1950s and presented to her by her second husband, Mike Todd, in August 1957, when she was expecting their child (fig. 270 and opposite). The necklace could also become a tiara, as worn by artist Niki de Saint Phalle in a photograph taken by Henry Clarke in May 1953 for *Vogue*. Taylor also wore a ring in the form of a gold snake with a diamond-studded head (fig. 268) and a gold cuff bracelet with pavé-set diamonds (fig. 267).

But Taylor's most well-known and highly publicized romance was the one she carried on with fellow actor Richard Burton. This tumultuous love story resulted in divorce and remarriage as well as innumerable gifts of jewelry. The most iconic was the necklace designed by Cartier to support the historic Peregrina pearl. Bought at auction on January 23, 1969, by Richard Burton, this perfect drop-shaped pearl boasted a history that reached back to King Philip II of Spain in the 1500s. Napoleon's brother Joseph Bonaparte removed it from Spain, and it was subsequently sold to the Duke of Abercorn, whose family owned it until it ended up on the décolleté of the famous movie actress. The collaboration between Elizabeth Taylor and Cartier designer Al Durante

LEFT TO RIGHT

267. **Cuff bracelet** Cartier New York, about 1976. Gold, platinum, circular-cut diamonds. 5.2 × 6 × 4 cm. Cartier Collection BT 138 C76. Provenance: Elizabeth Taylor.

268. ***Snake* ring** Cartier Paris, 1966. Chased and polished gold, platinum, single-cut diamonds, two faceted emeralds. 2.3 × 2.2 × 0.5 cm. Cartier Collection RG 43 A66. Provenance: Elizabeth Taylor.

269. ***Tank* wristwatch** Cartier Paris, 1959. Yellow and pink gold, one faceted sapphire. Round LeCoultre caliber 821 movement, Côtes de Genève decoration, rhodium-plated, 2 adjustments, 18 jewels, Swiss lever escapement, monometallic balance, flat balance spring. Case 3 × 2.3 cm. Cartier Collection WCL 37 A59. Sold to Elizabeth Taylor.

Elizabeth Taylor wearing the ruby-and-diamond necklace and pendant earrings given to her by Mike Todd in 1957.

But the most publicized acquisition of this glamorous couple was the Cartier diamond of 69.42 carats, bought at auction in 1969 for $1,050,000 by Cartier, outbidding Richard Burton by $50,000. Burton contacted Cartier, and they reached an agreement: the diamond was his for $1.1 million with the proviso that Cartier could display the stone for a limited period in its Fifth Avenue shop in New York. An advertisement in the *New York Times* publicized the exhibition, mentioning that the diamond had been acquired by Elizabeth Taylor and Richard Burton, and the public response was huge. It was renamed the Taylor-Burton diamond, and Taylor wore it for the first time at the Zodiac-themed ball celebrating Princess Grace's fortieth birthday in Monte Carlo on November 17, 1969. For this occasion, as for many others, the stone was mounted on a pear-shaped diamond rivière, but it could also be detached and worn as a ring. Princess Grace, for her part, wore her exquisite ruby-and-diamond Cartier clips.

The who's who of Cartier's illustrious champions is extensive, and inevitably not all of them can be discussed here. Although it is easy to think of them as mere beneficiaries of the master designers' innovation, their own contributions to the Cartier legend were considerable: not only did their financial power ensure the best-quality jewels and materials, but their flair for beauty and style also resulted in collaborations with Cartier that gave birth to some of the house's most important creations. Indeed, an examination of a Cartier artifact is impossible without referring in some way to the remarkable person or persons who inspired and wore it.

resulted in a spectacular necklace that would display this historic pearl to great advantage.

This was not the only gift bestowed on Elizabeth Taylor during her long and sometimes tortuous relationship with Richard Burton. For her fortieth birthday, in 1972, she received another historic gem: the heart-shaped table-cut Taj Mahal diamond, which dated from the early seventeenth century. For Taylor, Cartier set the jewel as a pendant in a necklace of Indian inspiration.

270. Necklace Cartier Paris, 1951, altered in 1953. Platinum; gold; round brilliant-, baguette-, and fancy-cut diamonds; eight cushion-shaped and oval faceted Burmese rubies. Length 37.5 cm. Cartier Collection NE 49 A51. Provenance: Elizabeth Taylor.

A tiara fitting allows the necklace to be worn as a head ornament (above).

NOTES

ARISTOCRACY AND ASPIRATION: CARTIER IN THE EARLY TWENTIETH CENTURY

1 Consuelo Vanderbilt Balsan, *The Glitter and the Gold* (New York: Harper & Brothers, 1952), 137.
2 Cartier used the term *kokoshnik* rather indiscriminately—not strictly for tiaras that rise to a central point.
3 Previously, European precious jewelry was customarily set in gold or gold topped with silver. Silver's whiteness was desirable for mounting colorless diamonds, but its tendency to tarnish was a disadvantage. The weight and malleability of both gold and silver required the construction of comparatively heavy settings.
4 Hans Nadelhoffer, *Cartier: Jewelers Extraordinary* (New York: Harry N. Abrams, 1984), 127.
5 Ibid., 126, 297n5.
6 1917 deed of sale in the Cartier archives. A slightly different version of events (perhaps based on a 1916 *New York Times* notice, but contradicted by the 1917 deed of sale) is provided by Wayne Craven. According to him, Plant sold the house to William K. Vanderbilt (who had sold the lot to Plant in the first place) in 1916. Vanderbilt in turn leased it to Cartier. See Wayne Craven, *Gilded Mansions* (New York and London: W. W. Norton, 2009), 321–22. Regardless, it indicates the high value ascribed to natural pearls at the time.
7 Greg King, *A Season of Splendor: The Court of Mrs. Astor in Gilded Age New York* (Hoboken, NJ: John Wiley & Sons, 2009), 224, 227.
8 Geoffrey C. Munn, *Tiaras: A History of Splendour* (Woodbridge, Suffolk: Antique Collectors' Club, 2001), 309, 310.
9 Hundreds of new titles were issued by the English government in the first three decades of the twentieth century. See Munn, *Tiaras*, 127.
10 Ibid., 101.
11 Balsan, *The Glitter and the Gold*, 152.
12 Stefano Papi, *Jewels of the Romanovs: Family & Court* (London and New York: Thames & Hudson, 2010), 112, 114, 115, 116.
13 Nadelhoffer, *Cartier: Jewelers Extraordinary*, 121.
14 Gilberte Gautier, *Cartier: The Legend* (London: Arlington Books, 1983), 123.
15 Munn, *Tiaras*, 11.
16 Evalyn Walsh McLean, *Father Struck It Rich* (Boston: Little, Brown and Company, 1936), 156.
17 Gautier, *Cartier: The Legend*, 130; Nadelhoffer, *Cartier: Jewelers Extraordinary*, 284.
18 Nadelhoffer, *Cartier: Jewelers Extraordinary*, 37.
19 Gautier, *Cartier: The Legend*, 93, 94.
20 Eric Nussbaum, "The Creation of the Cartier Collection," in "Cartier: Papers of the Symposium Held Jointly by the British Museum and the Society of Jewellery Historians at the British Museum in 1997," ed. Judy Rudoe, special issue, *Jewellery Studies* 9 (2001): 8, fig. 2.
21 Mary E. Davis, *Ballets Russes Style: Diaghilev's Dancers and Paris Fashion* (London: Reaktion Books, 2010), 119.
22 Nadelhoffer, *Cartier: Jewelers Extraordinary*, 83–85.
23 Gabriel-Louis Pringué, *30 ans de dîners en ville* (Paris: Lacurne, 2012), 186–87.
24 "Ball in Paris Like Arabian Night Tale," *New York Times*, May 31, 1912.
25 Balsan, *The Glitter and the Gold*, 226.
26 Gautier, *Cartier: The Legend*, 151, 153.

NEW OUTLOOK: ART DECO 1918–1939

1 Violette Petit, "The Foundations of an Empire: Cartier Paris, London, New York 1899–1939," in *Cartier: Style and History* (Paris: Réunion des musées nationaux—Grand Palais, 2013), 21.
2 Ibid., 22.
3 Louis Cartier married Andrée-Caroline Worth, daughter of Jean-Philippe Worth, while the Cartier brothers' sister, Suzanne, married Jacques Worth.
4 Judy Rudoe, *Cartier: 1900–1939* (New York: Harry N. Abrams, 1997), 284. Twenty-seven tiaras and head ornaments were made in 1937.
5 In 1937 Chips Channon—writing in his diary about a dinner he gave in London on February 26—remarked that "Lady Granard could scarcely walk for jewels." Henry Channon, *'Chips': The Diaries of Sir Henry Channon* (London: Weidenfeld & Nicolson, 1993), 116. Lady Granard, born Beatrice Mills, daughter of wealthy financier Ogden Mills, was a devoted customer of Cartier in the 1930s.
6 Hans Nadelhoffer, *Cartier*, rev. ed. (London: Thames & Hudson, 2007), 131–40.
7 Rudoe, *Cartier: 1900–1939*, 316–19. In all likelihood, it was never expected that this daring tour de force of the jeweler's art would be sold.
8 Channon, *'Chips,'* 65–66. The cigarette case was sold most recently at Sotheby's in London on November 30,

2010 (lot 16). The American-born Channon was a great admirer of jewelry and mentions it often in his published diaries. He was wittily described by Jean Cocteau as having eyes set by Cartier (*'Chips,'* 5). In 1935–36 he befriended Mrs. Simpson (later the Duchess of Windsor and one of Cartier's most enduring customers), whom he describes as being increasingly bejeweled, "smothered in rubies" or "dripping in emeralds," many of which were bought for her at Cartier London by the king (*'Chips,'* 43, 73, 77).

9 Nadelhoffer, *Cartier*, rev. ed., 253.

10 Ibid., 248.

11 Ibid., 214, 216.

12 Martin Chapman, *Cartier and America* (San Francisco and Munich: Fine Arts Museum and DelMonico/Prestel, 2009), 32, fig. 24. Rudoe, *Cartier 1900–1939*, 31, fig. 25.

13 See Chapman, *Cartier and America*, 42n32.

14 In a 1964 issue of American *Vogue*, James Pope-Hennessy described Daisy Fellowes as having "very great beauty, a subtle exquisite barbed sense of humour, an inborn taste for dress, and a considerable fortune." Quoted in Stefano Papi and Alexandra Rhodes, *Famous Jewelry Collectors* (London: Thames & Hudson, 1999), 158. Cocteau's comment that Mrs. Fellowes "launched more fashions than any other woman in the world" is much cited; among other places, it appears in the Metropolitan Museum of Art's Heilbrunn Timeline of Art History in connection with an Elsa Schiaparelli evening ensemble (http://www.metmuseum.org/toah/works-of-art/C.I.46.4.3a-e).

15 Chapman, *Cartier and America*, 46, fig. 33.

16 Ibid., fig. 1.

FOREIGN FASCINATION

1 Hans Nadelhoffer, *Cartier: Jewelers Extraordinary* (New York: Harry N. Abrams, 1984), 142.

2 Susan Stronge, "Cartier and the East," in "Cartier: Papers of the Symposium Held Jointly by the British Museum and the Society of Jewellery Historians at the British Museum in 1997," ed. Judy Rudoe, special issue, *Jewellery Studies* 9 (2001): 68.

3 From a high in 1918 of 77 percent on incomes over $1,000,000 to just 25 percent on incomes over $100,000 in 1925.

4 Janet Zapata, *From Here to Antiquity*, exh. cat. (New York: DK Bressler, with S. J. Shrubsole, 2013).

5 Ibid., 146.

6 Judy Rudoe, *Cartier: 1900–1939* (New York: Harry N. Abrams, 1997), 136.

7 Michel Aliaga, François Chaille, et al., *Cartier: Innovation through the 20th Century*, exh. cat. (Paris: Flammarion, 2007), 143.

8 George E. Harlow, "Following the History of Diamonds," in *The Nature of Diamonds* (Cambridge, UK, and New York: Cambridge University Press in association with the American Museum of Natural History, 1998), 127.

9 For a fuller discussion of the Hope diamond's history and transformations, see Alfred A. Levinson, "Diamond Sources and Their Discovery," in *The Nature of Diamonds*, 105.

10 Rudoe, *Cartier: 1900–1939*, 158.

11 Anna Jackson and Amin Jaffer, "Indian Princes and the West," in *Maharaja: The Splendour of India's Royal Courts* (London: V & A Publications, 2009), 194–227.

12 "Vogue Sketches: The Beautiful New Jewels of the Smartest Women in Paris," *Vogue*, November 15, 1927, 68.

13 Carol Michaelson, "Chinese Inspiration in Cartier's Work," in "Cartier: Papers of the Symposium," 51–64.

14 Ibid., 51–55.

15 Hae Jeon Kim and Marilyn R. Delong, "Sino-Japanism in Western Women's Fashionable Dress in *Harper's Bazaar*, 1890–1927," *Clothing and Textiles Research Journal* 11, no. 1 (1992): 24–30.

16 Anna Jackson, "Inspiration from the East," and Valerie Mendes, "Art Deco Fashion," in *Art Deco 1910–1939* (London: V & A Publications, 2003), 69 and 262.

17 Although both were produced by Diaghilev, the 1920 ballet *The Song of the Nightingale* was distinct from the 1914 opera *The Nightingale*.

18 Rudoe, *Cartier: 1900–1939*, 112.

19 A similar clock was owned by George Blumenthal (who later donated it to the Musée des arts décoratifs in Paris), whose wife owned the *laque burgauté* vanity set illustrated on page 102.

20 Katherine Prior and John Adamson, *Maharajas' Jewels* (New York: Vendome Press, 2000), 12.

THE ART OF SMOKING

1 It should be noted that while many of the items discussed in this chapter are interpreted as masculine or feminine in style, Cartier's archival records rarely specify an intended gender.

2 Iain Gately, *Tobacco: A Cultural History of How an Exotic Plant Seduced Civilization* (New York: Grove Press, 2001), 206–7.

3 Edith Wharton, *The House of Mirth* (New York: Charles Scribner's Sons, 1922), 14, 37.

4 Elizabeth Drexel Lehr, *"King Lehr" and the Gilded Age* (Bedford, MA: Applewood Books, 2005).

5 Gerard S. Petrone, *Tobacco Advertising: The Great Seduction* (Atglen, PA: Schiffer Publishing, 1996), 214, 218.

6 Stefano Papi, *Jewels of the Romanovs: Family and Court* (London and New York: Thames & Hudson, 2010), 126–27, 129, 289, 292–93. Sotheby's London, *Romanov Heirlooms: The Lost Inheritance of Grand Duchess Maria Pavlovna*, November 30, 2009.

7 A 1915 cigarette holder of similar form, with an albatross-bone tube and an enamel-trimmed white gold cup, was a treasured possession of Russian composer Igor Stravinsky. It was presented to him as a gift by the Princesse de Polignac (Daisy Fellowes's aunt). Eric Nussbaum, "The Creation of the Cartier Collection," in "Cartier: Papers of the Symposium Held Jointly by the British Museum and the Society of Jewellery Historians at the British Museum in 1997," ed. Judy Rudoe, special issue, *Jewellery Studies* 9 (2001): 11.

8 Janet Zapata, "Art Deco Vanity Case," in *The Legacy of Elma Rumsey Cartier*, ed. Sylvia Neely and David E. Cassens (St. Louis, MO: Saint Louis University, 1995), 27.

9 Judy Rudoe, *Cartier: 1900–1939* (New York: Harry N. Abrams, 1997), 218.

THE MASCULINE VIEW

1 Quoted in Hans Nadelhoffer, *Cartier: Jewellers Extraordinary* (London: Thames & Hudson, 1984), 197.

2 *Cartier 1899–1949: The Journey of a Style*, exhibition catalog (Lisbon: Calouste Gulbenkian Foundation, 2007), 95, no.13, for a mustache comb about 1907; Harry St. Clair Fane, Hans Nadelhoffer, et al., *Reflections of Elegance: Cartier Jewels from the Lindemann Collection*, exh. cat. (New Orleans: New Orleans Museum of Art, 1988), 150, pl. LIV, for a Cartier opisometer of about 1911.

3 François Chaille and Franco Cologni, *The Cartier Collection: Timepieces* (Paris: Flammarion, 2006), 144–52, 196–256.

4 Philip Van Rensselaer, *Million Dollar Baby: An Intimate Portrait of Barbara Hutton* (New York: G. P. Putnam's Sons, 1979), 83.

5 John Culme and Nicholas Rayner, *The Jewels of the Duchess of Windsor* (New York and London: Vendome Press in association with Sotheby's, 1987), 129–31.

6 Ibid., 156; Gilberte Gautier, *Cartier: The Legend* (London: Arlington Books, 1983), 157, where it is claimed that the commander of the American Expeditionary Forces in Europe, General John Pershing, was presented by Cartier with the first Tank watch. See also *The Cartier Museum at the Goldsmiths' Hall, Foster Lane, London*, exh. cat. (London: Goldsmiths, 1988), 37.

7 Cartier took out a patent on the Basculante, which required the wearer to take the watch off in order to reverse the face. Jaeger and LeCoultre took out a patent for the Reverso, which didn't need to be removed from the wrist in order to be reversed. Cartier and Jaeger sometimes took out patents together.

8 Judy Rudoe, *Cartier: 1900–1939* (New York: Harry N. Abrams, 1997), 133, nos. 72 and 73.

9 Toussaint was never a designer herself—she couldn't even draw—but her ability to offer splendid suggestions and her brilliant analysis of current tastes was vital to the success of Cartier's lines of men's accessories long before and well after World War II. Toussaint had joined the firm in Paris as Louis Cartier's assistant in 1918 and was still *en poste* after World War II; she died in 1978.

10 François Chaille, Eric Nussbaum, and Franco Cologni, *The Cartier Collection: Jewelry* (Paris: Flammarion, 2004), 278.

11 François Chaille and Franco Cologni, *The Cartier Collection: Precious Objects* (Paris: Flammarion, 2011), 415.

12 Martin Chapman, *Cartier and America* (San Francisco and Munich: Fine Arts Museum and DelMonico/Prestel, 2009), 145, no. 153.

13 For an agate letter-opener set including a watch with a kingfisher-feather face of about 1930, see Fane et al., *Reflections of Elegance*, 134, pl. XLVII.

14 See Nadelhoffer, *Cartier: Jewellers Extraordinary*, 92, for purpurine, and Sotheby's New York, September 28, 2010, lot 162, for a Cartier Bakelite clip watch of 1935.

15 Nadelhoffer, *Cartier: Jewellers Extraordinary*, 205.

16 Ibid., 138.

17 The baguette cut was known in medieval times, but was reinvented for Cartier in 1912 as a way of using waste material from a natural diamond octahedron. See Janet Zapata, "Diamond Jewelry for Everyone," in George E. Harlow, ed., *The Nature of Diamonds* (Cambridge, UK, and New York: Cambridge University Press in association with the American Museum of Natural History, 1998), 190.

18 Fane et al., *Reflections of Elegance*, 94, plate XXIX.

19 Quoted in Nadelhoffer, *Cartier: Jewellers Extraordinary*, 277.

THE AGE OF GLAMOUR

1 According to Elizabeth Drexel Lehr, the Castles made their sensational Paris debut at a dinner in honor of Grand Duchess Vladimir (Maria Pavlovna) hosted by Lehr and her husband at the Ritz Hotel. Elizabeth Drexel Lehr, *"King Lehr" and the Gilded Age* (Bedford, MA: Applewood Books, in cooperation with the Preservation Society of Newport County, 2005), 239–40.

2 Quoted in Carolyn Hall, *The Thirties in Vogue* (New York: Harmony Books, 1985), 94.

3 Quoted in Judy Rudoe, *Cartier: 1900–1939* (New York: Harry N. Abrams, 1997), 263.

4 Quoted in *Magnificent Jewels from the Collection of Mrs. Charles Wrightsman*, Sotheby's New York, December 5, 2012.

5 Quoted in Sylvie Raulet, *Jewelry of the 1940s and 1950s* (New York: Rizzoli International Publications, 1988), 16, 18.

6 Illustrated in *Vogue*, November 15, 1946, 8.

7 All illustrated in *Vogue*, November 15, 1948, 4; February 1, 1949, 9; November 15, 1950, 17; May 15, 1947, 6.

8 Diana Vreeland, introduction, *The Magnificent Jewels of the late Countess Mona Bismarck*, Sotheby's Geneva, May 13, 1986, 5.

9 The sapphire, mounted on the necklace, was unnamed at the time it was given to the Smithsonian. It was dubbed the Bismarck Sapphire Necklace in memory of its former owner.

ICONS OF STYLE

1 Greg King, *A Season of Splendor: The Court of Mrs. Astor in Gilded Age New York* (Hoboken, NJ: John Wiley & Sons, 2009), 345.

2 George Eells, *The Life That Late He Led: A Biography of Cole Porter* (New York: G. P. Putnam's Sons, 1967), 88.

3 Cole Porter, *The Complete Lyrics of Cole Porter*, ed. Robert Kimball (New York: Alfred A. Knopf, 1983; reprinted 1992, DaCapo Press), 210–11.

4 Cecil Beaton, *The Glass of Fashion* (London: Weidenfeld & Nicolson, 1954), 185.

5 Stefano Papi and Alexandra Rhodes, *Famous Jewelry Collectors* (London and New York: Thames & Hudson, 2004), 183.

6 Ibid., 179, 182.

7 Hans Nadelhoffer, *Cartier: Jewelers Extraordinary* (New York: Harry N. Abrams, 1984), 125.

8 John Culme and Nicholas Rayner, *The Jewels of the Duchess of Windsor* (New York and London: Vendome Press in association with Sotheby's, 1987), 174–76.

9 Ibid., 197.

10 Papi and Rhodes, *Famous Jewelry Collectors*, 155.

11 For a full discussion of the necklace's creation and transformations, see Judy Rudoe, "The Taste for 'Barbaric Splendour': Daisy Fellowes and Her 'Hindu' Necklace," in "Cartier: Papers of the Symposium Held Jointly by the British Museum and the Society of Jewellery Historians at the British Museum in 1997," ed. Judy Rudoe, special issue, *Jewellery Studies* 9 (2001): 78–94.

SELECTED BIBLIOGRAPHY

Aliaga, Michel, et al. *Cartier: Innovation through the 20th Century*. Paris: Flammarion, 2007.

Balfour, Ian. *Famous Diamonds*. London: Collins, 2009.

Benton, Charlotte, Tim Benton, and Ghislaine Wood, eds. *Art Deco 1910–1939*. Boston: Bulfinch Press, 2003.

Cartier 1899–1949: The Journey of a Style. Exhibition catalog. Lisbon: Calouste Gulbenkian Foundation, 2007.

The Cartier Museum at the Goldsmiths' Hall, Foster Lane, London. Exhibition catalog. London: Goldsmiths, 1988.

Cartier: Style and History. Exhibition catalog. Paris: Réunion des musées nationaux–Grand Palais, 2013.

Chaille, François, and Franco Cologni. *The Cartier Collection: Timepieces*. Paris: Flammarion, 2006.

Chapman, Martin. *Cartier and America*. San Francisco and Munich: Fine Arts Museum and DelMonico/Prestel, 2009.

Cologni, Franco. *Cartier: The Tank Watch—Timeless Style*. Paris: Flammarion, 2012.

Cologni, Franco, and François Chaille. *The Cartier Collection: Precious Objects*. Paris: Flammarion, 2011.

Cologni, Franco, and Ettore Mocchetti. *Made by Cartier: 150 Years of Tradition and Innovation*. New York: Abbeville Press, 1993.

Cologni, Franco, and Eric Nussbaum. *Platinum by Cartier: Triumphs of the Jeweler's Art*. New York: Harry N. Abrams, 1996.

Cologni, Franco, Eric Nussbaum, and François Chaille. *The Cartier Collection: Jewelry*. Paris: Flammarion, 2004.

Craven, Wayne. *Gilded Mansions*. New York and London: W. W. Norton, 2009.

Culme, John, and Nicholas Rayner. *The Jewels of the Duchess of Windsor*. New York and London: Vendome Press in association with Sotheby's, 1987.

Davis, Mary E. *Ballets Russes Style: Diaghilev's Dancers and Paris Fashion*. London: Reaktion Books, 2010.

Fane, Harry St. Clair, Hans Nadelhoffer, et al. *Reflections of Elegance: Cartier Jewels from the Lindemann Collection*. Exhibition catalog. New Orleans, LA: New Orleans Museum of Art, 1988.

Gautier, Gilberte. *Cartier: The Legend*. London: Arlington Books, 1983.

Harlow, George E., ed., *The Nature of Diamonds*. Cambridge, UK, and New York: Cambridge University Press in association with the American Museum of Natural History, 1998.

Harrison, Stephen, Emmanuel Ducamp, and Jeannine J. Falino. *Artistic Luxury: Fabergé Tiffany Lalique*. Cleveland, OH, and New Haven, CT: Cleveland Museum of Art in association with Yale University Press, 2008.

Jackson, Anna, and Amin Jaffer. *Maharaja: The Splendour of India's Royal Courts*. London: V & A Publications, 2009.

Jaffer, Amin, Vivienne Becker, et al. *Beyond Extravagance: A Royal Collection of Gems and Jewels*. New York: Assouline, 2013.

King, Greg. *A Season of Splendor: The Court of Mrs. Astor in Gilded Age New York*. Hoboken, NJ: John Wiley & Sons, 2009.

Menkes, Suzy. *The Royal Jewels*. Revised edition. London: Grafton Books, 1986.

Munn, Geoffrey C. *Tiaras: A History of Splendour*. Woodbridge, Suffolk, UK: Antique Collectors' Club, 2001.

———. *Tiaras: Past and Present*. London: V & A Publications, 2002.

Nadelhoffer, Hans. *Cartier: Jewelers Extraordinary*. New York: Harry N. Abrams, 1984.

———. *Cartier*. Revised edition. London: Thames & Hudson, 2007.

Neely, Sylvia, and David E. Cassens. *The Legacy of Elma Rumsey Cartier*. Exhibition catalog. St. Louis, MO: Saint Louis University, 1995.

Odom, Anne. *Hillwood: Thirty Years of Collecting, 1977–2007*. Washington, DC: Hillwood Estate, Museum & Gardens, 2007.

Papi, Stefano. *Jewels of the Romanovs: Family & Court*. London and New York: Thames & Hudson, 2010.

Papi, Stefano, and Alexandra Rhodes. *Famous Jewelry Collectors*. London and New York: Thames & Hudson, 1999.

Post, Jeffrey E., and Chip Clark. *The National Gem Collection*. Washington, DC, and New York: National Museum of Natural History, Smithsonian Institution, in association with Harry N. Abrams, 1997.

Prior, Katherine, and John Adamson. *Maharajas' Jewels*. New York: Vendome Press, 2000.

Raulet, Sylvie. *Jewelry of the 1940s and 1950s*. New York: Rizzoli International Publications, 1988.

Rudoe, Judy. *Cartier: 1900–1939*. New York: Harry N. Abrams, 1997.

———, ed. "Cartier: Papers of the Symposium Held Jointly by the British Museum and the Society of Jewellery Historians at the British Museum in 1997." Special issue, *Jewellery Studies* 9. London: Society of Jewellery Historians, 2001.

Sotheby's New York. *The F.D.R. Cartier Victory Clock*. Auction catalog. December 4, 2007.

Zapata, Janet. *From Here to Antiquity*. Exhibition catalog. New York: DK Bressler with S. J. Shrubsole, 2013.

Zapata, Janet, Ulysses Dietz, and Zette Emmons. *Gems from the East and West: The Doris Duke Jewelry Collection*. New York and Newport, RI: Doris Duke Charitable Foundation and Newport Restoration Foundation, 2003.

IMAGE CREDITS

In reproducing the images in this publication, the publisher obtained permission of the rights holders where possible. In those instances where the publisher could not locate the rights holders, notwithstanding good faith efforts, it requests that those parties submit contact information so permissions can be secured for future editions.

Vincent Wulveryck, Cartier Collection © Cartier: pp. 1, 2, 22, 24, 27, 33, 53, 58, 61, 89, 90, 99, 100 fig. 93, 112 figs. 105 and 108, 117, 122, 127, 154, 199, 202, 222, 234 fig. 244, 237, 239, 240, 246, 248 top, 259, back cover · **Nils Herrmann, Cartier Collection © Cartier:** pp. 4, 21 fig. 4, 26 fig. 9, 39 fig. 24, 59, 64, 67, 81 fig. 70, 82, 83 fig. 73, 84 fig. 74, 91, 93, 94 figs. 84 and 85, 97, 104, 105, 108 figs. 101 and 102, 113 fig. 110, 114 fig. 114, 115, 118 fig. 122, 123, 124, 132 figs. 132 and 133, 133, 134, 136 fig. 138, 138 figs. 140 and 141, 141, 142, 143, 145, 147, 148 figs. 154 and 156, 150–51, 153, 155, 162 fig. 165, 173 figs. 188 and 190, 176, 181, 182, 183, 184 fig. 200, 185, 186 fig. 202, 211, 212, 213, 218, 232, 234 fig. 245, 243, 245 · **© Bettmann/CORBIS:** pp. 6, 51, 168 left, 229 right · **© Cartier:** pp. 9, 12, 13, 14 top, 20, 23 bottom, 25 right, 26 top, 30, 31, 32, 35, 49 top, 52 right top and bottom, 62 top right, 63, 66, 69, 71 left, 76, 78 bottom, 80 top left, 83 left, 88, 92 bottom, 95 left, 110, 111, 125 right, 152 top, 161 top, 178, 188, 191, 219, 223, 227, 231 bottom, 236 left · **Jean-Philippe Charbonnier © Gamma – Rapho/Getty Images:** p. 10 · **Nick Welsh, Cartier Collection © Cartier:** pp. 14 bottom, 17 bottom, 21 figs. 1–3, 28 figs. 12 and 13, 37, 38, 39 figs. 23 and 25, 40 fig. 26, 41 fig. 29, 49 fig. 33, 50, 52 figs. 35–38, 54, 55 fig. 45, 56, 60, 62 figs. 56–58, 65 fig. 61, 72 fig. 65, 79 figs. 66 and 67, 80 fig. 69, 81 fig. 71, 84 fig. 75, 85, 86, 92 fig. 81, 98, 101 fig. 95, 103, 106–107, 108 fig. 103, 109, 112 fig. 107, 118 fig. 123, 121, 125 fig. 130, 139, 144, 146, 148 fig. 155, 149, 152 fig. 158, 161 fig. 164, 162 fig. 167, 164, 165, 167, 168 right, 169 fig. 179, 173 figs. 186, 187, and 189, 174, 175, 176–177, 180, 186–87 bottom, 194 figs. 206–207, 195, 196 fig. 210, 198 fig. 213, 200, 201, 203, 204 fig. 220, 206, 207 fig. 224, 208 fig. 227, 220, 221, 241, 248–249 bottom, 249 top, 250, 256 fig. 269 · **Private Collection © Cartier:** p. 15 · **John Rawlings © Condé Nast:** pp. 16, 210 · **Luc Fournol, Cartier Collection © Cartier. Comité Jean Cocteau:** p. 17 top · **Photo Boissonnas & Taponier 1912:** p. 18 · **Marian Gérard, Cartier Collection © Cartier:** pp. 23 top, 68, 72 fig. 64, 96, 100 fig. 92, 114 fig. 113, 132 fig. 134, 136 fig. 139, 140, 157, 169 fig. 180, 186 fig. 203, 207 fig. 225, 214, 216–217, 256 figs. 267–268, 258 · **Courtesy Siegelson, New York:** pp. 25 fig. 8, 79 fig. 68, 94 fig. 83, 101 fig. 94, 112 fig. 106, 114 fig. 111, 120, 126, 162 fig. 166, 194 fig. 208, 205 · **David Behl:** pp. 28 fig. 11, 40 fig. 27, 41 figs. 28 and 30, 49 fig. 32, 65 fig. 60, 113 fig. 109, 114 figs. 112 and 115, 118 fig. 121, 160, 163, 170 fig. 182, 172, 198 fig. 212, 208 fig. 226 · **Qatar Museums Authority, Albion Art Tokyo:** pp. 34, 197 · **Photo Les Arts décoratifs, Paris/Jean Tholance. All rights reserved:** p. 42 · **Qatar Museums Authority, © courtesy of Christie's:** p. 45 · **© Condé Nast Archive/CORBIS:** pp. 46, 171 top left · **© 2013 Hearst Communications, Inc. All Rights Reserved:** p. 48 · **© E.O. Hoppe/CORBIS:** p. 55 top · **Ken Larsen/Smithsonian:** p. 57 · **Rehbinder/*Vogue* © Condé Nast:** p. 70 · **Courtesy of Hillwood Estate, Museum & Gardens:** p. 71 right · **© André Ostier:** p. 73 · **© John Fasal Collection:** p. 74 · **Photograph © 2014 Museum of Fine Arts, Boston:** p. 78 top · **Peter Lynde:** p. 102 · **Nils Herrmann © Cartier/Private Collection:** pp. 116, 119, 192 fig. 204 · **© Hulton-Deutsch Collection/CORBIS™ & © 2014 Marlene, Inc. All Rights Reserved:** p. 128 · **© National Portrait Gallery, London:** p. 130 · **Bibliothèque des arts décoratifs, Paris:** p. 135 · **© Steichen/Condé Nast:** pp. 137, 190 · **© Man Ray Trust/Artists Rights Society (ARS), NY/ADAGP, Paris, 2014:** p. 138 right · **Photograph by A. Aubrey Bodine. © Jennifer B. Bodine. Courtesy of AAubreyBodine.com:** p. 156 · **Eric Sauvage, Cartier Collection © Cartier:** p. 170 figs. 181, 183–184 · **© Hulton Archive/Getty Images:** p. 171 top right · **Courtesy of The Andy Warhol Foundation for the Visual Arts, Inc. © Arnold Newman/Getty Images:** p. 171 bottom right · **© United Artists/Collection Suns/Sunset Boulevard/Corbis:** p. 171 bottom left · **Courtesy of Sotheby's, Inc.:** pp. 179, 204 fig. 221, 208 fig. 228, 238, 244 · **© Underwood & Underwood/CORBIS:** p. 184 right · **© Time & Life Pictures/Getty Images. Comité Jean Cocteau:** p. 187 · **John Phillips © Time & Life Pictures/Getty Images:** p. 192 right · **© Cartier Archives at Cartier:** p. 193 · **Horst/*Vogue* © Condé Nast:** pp. 196 left, 209 · **© Ministère de la Culture/Médiathèque du Patrimoine, Dist.:** p. 215 · **© Her Majesty Queen Elizabeth II 2013:** p. 226 · **Photo by Chip Clark/Smithsonian:** p. 231 top left · **© Permission of the Estate of Edward Steichen:** p. 231 top right · **Bouché/*Vogue* © Condé Nast:** p. 235 · **© Robert Doisneau/Rapho:** p. 242 · **© Photograph by Snowdon, Camera Press London:** p. 247 · **Nils Herrmann © Palais Princier de Monaco:** pp. 252 figs. 259–261, 253 fig. 262, 254, 255 · **© Palais Princier de Monaco:** p. 252 bottom right · **G. Lukomski © Palais Princier de Monaco:** p. 253 bottom · **© Photofest:** p. 257

INDEX

Italic page numbers refer to illustrations.

S

T

V

W

Y

Z

PAGE 1 *Tutti Frutti* double clip brooch (see page 117 top).

PAGE 2 *Hindu* necklace (see page 243).

PAGE 4 *Persian* cigarette case (see page 143).

PAGE 5

TOP Olga, Countess Hohenfelsen (see page 18).

SECOND ROW LEFT Actress and model Alden Gay, photographed by Edward Steichen (see page 46).

SECOND ROW RIGHT The Maharaja of Patiala (see page 74).

THIRD ROW LEFT Actress Marlene Dietrich (see page 128).

THIRD ROW RIGHT Clark Gable wearing a Cartier Tank watch (see page 158).

FOURTH ROW LEFT Model wearing Cartier diamond earrings and brooch (see page 188).

FOURTH ROW RIGHT Daisy Fellowes wearing her Hindu necklace (see page 224).

This publication accompanies the exhibition *Brilliant: Cartier in the 20th Century*, organized by and on view at the Denver Art Museum, November 16, 2014–March 15, 2015.

Brilliant: Cartier in the 20th Century is presented by:

Joy and Chris Dinsdale

Exhibition support is also provided by the generous donors to the Annual Fund Leadership Campaign and the citizens who support the Scientific and Cultural Facilities District (SCFD). Promotional support is provided by *5280 Magazine*, CBS4, and *The Denver Post*. We regret the omission of sponsors confirmed after April 1, 2014.

Published by the Denver Art Museum in association with The Vendome Press

DENVER ART MUSEUM
100 W. 14th Ave. Pkwy
Denver, CO 80204
denverartmuseum.org

THE VENDOME PRESS
1334 York Avenue
New York, NY 10021
vendomepress.com

Library of Congress Cataloging-in-Publication Data available upon request

ISBN 978-0-914738-93-0 (hardcover without slipcase)
ISBN 978-0-86565-311-5 (hardcover with slipcase)

Pierre Rainero's essay was translated from the French by Helge Dascher

EDITING AND PROJECT MANAGEMENT, DENVER:
Laura Caruso, Senior Editor & Manager of Publications
EDITORS: Jacqueline Decter and Barbara Clark
PRODUCTION COORDINATOR: Irene Convey
DESIGNER: Celia Fuller

PRINTED IN CHINA BY OGI
FIRST PRINTING